THE CONSULTANT'S
PROBLEM-SOLVING WORKBOOK

THE CONSULTANT'S
PROBLEM-SOLVING WORKBOOK

Ron Tepper

JOHN WILEY & SONS

New York • Chichester • Brisbane • Toronto • Singapore

This publication is designed to provide accurate and
authoritative information in regard to the subject
matter covered. It is sold with the understanding that
the publisher is not engaged in rendering legal, accounting,
or other professional service. If legal advice or other
expert assistance is required, the services of a competent
professional person should be sought. *From a Declaration
of Principles jointly adopted by a Committee of the
American Bar Association and a Committee of Publishers.*

Library of Congress Cataloging in Publication Data:

Tepper, Ron, 1937–
    The consultant's problem-solving workbook.

    "A Wiley-Interscience publication."
    Bibliography: p.
    1. Business consultants.   I. Title.

HD69.C6T47   1987   658.4′6   86-24728
ISBN 0-471-84682-1

Printed in the United States of America

10 9 8 7 6 5 4 3 2 1

PREFACE

There are elements of business that are, at best, difficult for consultants to master because of the intangible nature of the profession and the psychology involved in dealing with clients, regardless of how knowledgeable a consultant may be in his or her field. These elements must be mastered if the consultant is to have a practice that is not only profitable but growth-oriented as well.

This workbook is designed to give consultants a practical answer and direction to take with everyday problems ranging from establishing fees to marketing services.

It answers questions such as:

How do you structure an agreement with a client? How do you word an agreement with partners, especially if they are friends?

How do you arrive at a fee? How do you explain and rationalize that fee to your client, and more important, what technique do you utilize to get your client to agree to raise your fee when the time comes?

What are the pitfalls of incorporation? What protection does it afford the consultant? Should you incorporate? Are you familiar with the other forms of business and the weaknesses (and advantages) of each?

How do you develop a brochure, newsletter, audio/visual presentation, or sales letter, especially if you do not have the faintest idea of how to write or what elements go into them?

What are the most effective methods for building your business?

The workbook also introduces a number of concepts such as:

The low-cost alternative to advertising, one that is 10 times more effective.

"Venture Consulting," where consultants share in the increased profits or production of their client companies.

v

The billing multiplier.

A business building technique that is an alternative to telephone cold calling.

Methods for making sales letters more effective and results oriented.

The Consultant's Problem-Solving Workbook answers every conceivable question about consulting and running a practice. This book is a "practical, how to" guide complete with forms, checklists, samples, detailed instructions, and procedures that any consultant can follow to either launch his or her business or build it.

The Consultant's Problem-Solving Workbook is not a book of theories, but of practical, useful information and inside tips on how to build and run a successful practice. It is more than a problem solver, it is a guide; a guide that not only explains the techniques utilized by these successful consultants but also shows how those methods can be emulated by consultants in any field.

RON TEPPER

Torrance, California
January 1987

ACKNOWLEDGMENTS

The idea for this book came from John Wiley & Sons editor Michael Hamilton, who saw the need for a consultant's workbook that would not only contain forms and checklists but would also enable any consultant, newcomer, or established practitioner to improve his or her business by simply adopting existing procedures that have proved successful for consultants throughout the country.

Compiling the forms, procedures, and obtaining permission for the material in this book took countless hours. The organization and structure would not have been possible without the dedicated efforts of Janet Haynes Tepper.

Also, a special thanks to Marilyn Dibbs from John Wiley who spent many hours painstakingly working on this book as well.

RON TEPPER

CONTENTS

TABLE OF CHECKLISTS

THE CONSULTANT'S
PROBLEM-SOLVING WORKBOOK

CHAPTER 1

CORPORATE STRUCTURE, AGREEMENTS, AND CLIENT CONTRACTS

Taxes and liability. Those are the two most important considerations when organizing your business today.

Of the three basic ways to form a business (sole proprietor, partnership, corporation) a corporation offers the best protection (liability).

Which one offers the best tax breaks? The verdict is mixed. Although many certified public accountants (CPAs) will say the corporation is taxed twice— once on its income and once on the dividends (or salary) derived from it, the corporate structure offers other advantages.

For example, a corporation can virtually pay for all your business needs (entertainment, car, insurance), and provide a minimal salary. By keeping your salary low, and not listing any business deductions, the chance of being queried by the Internal Revenue Service (IRS) diminishes.

On the other hand, the consultant who opens a practice as a sole practitioner (or with a partner) and deducts everything from his or her income (tickets, entertainment, car, clothing, etc.) is often audited. There are tradeoffs, advantages, and disadvantages in each of these forms.

Sole proprietorships are not taxed by the federal government. The income from the business flows directly through to you and is taxed as ordinary income by the government.

As a general rule partnerships are not subject to federal income tax. Instead each partner must report on his or her individual income tax return the pro rata share of each item of partnership gain, loss, income, deduction, or credit—and pay tax accordingly. It would seem that sole proprietors and partnerships have an advantage over the corporation because income is taxed only once. There is, however, that important consideration—liability. If you operate your business as a corporation, your liability is usually limited to the assets of the corporation. In most cases, your personal assets cannot be attached in a lawsuit. With partnerships and sole proprietorships, there is usually no limit to your liability. Your home, car, and personal belongings can easily become part of any lawsuit.

In fact, with a partnership, you may find yourself faced with debts you knew nothing about. For example, in most partnerships when one partner buys something in the name of the business, the other partner is automatically encumbered with the debt—even if he or she knew nothing about the purchase, or even objected to it.

With the prevalence of lawsuits in today's society, consultants should carefully consider each of these three forms of business, the advantages and disadvantages, when opening their doors. Lawsuits in business go far beyond product liability. Today, there can be malpractice suits in virtually any profession.

FILING DOING BUSINESS AS (DBA) FORM

If you are a sole proprietor, you can start your business by filing a Doing Business As (DBA). DBAs are fictitious business statements that are filed with your local newspaper.

Newspapers charge a modest fee (usually under $100) to publish your DBA, and file it with the state. In most states, a DBA is good for five years before refiling is needed.

If your name is John Smith and you want to establish Smith Management Consulting Services, this requires a DBA. The newspaper carries a form similar to the one in this workbook. Prior to opening a business bank account, most banks will require proof of your DBA filing. When filing, do so with a small local newspaper, not a large metropolitan daily. The rates will be cheaper.

Remember, filing a DBA does not separate the company from your personal assets. From a tax standpoint, the income the company derives will have to be declared on your personal tax return.

A DBA could fall into either the sole proprietor or partnership category, since two businesspeople could get together, agree to be partners, and file a DBA. For an example of a DBA see Figure 1-1.

ABANDONING DBA FORM

Figure 1-2 is a "Statement of Abandonment of the Use of the Fictitious Name." In the event you decide to change the name of the business or close it, make sure you file this (or a similar) form supplied by the newspaper. If you do not abandon it, there is always the possibility of confusion and legal problems with an active name and an inactive business and businessperson.

GENERAL PARTNERSHIP AGREEMENT

There are a variety of partnerships you can form when opening a consulting practice. The important thing is to ensure that each partner's duties are clearly spelled out and the partnership agreement contains a buyout and survival clause. Thus in the event of a death or a disagreement, the company can continue to function without any long, protracted legal problems.

PUBLISH IN:

COUNTY CLERK'S FILING STAMP

FICTITIOUS BUSINESS NAME STATEMENT

THE FOLLOWING PERSON(S) IS (ARE) DOING BUSINESS AS:

1. Fictitious Business Name(s)

2. Street Address, City & State of Principal place of Business in California   Zip Code

3. Full name of Registrant   (if corporation - show state of incorporation)

Residence Address	City	State	Zip Code

Full name of Registrant   (if corporation - show state of incorporation)

Residence Address	City	State	Zip Code

Full name of Registrant   (if corporation - show state of incorporation)

Residence Address	City	State	Zip Code

Full name of Registrant   (if corporation - show state of incorporation)

Residence Address	City	State	Zip Code

4. This business is conducted by ( ) an individual (.) a general partnership ( ) a limited partnership
( ) an unincorporated association other than a partnership ( ) a corporation ( ) a business trust (CHECK ONE ONLY)

5.   If Registrant a corporation sign below:

Signed_____   Corporation Name_____

Typed or Printed_____   Signature & Title_____

This statement was filed with the County Clerk of _____ County on date indicated by file stamp above.

6. New Fictitious Business Name Statement [ ]

7. Refile — Statement expires December 31. [ ]

File No. _____

I HEREBY CERTIFY THAT THIS COPY IS A CORRECT COPY OF THE ORIGINAL STATEMENT ON FILE IN MY OFFICE.

_____
COUNTY CLERK

BY _____ DEPUTY

File No._____

FIG. 1-1. DBA fictitious name statement. (Figure continued on p. 4.)

INSTRUCTIONS FOR COMPLETION OF STATEMENT

Box 1. Insert the new business name here. (Type or print clearly)

Box 2. Insert the street address of the principal place of business (Post Office boxes are **not** acceptable).

Box 3. If the owner is an individual, insert the full name and residence address. If the owner is a partnership or other association of persons, insert the full name and residence address of each general partner. If the owner is a corporation, insert the name of the corporation and business address as set forth in its articles of incorporation and the state of incorporation. (Post Office boxes are **not** acceptable).

Box 4. Check off the one item which best describes the nature of the business.

Box 5. Sign the form. Use the right box for corporations who are the sole owner and the left box for all other types of ownerships. Only one owner, partner or corporate officer signs.

Boxes 6. and **7.** Check one box only. Check six if a new filing, and seven if refiling.

CALIFORNIA BUSINESS AND PROFESSIONS CODE

SECTION 17910-**Every person who regularly transacts business in this state for profit under a fictitious business name shall:**
(a) File a fictitious business name statement in accordance with this chapter not later than 40 days from the time he commences to transact such business; and
(b) File a new statement in accordance with this chapter on or before the date of expiration of the statement on file.

SECTION 17917-(a) **Within 30 days after a fictitious business name statement has been filed pursuant to this chapter, the registrant shall cause a statement in the form prescribed by subdivision (a) of Section 17913 to be published pursuant to Government Code Section 6064 (once per week for four successive weeks) in a newspaper of general circulation in the county in which the principal place of business of the registrant is located** or, if there is no such newspaper in that county. then in a newspaper of general circulation in an adjoining county. If the registrant does not have a place of business in this state. the notice shall be published in a newspaper of general circulation in Sacramento County. **(The Los Angeles DAILY JOURNAL and the DAILY COMMERCE are qualified for publication of fictitious business names in Los Angeles County.)**

Section 17920-(a) Unless the statement expires earlier under subdivision (b) or (c), a fictitious business name statement expires at the end of five years from December 31 of the year in which it was filed in the office of the county clerk.
(b) Except as provided in Section 17923. a fictitious business name statement expires 40 days after any change in the facts set forth in the statement pursuant to Section 17913, except that a change in the residence address of an individual. general partner, or trustee does not cause the statement to expire.
(c) A fictitious business name statement expires when the registrant files a statement of abandonment of the fictitious business name described in the statement.

Section 17900-**(a) As used in this chapter, 'fictitious business name' means:**
(1) In the case of an individual. a name that does not include the surname of the individual or a name that suggests the existence of additional owners.
(2) In the case of a partnership or other association of person, a name that does not include the surname of each general partner or a name that suggests the existence of additional owners.
(3) In the case of a corporation, any name other than the corporate name stated in its articles of incorporation.
(b) A name that suggests the existence of additional owners within the meaning of subdivision (a) is one which includes such words as 'Company,' 'and Company,' 'and Son,' 'and Sons,' 'and Associates,' 'Brothers,' and the like, but not words that merely describe the business being conducted.

Section 17910.5-(a) No person shall adopt any fictitious business name which includes 'Corporation,' 'Corp.,' 'Incorporated,' or 'Inc.' unless such person is a corporation organized pursuant to the laws of this state or some other jurisdiction.

FIG. 1-1. (*continued*)

Mail materials to:

County Filing Fee-$5.00

_____

_____

_____

File No. _____
            (If not known, leave blank)

STATEMENT OF ABANDONMENT OF
USE OF FICTITIOUS BUSINESS NAME

The following person (persons) has (have) abandoned the use of the fictitious business

name _____
               (Fictitious Name Being Abandoned-Type or print clearly)

at _____.
               (Street Address of Principal Place of Business)

The fictitious business name referred to above was filed in the County Clerk's office

on _____.
     (If date not known, leave blank)

1. _____   3. _____
   (Full Name-Type or print clearly)

  _____   _____
   (Address)

  _____   _____
   (City, State, Zip Code)

2. _____   4. _____

  _____   _____

  _____   _____

The business was conducted by (check one) ____ an individual, ____ a general partnership, ____ a limited partnership, ____ an unincorporated association other than a partnership, ____ a corporation, ____ a business trust.

Signed: _____
                       (By general partner or corporate officer)

This statement was filed with the County Clerk of Los Angeles County on date indicated by file stamp above.

SEE REVERSE SIDE FOR INSTRUCTIONS

THE LOS ANGELES DAILY JOURNAL
Established 1888
210 South Spring St., Los Angeles, Ca 90012
P.O. Box 54026, Los Angeles, Ca 90054
Telephone (213) 625-2141

DAILY COMMERCE
Established 1917
210 South Spring St., Los Angeles, Ca 90012
P.O. Box 54026, Los Angeles, Ca 90054
Telephone (213) 624-3111

FIG. 1-2. Statement of abandonment of use of fictitious business name. (_Figure continued on p. 6._)

INSTRUCTIONS FOR COMPLETION OF FORM

Type or clearly print the required information in the spaces provided on reverse side. Please note directions in parentheses below each line. Post office boxes are not acceptable for addresses.

The information on this Abandonment form must be the same as was on your original Fictitious Business Name Statement.

If you can not determine the filing date or number assigned by the County Clerk for the Fictitious Business Name being abandoned, we will look up the information for you in the county's records. Leave the space blank.

If you have any questions please call (213) 625-2141 extension 250, 251 or 252. We will be happy to assist you.

CALIFORNIA BUSINESS AND PROFESSIONS CODE

Abandonment of Use of Fictitious Business Name

Section 17922-(a) **A person who has filed a fictitious business name statement may, upon ceasing to transact business in this state under that fictitious business name, file a statement of abandonment of use of fictitious business name.** The statement shall be executed in the same manner as a fictitious business name statement and shall be filed with the county clerk of the county in which the person has filed his fictitious business name statement. **The statement shall be published in the same manner as a fictitious business name statement (once per week for four weeks in a newspaper of general circulation)** and an affidavit showing its publication shall be filed with the county clerk after the completion of publication.

    (b) The statement shall include:

        (1) The name being abandoned and the street address of the principal place of business.

        (2) The date on which the fictitious business name statement relating to the fictitious business name being abandoned was filed and the county where filed.

        (3) In the case of an individual, the full name and address of the individual.

        (4) In the case of a partnership or other association of persons, the full names and residence addresses of all the general partners.

        (5) In the case of a corporation, the name of the corporation as set forth in its articles of incorporation.

        (6) In the case of a business trust, the full name and residence address of each of the trustees.

Section 17930-Any person who executes, files, or publishes any statement under this chapter, knowing that such statement is false, in whole or in part, shall be guilty of a misdemeanor and upon conviction thereof shall be punished by a fine not to exceed five hundred dollars ($500).

FIG. 1-2. (continued)

There are more "horror" stories about partnerships than any other form of business. Friends shake hands, open their doors, and six months later they are enemies. Most problems arise because friends, acquaintances, and associates forget that no matter how strong their relationship is, when you open a business it is a *business*, and it should be treated as one. Handshakes may be fine between contestants in an athletic event, but they are insufficient when it comes to business. If someone is willing to shake your hand on a business deal, they should be ready to sign a piece of paper as well.

Too many friends let personal feelings get in the way of business. They decide to go into business together, and then say, "Well, we've always gotten along . . . we do not need any partnership papers or an agreement." That thought can lead to disaster. There is no way to predict how another person will react when you work side-by-side, 8 to 10 hours a day. Nor is there any way to predict what will happen to the personality of a good friend when money enters the picture.

Be sure and protect yourself and your friend. Make sure there are partnership papers prepared by an *attorney*. Although businesspeople can do many things for themselves, this is one area that should be handled by an attorney.

Regardless of the initial capital contribution made to get the company off the ground, compensation for each partner should be spelled out as part of the agreement. For example, let's suppose two people went into business together and formed a consulting partnership. Partner 1 put up $1000; partner 2 $500. The partnership agreement can be structured so that 1 gets twice the income of 2, or 1 gets his $1000 out before any salaries are taken.

Often partners decide that one will take a greater salary than the other. Partners might decide this for tax purposes (suppose one partner has other income and does not need the additional salary). These considerations and conditions should be spelled out in the agreement.

Figure 1-3 is an example of a partnership agreement. The necessary wording for a buyout or survival clause is found within this agreement. In structuring a partnership agreement there are a number of things partners should address—with the aid of an attorney. The following checklist covers the most critical ones.

Partnership Agreement Checklist

1. Financial obligations of each partner.

2. Buyout clause—in the event of disagreement or similar situations.

3. Survival clause—in the event of death or incapacitating accident.

4. Salaries or income—Who takes what and when?

5. Profits—are they distributed, reinvested, when?

6. Check signing privileges—are there restrictions? Two signatures for checks over certain amount?

7. Purchasing—Who can purchase what? For how much? Does it require partner approval?

8. Hiring/firing—Who has the authority?

9. Raises—When? To whom? Under what conditions? What if there is a disagreement?

10. Resignation—How is it handled? Can a partner resign? What liabilities will they still have if they do? What assets?

11. Duties and obligations—What are partners responsible for . . . is there a division of responsibilities?

12. Failure to perform—Is there recourse against the partner who fails to hold up his or her end of the bargain? If so, what?

13. Selling the business—How many partners have to agree? If there is a disagreement, does a partner have recourse or some way to appeal?

14. Hours—Are there specific hours when partners have to be at work?

GENERAL PARTNERSHIP AGREEMENT

ROBERT GARCIA and JOHN SMITH, hereinafter called the partners, do hereby form a General Partnership pursuant to the laws of the State of California.

1.

NAME

The name of the partnership shall be: AU DESIGN.

2.

PURPOSE

The purpose of the Partnership is to operate a jewelry design and manufacturing center.

3.

TERM

The term of the partnership shall be five (5) years commencing with the date of the execution of this Agreement by all the partners unless sooner terminated by mutual agreement of the partners or by operation of law.

4.

PRINCIPAL PLACE OF BUSINESS

The address of the principal place of business of the Partnership shall be: 512 Elm Street, Anytown, USA.

5.

PARTNERS, ADDRESSES, INTERESTS AND INITIAL CAPITAL CONTRIBUTIONS

The names, addresses, interests and initial capital contributions of the partners are listed on Exhibit "A" attached hereto and made a part hereof.

6.

RECORDING

The partners shall cause an executed and acknowledged duplicate original of this Agreement to be recorded in the Office of the Recorder of the County in which the principal office of business of the partnership is situated, of the County in which the partnership has places of business situated, and of the County in which real property to which the partnership holds title is located.

FIG. 1-3. General partnership agreement.

7.

ADDITIONAL CAPITAL CONTRIBUTIONS

No partner shall be required to make additional contributions to the capital of the partnership and no partner shall be permitted to voluntarily make an additional contribution to the capital of the Partnership without the written consent of all the other partners.

8.

WITHDRAWAL OF CAPITAL

No portion of the capital of the Partnership may be withdrawn at any time without the express written consent of all the partners.

9.

INTEREST ON CAPITAL

No partner shall be entitled to interest on his contributions to the capital of the Partnership.

10.

LOANS TO PARTNERSHIP

No partner may loan or advance money to the Partnership without the written consent of the remaining partners. Any such loan by a partner to the Partnership shall be separately entered in the books of the Partnership as a loan to the Partnership, shall bear interest at such rate as may be agreed on by the lending partner and the remaining partners, and shall be evidenced by a promissory note delivered to the lending partner and executed in the name of the Partnership by the remaining partners.

11.

ACCOUNTING PROCEDURE

The cash method of accounting is hereby adopted. A set of books shall be maintained at the principal place of business of the Partnership and shall be available for inspection by any partner during business hours. It is expected that initially the accounting shall be done on a calendar year basis in a practice generally acceptable for the purposes of satisfying the requirements of Federal and State Income Taxing agencies.

12.

ANNUAL ACCOUNTING

As soon after the close of each fiscal year as is reasonably practicable, a full and accurate inventory and accounting shall be made of the affairs of the Partnership as of the close of such fiscal year. On such accounting being made, the net profit or net loss sustained by the Partnership during such fiscal year shall be ascertained and credited or debited, as the case may be, in the books of account of the Partnership to the respective partners in the proportions specified in Paragraph 14 of this Agreement.

13.

DEFINITION OF PROFITS AND LOSSES

The terms "net profits" and "net losses" as used in this Agreement shall mean the net profits and net losses of the Partnership as determined by generally acceptable accounting principals for each accounting period provided for in this Agreement.

FIG. 1-3. (*continued*) (*Figure continued on p. 10.*)

PROFITS AND LOSSES

Profits and losses are to be distributed on a calendar basis but profits are to be distributed only after the Partnership has returned or repaid capital cash contributions or loans to partners who have contributed or loaned cash to the Partnership in accordance with the agreement between the Partnership and the lending or contributing partner.

In any event, there shall be no distribution of profits to the extent that such distribution would cause the combined balances of the Partnership bank accounts to fall below the sum of $500.00 unless a specific lesser amount is agreed to in writing by all of the partners.

The net profits or losses of the Partnership shall be shared as follows: 50% for each partner.

15.

CAPITAL ACCOUNTS

An individual capital account shall be maintained for each partner consisting of his contribution to the initial capital of the Partnership, any additional contributions to the Partnership capital made by him pursuant to this Agreement, and any amounts transferred from his income account to his capital account pursuant to this Agreement.

16.

INCOME ACCOUNTS

An individual income account shall be maintained for each partner. At the end of each fiscal year each partner's share of the net profits or net losses of the Partnership shall be credited or debited to and his withdrawals during such fiscal year deducted from his income account. After such amounts have been credited or debited to and deducted from a partner's income account, any balance or deficit remaining in such account shall be transferred to or charged against such partner's capital account.

17.

BANK ACCOUNTS

All funds of the Partnership shall be deposited in accounts in the name of the partnership at such bank or banks in Los Angeles County, California, as may from time to time be selected by a majority vote of the partners. All withdrawals from any such account or accounts shall be made only by check or other written instrument executed by both partners.

18.

DEVOTION OF TIME AND EFFORT

Each partner shall devote such time and effort to the Partnership as is reasonably necessary to the proper conduct of the Partnership business.

19.

OUTSIDE ACTIVITIES

A partner shall not engage in or invest in any other business ventures which would interfere with or compete with the purpose of this Partnership without the prior written consent of the remaining partners.

FIG. 1-3. (continued)

20.

SALARIES

No partner shall be entitled to any salary or other compensation for his services to the Partnership business.

21.

DRAWS

Each partner shall be permitted to withdraw from the funds of the Partnership for his own use an amount to be agreed upon by all of the partners. Any such withdrawal by a partner shall be charged against his share of the net profits of the Partnership for the fiscal year in which such withdrawal is made. If the total withdrawals by a partner during a given fiscal year exceed his share of the net profits for such year, the partner shall not be permitted to make further withdrawals until such deficiency has been repaid to the Partnership.

22.

AUTHORITY OF THE PARTNERS

Each of the partners shall have authority to act on behalf of the Partnership in all matters respecting the Partanership, its business and its property except as provided in Paragraph 17 above and except as follows:

    a. No partner shall incur an obligation on behalf of the Partnership in excess of $500.00 without the consent of all the partners;

    b. Acts prohibited by law; and

    c. Acts prohibited elsewhere in this Agreement.

23.

MANAGEMENT

Each partner shall have an equal voice in the management and conduct of the Partnership business and all disagreements or issues arising shall be decided by a majority vote of the partners, each partner having one vote.

No act in contravention of this Agreement may be legally done without the consent in writing of all the partners.

24.

LIMITATION ON LIABILITY AMONG PARTNERS

A partner shall not be liable, responsible or accountable in damages or otherwise to the other partners for any acts performed or for any omission to act within the scope of the authority conferred on him by this Agreement or by law, except for acts of bad faith, willful misfeasance, gross negligence or reckless disregard of his duties.

25.

ARBITRATION

Any dispute or controversy arising under, out of, in connection with, or in relation to this Agreement, and any amendment thereof, or the breach thereof, or in connection with the dissolution of the Partnership, shall be determined and settled by arbitration to be held in Thousand Oaks, California, in accordance with the rules than obtaining, of the American Arbitration Association. Any

FIG. 1-3. (*continued*) (*Figure continued on p. 12.*)

award rendered therein shall be final and binding on each and all partners and judgment may be entered thereon in the Superior Court of the State of California for the County of Ventura.

26.

PARTIES BOUND

Except as otherwise herein provided, this Agreement shall be binding upon and inure to the benefit of the parties hereto, their heirs, executors, administrators, successors, and all persons hereafter having or holding an interest in this Partnership, whether as assignees, substituted partners, or otherwise.

27.

ADDITIONAL DOCUMENTS

The partners shall execute, acknowledge, publish, file and record as required by law, a Fictitious Business Name Statement, a Statement of Partnership, a Notice of Dissolution (when applicable) and all other certificates or instruments which the Partnership may be required to file under the laws of the State of California and all cancellations of and amendments to any of the foregoing. In addition, and whether included or not in the above, each party hereto agrees to execute any further documents and writings which may be necessary to this Partnership or to carry out the provisions or intent hereof.

28.

DEATH, INCAPACITY OR WITHDRAWAL OF A PARTNER

Upon the death, legal incapacity or withdrawal of a partner the remaining or surviving partners shall have the right to purchase the interest of the deceased, incapacitated or withdrawing partner at the appraised value reached by the following procedure:

Within sixty (60) days after appointment of a personal representative of a deceased or incapacitated partner or of written notice by a partner of intent to withdraw, the remaining partners and the personal representative or the withdrawing partner shall either (a) jointly appoint an appraiser to value the interest to be sold or (b) failing this joint action, shall each separately designate an appraiser who within thirty (30) days after their appointment shall jointly designate a third appraiser. The failure of the remaining partners, the personal representative of the deceased or incapacitated partner or the withdrawing partner to appoint an appraiser within the time period allowed shall be deemed equivilant to appointing the appraiser selected by the other party.

If within thirty (30) days after the appointment of all appraisers, a majority of the appraisers concur on the value of the interest being appraised, that appraisal shall be deemed binding and conclusive. If the majority of the appraisers do not concur within that period, the determination of the appraiser whose appraisal is neither highest nor lowest shall be deemed binding and conclusive. The expense of the appraisal shall be shared equally by the remaining partners and the withdrawing partner or the estate of the deceased or incapacitated partner.

If within thirty (30) days after receipt of the appraisal the remaining partners elect to purchase the interest in question, they shall pay for that interest as follows: Twenty-five percent (25%) of the purchase price shall be paid within ninety (90) days of the date the purchase price is ascertained and the remaining

FIG. 1-3. (continued)

principle balance shall be paid together with interest thereon at the rate of ten (10) percent per annum, in four equal annual installments, the first of such installments being due within one (1) year from the date of the initial payments.

In the event the remaining partners fail to elect to purchase the interest in question, then the remaining partners shall cause the assets of the Partnership to be sold and the proceeds thereof distributed among the partners according to their respective interests in the Partnership.

Should any one or more of the remaining partners be unable or unwilling to purchase a portion of the interest in question, such interest may then be purchased by the other remaining partners. For purposes of this section the term "personal representative" with respect to a deceased partner shall also include the person or persons taking the interest in the partnership from such deceased partner in a manner not requiring administration of the decedent's estate and appointment of a personal representative.

29.

INTERPRETATION AND CONTENTS

When the context in which words are used in this Agreement indicates that such is the intent, words in the singular number shall include the plural and vice-versa. This Agreement shall be governed and construed in accordance with the laws of the State of California.

30.

PARTIAL INVALIDITY

In the event that any provision of this Agreement shall be held to be invalid, the same shall not affect in any respect whatsoever the validity of the remainder of this Agreement

31.

COUNTERPARTS

This Agreement may be executed in any number of counterparts, each of which shall be deemed an original, but all of which together shall constitute one and the same instrument.

32.

CAPTIONS

The captions to the paragraphs of this Agreement are solely for the convenience of the parties, and in no way either define, limit, or describe the scope of this Agreement or individual paragraphs hereof or the intent of any provisions thereof, and are not to be used as an aid in the interpretation or construction of this Agreement.

33.

ENTIRE AGREEMENT

This instrument contains the entire agreement of the parties relating to the rights granted and obligations assumed in this instrument. Any oral representations or modifications concerning this instrument shall be of no force or effect unless contained in a subsequent written modification signed by the party to be charged.

FIG. 1-3. (**continued**) (Figure continued on p. 14.)

DATED: ROBERT GARCIA
_____

DATED: JOHN SMITH
_____

FIG. 1-3. (continued)

CONSENT OF SPOUSE

I CERTIFY THAT:

  1. I am the spouse of ROBERT GARCIA who has signed the foregoing General Partnership Agreement as a partner thereof.

  2. I have read and approved the provisions of that General Partnership Agreement.

  3. I agree to be bound by and accept the provisions of the General Partnership Agreement in lieu of all other interests I may have in the Partnership.

Executed on _____, 1986, at _____, California.

                              _____
                              BETTY GARCIA

CONSENT OF SPOUSE

I CERTIFY THAT:

  1. I am the spouse of JOHN SMITH who has signed the foregoing General Partnership Agreement as a partner thereof.

  2. I have read and approved the provisions of that General Partnership Agreement.

  3. I agree to be bound by and accept the provisions of the General Partnership Agreement in lieu of all other interests I may have in the Partnership.

Executed on _____, 1986, at _____, California.

                              _____
                              JAYNE SMITH

FIG. 1-3. (continued)

ARTICLES OF INCORPORATION

Corporations have paperwork as well. Figure 1-4 is an example of a typical "Articles of Incorporation." There is nothing complex; however, they must be filed with the state, and their purpose stated. Within the articles is an "Agent for Services," which is usually the attorney for the corporation, or the attorney responsible for the incorporation.

Corporations cannot be mere "shells." They must hold regular meetings or they can lose the corporate status, as well as the liability protection. Most states require that company directors meet once a year (as directors), and shareholders meet once a year (as shareholders).

WAIVER OF NOTICES AND MINUTES OF MEETINGS

To prove the corporation is legitimate, minutes (Figure 1-5, p. 20) should be kept and filed. For the first meeting, a waiver (of written notice), (Figure 1-6, p. 21) was entered, and regular business was transacted, including the election of officers and the issuance of stock. There was also a bank resolution filed.

A waiver is a document that says we are going to hold a meeting without written notice. Most closely held corporations (i.e., corporations that are held by just a few individuals) file waivers instead of formal written notices. These corporations are able to utilize the waiver because in most cases the directors and shareholders are involved in the day-to-day operation of the company, and can be personally contacted.

Waivers and additional minutes for a second meeting in March are shown in Figures 1-7 and 1-8 (pp. 29 and 30) respectively. In September, there is another waiver (Figure 1-9, p. 31), election, and a shareholders meeting as well. Figures 1-10, 1-11, and 1-12 (pp. 32–34) are examples of waivers and minutes of the September meeting. As is the case with most small companies, DSJM is closely held.

STOCKS

Figure 1-13 (pp. 35–36), a sample stock certificate follows, and is part of the 10,000 shares of common stock authorized.

In small, closely held companies (generally with a capitalization of less than $500,000), an attorney can save enormous stock issuance costs by filing the following stock issuance form (Figure 1-14, pp. 37–38) for closely held corporations. There are similar forms in every state. Stock transfer ledgers are part of every corporate record book (Figure 1-15, p. 39).

SAMPLE RESOLUTION FROM BOARD OF DIRECTORS AND SAMPLE CONTRACTS

Figure 1-16 (pp. 40–41) is the typical format for a resolution from a board of directors. This resolution can be copied, filled in, and filed in the corporate records.

Once you are in business, there are other contracts and agreements to consider. There should be one between you and your client. These agreements should be kept simple, easy-to-understand, and if possible limited to a one or two page letter of agreement. On the following pages you will find a collection of different agreements. They will give you an idea of the elements involved in a legal agreement and/or contract with a client.

The most important issues are duties, responsibilities, payment, nonpayment, and cancellation clauses. Each agreement handles these factors in a different way.

The short agreements are just as effective in court (in the event you have to sue) as an in-depth, 12 page document. The shorter letter of agreement (Figure 1-17, p. 42) also creates less anxiety for the client when he or she signs it.

The next five agreements (Figures 1-18 through 1-22, pp. 43–48) are all retainer-type contracts. One has hourly fees spelled out in addition to the retainer, and one is a "performance based" contract. These contain excellent verbage that can be transferred to any kind of agreement you might need.

Not all agreements can be made this simple. Figures 1-23 and 1-24 (pp. 49–53) represent agreement between an engineering consultant and a developer. It spells out their duties.

Figure 1-25 (pp. 54–55) is an agreement between a data processing consultant and a client. It is based on previous discussions, and the duties are spelled out, along with the fees involved. The company signs on page 2, and the agreement is then operative.

The next agreement (Figure 1-26, pp. 56–57) is from an accounting consultant who will perform services for a company. With the rising number of malpractice suits against attorneys and accountants, consultants in these areas are careful to indicate their duties and limitations.

The agreement shown in Figure 1-27 (pp. 58–60) ensures what the data processing firm will do for a client. This is strictly a study; no action, aside from recommendations will result.

Figures 1-28 and 1-29 (pp. 61–62) are a sample agreement divided into two phases, with the consulting firm limited to the first phase, and a recommendation for the second phase. If everything goes well, the client can retain the firm to handle Phase II. The hourly fees appear in Figure 1-29.

Figure 1-30 (p. 63) comes from the office of an attorney who specializes in real estate. There is a penalty clause for late payments.

Figure 1-31 (pp. 64–65) letter is from the same accounting consultant cited earlier. The duties of the firm differ in this agreement.

SAMPLE FORMS: NEW CLIENT INFORMATION; THIRD CPA CONSULTING

Figure 1-32 (p. 66) is a new client information form. It came from a legal firm, hence the area that allows for dissolution information.

The form in Figure 1-33 (pp. 67–69) is from the same accounting firm as Figure 1-31, note the different obligations.

1065157

ARTICLES OF INCORPORATION

OF

DSJM ENTERPRISES, INC.

ENDORSED
FILED
In the office of the Secretary of State
of the State of California

JAN 29 1982

MARCH FONG EU, Secretary of State
Camille M. Guy
Deputy

Name

One: The name of the corporation is: DSJM ENTERPRISES, INC.

Purpose

Two: The purpose of the corporation is to engage in any
lawful act or activity for which a corporation may be organized
under the General Corporation Law of California other than
the banking business, the trust company business or the
practice of a profession permitted to be incorporated by the
California Corporations Code.

Agent For Service

Three: The name and address in the State of California of
the corporation's initial agent for service of process is:

Hugh W. Holbert
171 E. Thousand Oaks Blvd.
Suite 205
Thousand Oaks, CA 91360

Authorized Shares

Four: The total number of shares which the corporation is
authorized to issue is 10,000.

Dated: January 19, 1982   *Hugh W Holbert*
                                 HUGH W. HOLBERT

The undersigned declares that the undersigned has executed
these Articles of Incorporation and that this instrument is
the act and deed of the undersigned.

Dated: January 19, 1982   *Hugh W Holbert*
                                 HUGH W. HOLBERT

FIG. 1-4. Articles of incorporation.

State of California

OFFICE OF THE SECRETARY OF STATE

I, *MARCH FONG EU*, Secretary of State of the State of California, hereby certify:

That the annexed transcript has been compared with the record on file in this office, of which it purports to be a copy, and that same is full, true and correct.

IN WITNESS WHEREOF, I execute this certificate and affix the Great Seal of the State of California this

JAN 2 9 1982

March Fong Eu

Secretary of State

SEC/STATE FORM CE-107 ① △ OSP

FIG. 1-4. (continued)

MINUTES OF FIRST MEETING OF

BOARD OF DIRECTORS OF

DSJM ENTERPRISES, INC.

A California Corporation

The Incorporator named in the Articles of Incorporation of the above named corporation, constituting the Board of Directors of said corporation, held the first meeting at the time, on the day and at the place set forth as follows:

TIME:	10:00 A.M.
DATE:	January 29, 1982
PLACE:	171 E. Thousand Oaks Blvd. Suite 205 Thousand Oaks, CA 91360

There were present at the meeting the following directors, constituting a quorum of the full board:

HUGH W. HOLBERT

HUGH W. HOLBERT then appointed the following persons to serve as Directors until the next regular meeting of the shareholders.

DIETER SAUER
JOYCE MORROW

All persons being present acknowledged and accepted their appointment.

On motion and by unanimous vote, the following named persons were elected Temporary Chairman and Secretary of the first meeting:

Temporary Chairman: DIETER SAUER

Temporary Secretary: JOYCE MORROW

FIG. 1-5. Board of director's minutes.

WAIVER OF NOTICE AND CONSENT TO HOLDING

OF FIRST MEETING OF DIRECTORS OF

DSJM ENTERPRISES, INC.

A California Corporation

The undersigned, being the Incorporator named in the Articles of Incorporation, and desiring to hold the first meeting of the Board of Directors of said corporation for the purpose of completing the organization of its affairs, DOES HEREBY waive notice of said meeting and consent to the holding thereof, at the time, on the date and at the place set forth as follows:

TIME:	10:00 A.M.
DATE:	January 29, 1982
PLACE:	171 E. Thousand Oaks Blvd. Suite 205 Thousand Oaks, CA 91360

Said meeting is to be held for the purpose of adopting By Laws, electing officers, adopting a form of corporate seal and bank account, authorizing issuance of shares in accordance with the provisions of the California Corporations Code and the filing of a statement of non-necessity for a permit, or the filing of an application for a permit as the case may be, with the California Commissioner of Corporations, and transacting such other business as may be brought before said meeting; the undersigned further agrees that any business transacted at said meeting shall be as valid and legal and of the same force and effect as though said meeting were held after notice duly given.

WITNESS my signature this 29th day of January, 1982.

HUGH W. HOLBERT
_____

FIG. 1-6. Waiver of notice for director's meeting. (*Figure continued on p. 22.*)

WAIVER

The Chairman announced that the meeting was held pursuant to written waiver of notice thereof and consent thereto signed by the incorporator of the corporation. Such waiver and consent was presented to the meeting and upon motion duly made, seconded and unanimously carried was made a part of the records of the meeting and now precedes the minutes of this meeting in the Book of Minutes of the Corporation.

ARTICLES FILED

The Chairman stated that the original Articles of Incorporation of the corporation had been filed in the office of the California Secretary of State in Sacramento.

Date of Filing Articles in Sacramento: January 29, 1982

The Chairman then presented to the meeting a certified copy of said Articles of Incorporation, showing filings as stated, and the Secretary was directed to insert said copy in the Book of Minutes of the corporation.

BY-LAWS

The matter of the adoption of By-Laws for the regulation of the corporation was next considered. The Secretary presented to the meeting a form of By-Laws which are duly considered and discussed. On motion duly made, seconded and unanimously carried, the following resolutions were adopted:

WHEREAS, the shareholders of this corporation have not as yet adopted any By-Laws for the regulation of its affairs; and

WHEREAS, there has been presented to this meeting a form of By-Laws for the regulation of the affairs of this corporation; and

WHEREAS, it is deemed to be in the best interests of this corporation and its shareholders that said By-Laws be adopted by this Board of Directors as and for the By-Laws of this Corporation;

NOW, THEREFORE, BE IT RESOLVED, that the By-Laws presented to this meeting and discussed hereat be and the same hereby are adopted as and for the By-Laws of this corporation.

FIG. 1-6 (continued)

RESOLVED FURTHER, that the Secretary of this corporation be and hereby is authorized and directed to execute a certificate of the adoption of said By-Laws and to insert said By-Laws as so certified in the Book of Minutes of this corporation and to see that a copy of said By-Laws, similarly certified, is kept at the principal office for the transaction of business of this corporation, in accordance with Section 502 of the California Corporations Code.

ELECTION OF OFFICERS

The meeting proceeded to the election of a President, a Vice President, a Secretary and a Treasurer. The following were duly nominated and elected to the office indicated after their names:

    DIETER SAUER, President
    JOYCE MORROW, Secretary
    JOYCE MORROW, Treasurer

Each officer so elected being present accepted his office, and thereafter the President presided at the meeting as Chairman and the Secretary acted as Secretary of the meeting.

CORPORATE SEAL

The Secretary presented for the approval of the meeting a proposed seal of the corporation, consisting of two concentric circles with the name of the corporation in one circle and the words and figures, "INCORPORATED", the date of incorporation, and "CALIFORNIA", in the form and figures as follows:

On motion duly made, seconded and unanimously carried, the following resolution was adopted:

FIG. 1-6. Waiver of notice for director's meeting. (*Figure continued on p. 24.*)

RESOLVED, that the corporate seal in the form, words and figures presented to this meeting be and the same hereby is adopted as the seal of this corporation.

SHARE CERTIFICATE

The Secretary presented to the meeting a proposed form of share certificate for use by the corporation. On motion duly made, seconded and unanimously carried, the followng resolution was adopted:

RESOLVED, that the form of share certificate presented to this Board be and the same hereby is approved and adopted, as the share certificate of this corporation.

The Secretary was instructed to insert a copy thereof in the Book of Minutes immediately following the minutes of the meeting.

ISSUANCE OF SHARES UNDER SMALL OFFERINGS EXEMPTION

The Chairman stated that the next order of business was to consider the issuance of the corporation's capital stock. He advised the Board that an exemption is provided for by Section 25102(h) of the California Corporations Code for closely held corporations. He advised that in order to qualify for this exemption the Board must establish certain facts and conditions. These facts must then be set forth on the notice form required by the Commissioner's office, together with an opinion of legal counsel based thereon.

The Chairman cautioned that while this initial issuance could thereby be exempt, the Commissioner's rules would require a legend condition restricting the subsequent transfer of these shares in the manner provided in those rules.

After considering the matter, upon motion being first duly made, seconded and carried, the following resolutions were adopted:

RESOLVED, that immediately after the sale and issuance of the share hereinafter proposed to be issued, the issuer will have only one class of stock outstanding which will be owned beneficially by no more than ten (10) persons, and all of the certificates evidencing such stock will contain the legend required by Section 260.102.6 of Title 10 of the California Administrative Code.

FIG. 1-6. *(continued)*

RESOLVED FURTHER, that the offer and sale of this stock will not be accompanied by the publication of any advertisement, that no selling expenses will be given, paid or incurred in connection therewith, and that no promotional consideration will be given, paid or incurred in connection therewith.

RESOLVED FURTHER, that the consideration received or to be received by the issuer for the stock to be issued consisted of or will consist of one of the kinds described in Section 21502(h).

RESOLVED FURTHER, that the notice required by Section 25102(h) (5) containing the above information, shall be filed by the Secretary of this corporation with the Commissioner of Corporations or shall be mailed for filing (with affidavit of service by mail retained by the issuer and its counsel) not later than the day on which the securities are issued.

RESOLVED FURTHER, that upon receipt of the consideration described herein, if not already received, the President and Secretary or Assistant Secretary of this corporation shall issue the following described shares to the following named persons for the consideration described herein:

NAME	NUMBER OF SHARES	CONSIDERATION
DIETER SAUER	1,000	$1,000.00
JOYCE MORROW	1,000	$1,000.00

FIG. 1-6. (continued) (Figure continued on p. 26.)

BANK RESOLUTION

To provide for a depositary for the funds of the corporation and to authorize certain officers to deal with the corporate funds, the following resolutions were duly adopted:

RESOLVED, that this corporation open an account or accounts with Bank of A. Levy, 137 E. Thousand Oaks Boulevard, Thousand Oaks, California.

RESOLVED FURTHER, that until such authority is revoked by sealed notification to said bank of such action by the Board of Directors of this corporation,

Names of Officers	Office Held
DIETER SAUER	President
JOYCE MORROW	Secretary/Treasurer

be, and are authorized acting together to execute checks and other items for and on behalf of this corporation.

FURTHER RESOLVED, that said account shall be governed by applicable banking laws, customs and clearing regulations and by the rules printed in the bank book, and shall be subject to the service charge schedule of the bank. If this is a checking account, the bank is requested to prepare and dispose of statements and cancelled checks monthly as instructed below. The bank assumes all risk of loss in transit of any statement or check.

Statement Instructions: Bank of A. Levy is instructed to mail the statement to the address shown on the bank records.

ACCOUNTING YEAR

The Chairman suggested that the meeting consider the adoption of an accounting year, either fiscal or calendar, so that the Franchise Tax Board could be notified thereof. On motion duly made, seconded and unanimously carried, the following resolution was adopted:

RESOLVED, that this corporation adopt an accounting year as follows:

FIG. 1-6. (continued)

Date Accounting Year Begins: January 1

Date Accounting Year Ends: December 31

INCORPORATION EXPENSES

In order to provide for the payment of the expenses of incorporation and organization of the corporation, on motion duly made, seconded and unanimously carried, the following resolution was adopted:

RESOLVED, that the President and the Treasurer of this corporation be, and they hereby are, authorized and directed to pay the expense of the incorporation and organization of this corporation.

PRINCIPAL OFFICE LOCATION

After some discussion, the location of the principal office of the corporation for the transaction of the business of the corporation was fixed pursuant to the following resolution unanimously adopted, upon motion duly made and seconded:

RESOLVED, that the county named in the Articles of Incorporation be and the same hereby is designated and fixed as the principal office for the transaction of the business of this corporation.

The meeting then proceeded to the matter of qualifying Shareholders of the corporation to receive the benefits of Section 1244 of the Internal Revenue Code of 1954, as amended. The Chairman reported that Section 1244 allows persons who purchase stock of the corporation to obtain an ordinary loss deduction under certain circumstances in the event they subsequently sell their stock at a loss or if their stock becomes worthless. The Chairman also reported that the corporation's stock qualifies for Section 1244 treatment in that (1) this corporation is a domestic corporation; (2) Section 1244 stock is common stock; (3) the aggregate amount of money and other property received for stock, as contribution to capital, and as paid in surplus by the corporation does not exceed $1,000.00; and (4) the issued stock was issued for money or property, but not for stock, securities or services.

After further discussion and upon motion duly made and seconded, the following recitals and resolutions were unanimously adopted:

WHEREAS, this corporation is a small businss corporation, as defined in Section 1244(c) (1) of said Code, as amended; and

FIG. 1-6. (*continued*) (*Figure continued on p. 28.*)

WHEREAS, the corporation has not heretofore received any gross receipts from any sources, and contemplates that in the future more than 50% of its aggregate gross receipts will be from sources other than royalties, rents, dividends, interest, annuities, and sales or exchanges of stock or securities.

WHEREAS, it is deemed advisable that the sale and issuance of shares of the stock of this corporation be effectuated in such a manner that qualified Shareholders may receive the benefits of Section 1244 of the Internal Revenue Code of 1954, as amended.

NOW, THEREFORE, BE IT RESOLVED, that the sale and issuance of shares of this corporation shall be made in compliance with the IRC Section 1244, as amended, so that qualified Shareholders may receive the benefits of Section 1244.

RESOLVED, FURTHER, that the officers of this corporation be and they hereby are authorized and directed to execute all documents and to take such action as they deem necessary and advisable in order to carry out the provisions of this resolution.

ADJOURNMENT

There being no further business to come before the meeting, upon motion duly made, seconded and unanimously carried, the meeting was adjourned.

_____
Temporary Chairman, DIETER SAUER

Attest:

_____
Temporary Secretary, JOYCE MORROW

_____
Secretary, JOYCE MORROW

FIG. 1-6. (continued)

WAIVER OF NOTICE AND CONSENT TO HOLDING OF
REGULAR MEETING OF THE BOARD OF DIRECTORS OF
DSJM ENTERPRISES, INC.
A CALIFORNIA CORPORATION

We, the undersigned, being all of the directors of DSJM
Enterprises, Inc., desiring to hold a regular meeting of the
Board of Directors of said Corporation for the purpose of
conducting the general business of said Corporation, hereby
waive notice of said meeting and consent to the holding thereof,
at the time, on the day and at the place set forth as follows:

TIME: 11:00 a.m.

DATED: March 4, 1982

PLACE: 171 E. Thousand Oaks Blvd.
                               Suite 205
                               Thousand Oaks, CA 91360

Said meeting is to be held for the purpose of conducting the
general business of the corporation, electing officers and
transacting such other business as may be brought before said
meeting; we do further agree that any business transacted at
said meeting shall be as valid and legal and of the same force
and effect as though said meeting were held after notice duly
given.

WITNESS our signatures this 4th day of March, 1982.

_____
DIETER SAUER
Director

_____
JOYCE MORROW
Director

FIG. 1-7. Waiver of notice for director's meeting.

MINUTES OF THE REGULAR MEETING OF
THE BOARD OF DIRECTORS OF
DSJM ENTERPRISES, INC.
A CALIFORNIA CORPORATION

Minutes of the regular meeting of the Board of Directors of
DSJM Enterprises, Inc., held at 171 E. Thousand Oaks Boulevard,
Suite 205, Thousand Oaks, California on March 4, 1982, at 11:00
A.M.:

There were present at the meeting the following directors,
constituting a quorum of the full Board:

    DIETER SAUER
    JOYCE MORROW

The meeting was called to order by the president Dieter Sauer.

The secretary then presented to the meeting the written waiver
of notice and consent to the holding of the meeting, signed by
all of the directors of the Corporation. On motion duly made,
seconded and unanimously carried, it was ordered that the
secretary file the waiver with the minutes of this meeting.

The minutes of the Board of Directors meeting held on January
29, 1982 were read and approved.

The treasurer made his report to the meeting and it was the
consensus that the financial affairs of the corporation are in
good order.

There being no further business to come before the meeting, upon
motion duly made, seconded and unanimously carried, the meeting
was adjourned.

                                    _____
                                    JOYCE MORROW
                                    Secretary

FIG. 1-8. Board of director's minutes.

WAIVER OF NOTICE AND CONSENT TO HOLDING OF
REGULAR MEETING OF THE BOARD OF DIRECTORS OF
DSJM ENTERPRISES, INC.
A CALIFORNIA CORPORATION

We, the undersigned, being all of the directors of DSJM
Enterprises, Inc., desiring to hold a regular meeting of the
Board of Directors of said Corporation for the purpose of
conducting the general business of said Corporation, hereby
waive notice of said meeting and consent to the holding thereof,
at the time, on the day and at the place set forth as follows:

TIME: 11:00 a.m.

DATED: September 2, 1982

PLACE: 171 E. Thousand Oaks Blvd.
                               Suite 205
                               Thousand Oaks, CA 91360

Said meeting is to be held for the purpose of conducting the
general business of the corporation, electing officers and
transacting such other business as may be brought before said
meeting; we do further agree that any business transacted at
said meeting shall be as valid and legal and of the same force
and effect as though said meeting were held after notice duly
given.

WITNESS our signatures this 2nd day of September, 1982.

                               _____
                               DIETER SAUER
                               Director

                               _____
                               JOYCE MORROW
                               Director

FIG. 1-9. Waiver of notice for director's meeting.

MINUTES OF THE REGULAR MEETING OF
THE BOARD OF DIRECTORS OF
DSJM ENTERPRISES, INC.
A CALIFORNIA CORPORATION

Minutes of the regular meeting of the Board of Directors of
DSJM Enterprises, Inc., held at 171 E. Thousand Oaks Boulevard,
Suite 205, Thousand Oaks, California on September 2, 1982, at
11:00 A.M.:

There were present at the meeting the following directors,
constituting a quorum of the full Board:

DIETER SAUER
JOYCE MORROW

The meeting was called to order by the president Dieter Sauer.

The secretary then presented to the meeting the written waiver
of notice and consent to the holding of the meeting, signed by
all of the directors of the Corporation. On motion duly made,
seconded and unanimously carried, it was ordered that the
secretary file the waiver with the minutes of this meeting.

The minutes of the Board of Directors meeting held on March 4,
1982 were read and approved.

The meeting then proceeded to the election of officers and the
following persons were duly nominated and elected to the offices
indicated after their names:

DIETER SAUER   President
JOYCE MORROW   Secretary
JOYCE MORROW   Treasurer

Each officer so elected being present accepted his office and
thereafter, the president presided at the meeting as chairman
and the secretary acted as secretary for the meeting.

The treasurer made his report to the meeting and it was the
consensus that the financial affairs of the corporation are in
good order.

There being no further business to come before the meeting, upon
motion duly made, seconded and unanimously carried, the meeting
was adjourned.

JOYCE MORROW
Secretary

FIG. 1-10. Board of director's minutes.

WAIVER OF NOTICE AND CONSENT
TO HOLDING OF ANNUAL SHAREHOLDERS MEETING OF
DSJM ENTERPRISES, INC.
A CALIFORNIA CORPORATION

We, the undersigned, being all the shareholders of DSJM
Enterprises, Inc., hereby waive notice and consent to the
holding of a meeting of the shareholders of said corporation for
the purpose of discussing the business operations of the
corporation and transacting such other business as may come up,
at the time, on the day and at the place set forth as follows:

TIME: 11:00 a.m.

DATE: September 2, 1982

PLACE: 171 E. Thousand Oaks Blvd.
                                Suite 205
                                Thousand Oaks, CA 91360

The undersigned further request that this waiver and consent be
made part of the minutes of such meeting for the purpose of
showing that any business transacted at the meeting is as valid
as though had at a meeting duly held after regular call and
notice.

WITNESS our signatures this 2nd day of September, 1982.

                                _____
                                DIETER SAUER
                                Shareholder

                                _____
                                JOYCE MORROW
                                Shareholder

FIG. 1-11. Waiver of notice and consent to holding of annual shareholders meeting of DSJM Enterprises, Inc. (a California company).

MINUTES OF ANNUAL SHAREHOLDERS MEETING OF
DSJM ENTERPRISES, INC.
A CALIFORNIA CORPORATION

The minutes of the annual shareholders meeting of DSJM
Enterprises, Inc., held at 171 E. Thousand Oaks Boulevard, Suite
205, Thousand Oaks, California, on September 2, 1982 at 11:00
A.M.:

There were present at the meeting the following shareholders:

    DIETER SAUER
    JOYCE MORROW

The meeting was called to order by president Dieter Sauer.

The secretary presented to the meeting the written waiver of
notice and consent to the holding of the meeting, signed by all
of the shareholders of the Corporation. On motion duly made,
seconded and unanimously carried, it was ordered that the
secretary file the waiver with the minutes of this meeting.

The meeting proceeded to the election of directors. The
following persons were duly nominated and elected as directors
of the Corporation:

    DIETER SAUER
    JOYCE MORROW

The financial affairs of the corporation as well as its general
condition were then reviewed and discussed. It was the
consensus that the Corporation is in good order.

There being no further business to come before the meeting, upon
motion duly made, seconded and carried, the meeting was
adjourned.

                                    _____
                                    JOYCE MORROW
                                    Secretary

FIG. 1-12. Minutes of annual shareholders meeting.

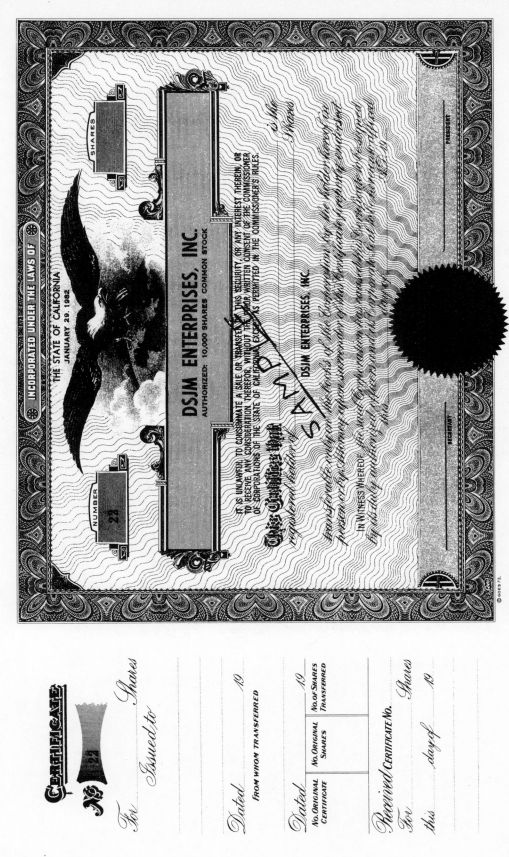

FIG. 1-13. Sample stock certificates. *(front)*

For Value Received,_____ hereby sell, assign and transfer unto_____ Shares represented by the within Certificate, and do hereby irrevocably constitute and appoint_____ Attorney to transfer the said Shares on the books of the within named Corporation with full power of substitution in the premises.

Dated_____ 19___

In presence of_____

FIG. 1-13. (back)

(Dept. of Corporations Use Only)

Fee Paid $_____

Receipt No. _____

         FEE: $25.00
_____

Dept. of Corporations
File No., If Any
_____

(Insert File Number(s) of
Previous Filings Before
the Department, If Any)

TO THE COMMISSIONER OF CORPORATIONS OF
THE STATE OF CALIFORNIA

Notice of Issuance of Shares Pursuant to Subdivision (h) of Section 25102
of the Corporations Code or Rule 260.103, Title 10, Cal. Admin. Code.

Check one of the following:
( ) Notice pursuant to Section 25102(h) as to an issuance subject to
    qualification under Corp. Section 25110, unless exempted.

( ) Notice pursuant to Rule 260.103 as to an issuance subject to qualification
    under Corp. Code Section 25120, unless exempted.

_____

Name of Issuer

_____

State of Incorporation

_____

Address of Principal Place of Business
      Number and Street   City   State   Zip Code

1. Is the issuer a "close corporation" as defined in Section 260.001,
    Title 10, California Administrative Code?   ( ) Yes   ( ) No

    Instruction: Review Corporations Code Section 158 and Rule 260.001,
    Title 10, California Administrative Code.

2. Under the exemption provided by Section 25102(h), shares of voting
    common stock have been or are proposed to be issued pursuant to this
    Notice beneficially to not more than 10 persons, whose names are set
    forth below; together with the names of the corresponding record
    shareholders if other than the beneficial shareholders:

    _____   _____

    _____   _____

    _____   _____

    _____   _____

    _____   _____

3. Immediately after the issuance and sale of such shares, the above-
    named issuer had or will have only one class of stock outstanding
    which was or will be owned beneficially by no more than 10 persons.

    Instruction: Review Sections 260.102.4 and 260.102.5, Title 10,
    California Administrative Code.

4. The offer and sale of such shares was not nor will be accompanied by
    the publication of any advertisement and neither selling expenses nor
    promotional considerations were or will be given, paid or incurred in
    connection therewith.

260.102.8(11-81)   -1-

FIG. 1-14. Stock issuance forms. *(Figure continued on p. 38.)*

5. To the best knowledge of the issuer, its shareholders (or proposed shareholders) have not entered into or granted, and presently do not intend entering into or granting, a shareholders' agreement, voting agreement, irrevocable proxy or other arrangement the effect of which would cause the statements contained herein to be incorrect.

    Instruction: Review Sections 260.001 and 260.102.4, Title 10, California Administrative Code.

6. Pursuant to the requirements of Section 260.102.6 of Title 10 of the California Administrative Code, all certificates evidencing such shares bear or will bear on their face the legend required by Section 260.141.11, and a copy of Section 260.141.11 has been or will be delivered to each issuee or transferee of the shares.

The undersigned officer of the issuer hereby declares that the foregoing is true under penalty of perjury. Executed at _____ , _____ , this _____ day of _____ , 198__ .

_____
Name

_____
Title

NOTE: If the officer signs this form in a jurisdiction which does not permit verifications under penalty of perjury, there must be attached a verification executed and sworn to before a notary public.

OPINION OF COUNSEL

I certify that I am an active member of the State Bar of California. On the basis of the facts stated in the foregoing Notice and other information, including representations as to the type of consideration received or to be received, supplied to me by officials and shareholders of the issuer and by proposed issuees, it is my opinion that the exemption from qualification with the Commissioner of Corporations provided by Subdivision (h) of Section 25102 of the California Corporations Code is available for the offer and sale of the shares referred to in this Notice.

_____   _____
Signature   Firm Name

_____   _____   _____
Name of Member of the State Bar   Address   Tel. No.
of California

(This opinion of counsel must be signed by an active member of the State Bar of California. Type name of attorney, address, phone number and firm name, if any.)

NOTE: If the issuer is a non-California corporation, a Consent to Service of Process as prescribed in the Commissioner's Rule 102.8(b) must be filed concurrently.
    Copies of Section 260.141.11 suitable for attachment to share certificates are available from the Department (see Item 6).

-2-

FIG. 1-14. (continued)

STOCK TRANSFER LEDGER

NAME OF STOCKHOLDER	PLACE OF RESIDENCE	DATE BECAME OWNER	FROM WHOM SHARES WERE TRANSFERRED (IF ORIGINAL ISSUE, ENTER AS SUCH)	CERTIFICATES SURRENDERED			CERTIFICATES ISSUED			AMOUNT PAID THEREON	BAL-ANCE SHARES HELD	DATE OF TRANSFER	TO WHOM TRANSFERRED
				NOS.	NO. OF SHARES		NO. OF SHARES	NOS.					

FIG. 1-15. Stock transfer ledger.

Resolution of Board of Directors

of

(Name of Company)

WHEREAS, the Board of Directors has considered the advisability of purchasing a membership in (organization/club) , for (whomever) and

WHEREAS, it was determined that such membership would be desirable and beneficial to this Company in that it would provide a place for entertaining business associates, visitors, customers, and the like, thereby increasing the Company's business and goodwill, and

WHEREAS,   (name of person) , officer in charge of marketing, will have the primary responsibility and duty of seeing to the accomodations of such visitors, and

WHEREAS, the expenses involved in such activities, are properly those of the Company's, and not a private individual, be it

RESOLVED, that as a step to increase the Company's business, (name) is hereby authorized to apply for membership in (name of org.) and to obtain reimbursement from the Company for

FIG. 1-16. Sample resolution from board of directors.

40

any fees therefy incurred, and

RESOLVED FURTHER, That ___(name)___ is authorized to obtain
reimbursement from the Company for all expenses incurred at
(name of organization) in connection with entertainment and
activities of the Company's guests, including, but not limited to
(spell out the type of expenses, such as meals, etc.) such
expenses.

I___(name)___ do hereby certify that I am the duly
elected and qualified Secretary and keeper of the records and
corporate seal of ___(name of company)___, a corporation
organized and existing under the laws of the State of
___(state)___, and that the above is a true and correct
copy of a resolution duly adopted at a meeting of the Board of
Directors thereof, convened and held in accordance with law and
bylaws of said Corporation on ___(date)___, and that such resolution
is now in full force and effect.

IN WITNESS WHEREOF, I have affixed my name as Secretary and have
caused the corporate seal of said Corporation to be hereunto
affixed this___(date)___

___(signature)___

Secretary

FIG. 1-16. (continued)

LETTER OF AGREEMENT

_____ hereby retains RON TEPPER & ASSOCIATES, INC. for public relations and marketing services commencing_____ and continuing monthly thereafter, until_____. Either party hereto may terminate this Agreement earlier by tendering a 30-day written notice of termination.

For these services,_____agrees to pay a monthly fee of_____dollars ($_____), plus expenses. The monthly fee shall be due and payable in advance and in the following manner: The first month's fee shall be due and payable upon the signing of this Agreement and a like amount on the same day of each subsequent month thereafter.

Expenses shall be billed by invoice and shall be due and payable within fifteen days of the invoice date. No expense in excess of seventy-five dollars ($75.00) shall be incurred by RON TEPPER & ASSOCIATES, INC. on the Client's behalf without the Client's prior approval.

In the event that any legal action is required to enforce this Agreement or any portion thereof, the prevailing party of such legal action shall be entitled to recover from the other party the reasonable attorney's fees and legal costs thereof.

RON TEPPER & ASSOCIATES, INC.

By:_____   _____
    RON TEPPER

DATE:_____, 1983   DATE:_____,1983

FIG. 1-17. Sample contract.

LETTER OF AGREEMENT

(Name of company) ("Client") hereby retains (name of company)
("Agency") for marketing services for its (name of project)
commencing (date) and continuing until either party hereto
terminates this agreement by tendering a 30-day written notice of
cancellation .

For these services, the Client agrees to pay a monthly retainer of
(write out) dollars ($0,000), from the effective date of this
contract through (date). The retainer will be increased to (write
out) dollars ($0,000) effective (date) and will remain at that level
through (date). On (date), the retainer shall be increased to
(write out) dollars ($0,000) per month and will remain at that
level until (date).

For the retainer, the Agency will provide to the Client account
services, meeting time, conceptual creatve time, PR, clerical time
(in preparing conference reports, ad schedules, marketing plans).
The Client will be billed separately for art design, art
production and creative copywriting time. The fees for these
services shall be:

    Creative copywriting ....$00 per hour

    Art design ....$00 per hour

    Art production...................$00 per hour

The Agency's responsibilities will be to provide the Client with a
marketing plan, media mix and breakdown; brochure design; copywriting; display design; arrange for any photography; ad placement; promotion and publicity.

The Agency will provide all ad placements and buyouts and will be
entitled to a (00%) advertising commission on all media and a
(00%) mark-up on all buy-outs. The Client will be billed on a
monthly basis with the retainer due the first of the month. For
all brochure and display work, one-half of the cost will be due
upon the Client's approval and one-half upon delivery and/or
installation.

For ads, one-half will be due upon final approval of ad and one-
half due upon invoice billing following publication. All brochures and display work will be put out on a competitive bid with
three bids for all work.

-More-

FIG. 1-18. Retainer letter of agreement. (*Figure continued on p. 44.*)

Letter of Agreement cont......

Expenses, creative copywriting, art design and art production fees
shall be billed monthly by invoice and shall be due and payable
within 15 days of the invoice date.

In the event that any legal action is required to enforce this
Agreement or any portion thereof, the prevailing party of such
legal action shall be entitled to recover from the other party the
reasonable attorney's fees and legal costs thereof.

AGREED TO:

(Name of company)   (Name of company)

By: (Signature)   By: (Signature)

(Date)   (Date)

FIG. 1-18. *(continued)*

LETTER OF AGREEMENT

(Name of company) and (name of company) agree to retain (name of company) for public relations services as outlined in a letter from (name of company) to (name of company)on March 19, 1985. The effective date of this agreement will be when (name of company) presents an acceptable plan and/or outline for publicity services for (name of company or person), and that plan and this contract is signed by all parties.

During the tenure of this agreement, (name of company) will be compensated on the basis of performance. The compensation shall be in the form of a (write out) dollar ($0,000) retainer that will be paid monthly on the condition that (name of company) secures for (name of company or person) one of the following three types of coverage during each (30) day period--

    A. National story and/or TV.
    B. TV or radio exposure on a top station in major market.
    C. Major editorial (print) coverage in top market.

Top or major markets shall be agreed to beforehand by the client and agency. Initial markets will be spelled out in the plan.

The fee shall also cover all normal expenses. Mass mailings requiring photo duplication shall be billed separately.

This agreement may be terminated by either party with a written, thirty (30) day notice.

In the event any legal action is taken to enforce this agreement or any portion thereof, the party which prevails in that suit shall be entitled to recover, from the other, its attorney's fees, in a reasonable amount, plus cost of said suit.

(Signature)
(Name of company)

(Date)

(Signature)
(Name of company)

(Date)

(Signature)
(Name of Company)

(Date)

FIG. 1-19. Retainer plus hourly fees agreement.

(This should be on your letterhead)

LETTER OF AGREEMENT

(Name of company) agrees to retain (name of company) for public
relations and marketing services commencing July 12, 1984 and
continuing until either party hereto terminates this agreement
by tendering a 30-day written notice of cancellation

During the length of this agreement, (name of company) will
perform publicity services for (name of company) as outlined in a
letter of June 19, 1984. For these services, (name of company)
agrees to pay a monthly retainer of (write-out amount of dollars)
(then put $0.000 in parenthensis), plus expenses. No expense in
excess of (write out) dollars, ($00.00) shall be incurred without
client's prior approval.

The fee shall be payable in the following manner: the first
month's fee shall be due and payable four weeks after the signing
of this agreement. The first month's fee shall be (write out)
dollars, ($0,000), which is a reduction of (write out) dollars
($000), reflecting credit for the client's previous payment for
consulting services. Subsequent retainers will be (write out)
dollars ($0,000) and will be due and payable upon invoicing. Each
subsequent billing cycle shall be moved up one week a month until
such time as the retainer is payable in advance. Expenses shall
be billed by invoice and shall be due and payable within fifteen
(15) days of the invoice date.

In the event any legal action is taken to enforce this agreement
or any portion thereof, the party which prevails in that suit
shall be entitled to recover, from the other, its attorney's fees,
in a reasonable amount, plus cost of said suit.

(Signature)   (Signature)
(Name of company)   (Name of company)

(Date)   (Date)

FIG. 1-20. Performance based letter of agreement.

(This should be on your letterhead)

LETTER OF AGREEMENT

(Name of company), a registered (state) political committee, agrees to retain (name of company) for (type of services) commencing January 1, 1983 and continuing until either party hereto terminates this agreement by tendering a 30-day written notice of cancellation.

During the length of this agreement, (name of company) will perform (type of) services for (name of person or committee) as outlined in a letter of November 12, 1982. For those service, the (name of person or committee) agrees to pay a monthly retainer of (write out) dollars ($0,000), plus expenses. No expense in excess of (write out) dollars ($00) shall be incurred without client's prior aproval.

The fee shall be payable in the following manner: Upon signing of this agreement, the first month's fee shall be due and payable, and every thirty (30) days thereafter an additional monthly fee, plus expenses incurred shall be due and payable until such time as the services are no longer required.

In the event any legal action is taken to enforce this contract or any portion thereof, the party which prevails in the suit shall be entitled to recover, from the other, its attorney's fees, in a reasonable amount, plus cost of said suit.

AGREED TO;

(Name of person or committee)　　　　(Name of company)

(Dated)　　　　(Dated)

(Note: This is an agreement with a political committee)

FIG. 1-21. Letter of agreement with variable payments.

(This should be on your letterhead)

LETTER OF AGREEMENT

(Name of company) agrees to retain (name of company) for (type of
services) commencing January 14, 1984, and continuing until either
party terminates this agreement by tendering a 30-day written
notice of cancellation.

During the tenure of this agreement, (name of company) will be
compensated on the basis of performance. The compensation shall
be in the form of a $0,000 (Write out dollars) fee for each feature
story that is published on (name of company) and his marketing
skills.

These stories will be targeted at various industries through trade
publictions. The industries shall be proposed by (name of
company) and approved by (name of company).

The performance fee shall be payable in the following manner: One
half ($0,000) shall be due and payable upon acceptance of the
publiaton of a feature and/or interview on (name of company). The
second half ($0,000) shall be due and payable upon publication of
the article.

Any expenses incurred in the form of long distance telephone calls
or special mailings shall also be paid by (name of company).
These expenses shall be approved in advance by the client and
will be due and payable upon billing.

In the event any legal action is taken to enforce this agreement
or any portion thereof, the party which prevails in that suit
shall be entitled to recover, from the other, its attorney's fees,
in a reasonable amount, plus cost of said suit.

AGREED TO:

(Name of company)   (Name of company)

(Date)   (Date)

(This is a performance based contract)

FIG. 1-22. Political letter of agreement.

Agreement Between Developer and Engineer

SECTION 1: ENGINEER AGREES to furnish and perform the various professional services hereinafter listed. Further it is the intent of this Agreement that a complete professional engineering job shall be done, and to that extent the scope of work is not necessarily limited to the services hereinafter listed:

OFFICE
1. Prepare preliminary land planning studies of property.
2. Attend meetings as required with DEVELOPER and the City of_____and other involved public agencies.
3. Prepare formal tract maps and perform all work required for recordation.
4. Prepare street improvement plans for construction purposes, effect cprrections, and obtain approval by the City of _____.
5. Prepare domestic water and sanitary sewer plans for construction purposes, effect corrections and obtain approval by the City
6. Prepare storm drain plans for construction purposes, effect corrections, and obtain approvals by the City of _____ and any other involved agencies.
7. Prepare rough grading plans and obtain approval of the City of _____.
8. Prepare 20-foot scale plot plan in accordance with the mylar system; prepare composite plot and grading plan; prepare 20-scale master utility plan.
9. Prepare sales map.
10. Perform necessary coordination work with utility companies.
11. Furnish three (3) sets of quantity and cost estimates:
   a. A preliminary estimate from tentative map.
   b. A preliminary estimate from unsigned plans.
   c. A final estimate from signed plans.
12. Prepare legal description and plat for each recorded unit.
13. Perform normal inspection of site improvements, required certifications and prepare "as-built" plans.

FIELDS
1. Prepare necessary grade sheets for inspectors, developers, etc.
2. Furnish one (1) set of stakes for rough grading of lots and streets.
3. Furnish one (1) set of "blue top" stakes for finish grading as required.
4. After the rough grading has been completed, ENGINEER

FIG. 1-23. Performance based agreement. (*Figure continued on p. 50.*)

shall verify that streets, pads, slopes, etc., have been graded in accordance with the approved plans. It shall be the responsibility of the grading contractor to protect the stakes until all verification work has been completed.

5. Furnish one (1) of stakes for sanitary sewer construction.
6. Furnish one (1) set of stakes for storm drain construction, drainage terraces and other drainage facilities as shown on the approved plans.
7. Furnish one (1) set of stakes defining building locations.
8. Furnish one (1) set of stakes for underground electrical and telephone utilities.
9. Furnish one (1) set of stakes for curb and gutter construction, cross gutters and any other improvements requird to complete the street construction.
10. After completion of improvements and landscaping, set final lot corners, tract boundary monuments, street centerline monuments and other survey controls as shown on the record map and required by the County of _____ and City of _____.
11. Prepare tie notes for street centerline monuments and furnish copies to the County of _____.
12. Prepare "as built" plans.

SECTION 2: DEVELOPER AGREES to pay ENGINEER as compensation for the above-named professional services as set forth in Section 1 a fee of:
$_____ per dwelling unit.

SECTION 3: THE DEVELOPER AGREES to pay ENGINEER interim compensation for work performed on the "Percentage-of-compensation" method. The attached Schedule "A" per unit cost estimate, based on an estimated _____ units, shall be used as a guide in determining the percentage of work completed by ENGINEER. The contract shall be adjusted for any changes in the number or recorded residential units. Progress billings will be made monthly by ENGINEER on forms supplied by DEVELOPER.

SECTION 4: .Revisions, variances or change orders needed to meet the requirements of the various jurisdictional agencies or good engineering practices, shall not be deemed extra work. Only revisions, variances of change orders requested by DEVELOPER after completion of the plans to the satisfaction of said jurisdictional agencies, legal descriptions not called for in the scope of the work, and plans for pumping stations, bridges and similar construction, shall be considered extra work. It shall be

FIG. 1-23. (continued)

the responsibility of ENGINEER to work with DEVELOPER and apprise
him of solutions to engineering problenms and the general details,
approach or technique to be used in preparing final improvement
plans. In any event, all orders for extra work shall be
authorized in writing by, DEVELOPER and acknowledged by ENGINEER.
With respect to extra work authorized by DEVELOPER as provided
above, ENGINEER shall be entitled to charge for his services the
following rates:

Office Technical Personnel $ _____ per hour
Three (3) Man Survey Party $_____ per hour
Two (2) Man Party $_____ per hour

SECTION 5: On August 1, 1984, and as appropriate thereafter,
the "per unit fee" as set forth in Section 2 and the rate for
"extra work" as set forth in Section 4 shall be increased by
eighty percent (%) of the percentage of wage and/or other
employee benefits granted surveyors under the Master Agreement
between the California Council of Civil Engineers and Land
Surveyors and the International Union of Operating Engineers Local
No. 12, AFL-CIO. These increases shall apply only to the
furnished work as of the date of increase.

SECTION 6: ENGINEER shall coordinate the planning of all
structures, utilities and other facilities which will affect the
tract and the subdivision development, including existing as well
as proposed facilities and regardless of whether plans for said
facilities are prepared by ENGINEER of third parties.

SECTION 7: All sketches, tracings, drawings, computations,
details and other original documents and plans are and shall
become and/or required to be filed with a governmental agency and
become public property, in which case ENGINEER is to furnish
duplicates to DEVELOPER upon its request.

SECTION 8: DEVELOPER reserves the right to terminate this
Agreement upon thirty (30) days written notice to ENGINEER. In
such event, for completed stages of the work, ENGINEER shall
receive that percentage of the fee set forth in the Schedule "A";
and in the case of partially completed stage of work, ENGINEER
shall receive an appropriately prorated percentage of the fee.

SECTION 9: DEVELOPER shall pay the cost of all fees, permits,
bond premium and title company charges not specifically covered by
the terms of this Agreement. All blueprinting and Xerox costs
will be included in the per unit cost as outlined in Schedule "A"
attached hereto.

FIG. 1-23. (continued) (Figure continued on p. 52.)

SECTION 10: ENGINEER and DEVELOPER each binds himself, his partners, executors and administrators of such other party in respect to all covenants of this Agreement. Neither party shall assign, sublet, or transfer his interest in this Agreement without the written consent of the other party hereto.

SECTION 11: Progress billings will be made monthly by the ENGINEER in accordance with rates set forth in Section 3 and Section 4. DEVELOPER will pay these billing within ten (10) days after receipt.

ENGINEER: DEVELOPER:

_____   _____

BY:_____   BY:_____

FIG. 1-23. (continued)

SCHEDULE "A"
TOWNHOUSE PROJECT

OFFICE
1. Quantity and Preliminary Cost Estimate $_____
2. Preparation of 20-scale Plot Plan $_____
3. Praparation of Composite and Grading Plan $_____
4. Preparation of 20-scale Master Utility Plan $_____
5. Preparation of 20-scale Water and Sewer Plan $_____
6. Preparation of Rough Grading Plan $_____
7. Preparation of Street Improvement Plan $_____
8. Preparation of final Quantity and Cost $_____
      Estimate
9. Blueprinting and Xeroxing $_____

                                  Subtotal $_____

FIELD
1. Rough Grade Staking $_____
2. Construction Corner Staking $_____
3. Curbs and Alley Cutter Staking $_____
4. Sewer Staking $_____
5. Undergroud Electrical Staking $_____
6. Storm Drain Staking $_____
7. Block Wall Staking $_____
8. Water Line Staking $_____

                                  Subtotal $_____

                                  GRANDTOTAL $_____

FIG. 1-24. Engineering consultant/developer agreement.

The JIA Management Group, Inc.

April 30, 1984

Dear

Based on our discussion of April 19, 1984, JIA submits the
following proposal to assist _____ in developing an Office
Automation/Business Data Service Strategy and Long-Range Plan.
JIA proposes to work with the established _____ Steering
Committee and its members in accomplishing the above goal.

The objectives of the plan are to:

* Identify and document the office automation and business
  data system needs of the _____ Group

* Determine the impact of the LOMM architecture on these
  needs, and identify the items that will be developed and
  supported by _____

* Develop a long-term office automation/business data
  services strategy and plan to support _____ current
  and future business requirements. This will include a
  strategy and plan for the following:

          - Business Applications
          - Office Automation Applications
          - Business Data Services Organization
          - Computer Hardware & Software

The plan will also identify personnel resource requirements,
costs, of the program, and the financial impact on _____
in the near-term, as well as over the long-term.

The approach recommended for the study was identified during our
previous discussions and JIA's presentation to you on April
18, 1984 (Attachment I). The key ingredient in that presentation
was a description of the proposed working relationship between
JIA and members of the Committee and their staff: JIA 's role
in the project is to assist the Committee in developing the future

1299 OCEAN AVENUE ● SUITE 333 ● SANTA MONICA, CALIFORNIA 90401 ● (213) 451-3041

FIG. 1-25. Data processing consultant agreement.

Page Two

strategy, not to develop a JIA recommended strategy for _____
which will then be presented to the Committee.

The implication of this approach is that the Committee members
must maintain significant involvement in all aspects of the study.
This does not necessarily imply a significant time commitment;
it does though require that the members provide the project with
guidance and ideas. A key element in this is the "three-day
strategy session" where the fundamental _____ office automa-
tion/business date services strategy will emerge and be agreed to.

Attachment II identifies study plan activities and schedule. We
estimate the effort to take approximately eleven weeks. Two and
a quarter JIA staff members will be involved in the study. The
schedule was developed assuming the availability of the Committee
members and their staff, including the possible involvement of a
new ___ hire who will be included as part of the study team.

The estimated cost for professional services is $ based
on the attached rate schedule (Attachment III). Expenses for
necessary travel, living and document preparation will be charged
as incurred. Invoices for professional services and expenses will
be billed at the end of each month. Payment is expected within
15 days after receipt of invoice.

We look forward to the opportunity to work with you and the Committee on this important engagement.

Sincerely,

Joseph E. Izzo
President

JEI/en

Attachments

Approved:_____

Date:_____

FIG. 1-25. (continued)

Zdonek ACCOUNTANCY CORPORATION

Date

Dear Mr. _____:

    This letter is to confirm the arrangements we discussed for you retaining our firm as the independent certified public accountants for The Company. As we informed you, our acceptance of this engagement is subject to the results of our firm's investigatory and approval procedures.

    We will examine the consolidated balance sheet of The Company, and subsidiaries as at December 31, 19__, and the related statements of income, retained earnings, and changes in financial position for the year then ended. Our examination will be in accordance with generally accepted auditing standards and will include such tests of the accounting records and such other auditing procedures as we consider necessary in the circumstances. Our examination will be for the purpose of expressing an opinion on the consolidated balance sheet as at December 31, 19__, and on the related statements of income, retained earnings, and changes in financial position for the year then ended. Since we were not the Company's auditors for the previous year, we will have to extend our procedures to satisy ourselves as to the opening balances for the current year, and the consistency of application of accounting principles and methods in the current year with those of the preceding year.

    We are not considering a detailed examination of all transactions nor do we expect that we will necessarily discover fraud, should any exist. We will, however, inform you of findings that appear to be unusual or abnormal.

    Your accounting department personnel will assist us to the extent practical in completing our engagement. They will provide us with the detailed trial balances and supporting schedules we deem necessary. A list of such schedules will be furnished you shortly after we begin the engagement.

25500 Hawthorne Blvd., Suite 2120, Torrance, CA 90505-6828 • (213) 378-9911 • (714) 638-2430

FIG. 1-26. CPA consultant agreement.

We will also be available to assist you, either in person or by telephone, with accounting, business or tax problems, and with planning. We will prepare the 19__ Federal and State income tax returns for The Company, and its subsidiaries.

Since this is our first examination of The Company, you requested that we review the Company's accounting system and procedures in detail and submit a separate report, including our evaluation, comments and recommendations. We will also review copies of the Company's income tax returns for the preceding three years and submit to you any comments we feel appropriate.

Fees for these services are at our standard rates and will be billed to you, plus out-of-pocket costs, monthly. These invoices are payable on presentation.

If this letter correctly expresses your understanding, please sign the enclosed copy where indicated and return it to us.

Thank you for the confidence you have placed in us by engaging us as your independent certified public accountants. We hope this proves to be the beginning of a long and mutually beneficial association.

Sincerely,

H. Zdonek

HZ:bjp

APPROVED:

By: _____

Date: _____

FIG. 1-26. (continued)

The JIA Management Group, Inc.

April 7, 1984

Senior Vice President, Finance
  and Administration

Dear

To evaluate the effectiveness of_____ MIS group, The JIA
Management Group, Inc. will peform the tasks listed below. The
objectives of the study are to:

* Assess the capability of the MIS group to support the
  business, both for the short-term and for the next several
  years. This is critical because of rapid business growth.

* Determine ways of improving communication between MIS
  and executive and user management to enhance the effectiveness of directing and controlling the MIS function at

Approach

After a brief orientation to acquaint study team members with the
operations and system environment, these activities will be undertaken:

* Interview the ten to twelve key users of MIS services in
  order to understand their perception of the quality of
  service being delivered.

* Conduct an MIS administration review to include planning
  and budgeting processes, project approval and priority
  assignmemt procedures, use of standards and product quality
  reviews, and management reporting.

* Conduct an MIS operations review to examine service
  delivery; problem identification, tracking, and resolution; production scheduling; library controls; production
  documentation and change control procedures; computer
  utilization, performance, capacity analysis and reporting.

1299 OCEAN AVENUE ● SUITE 333 ● SANTA MONICA, CALIFORNIA 90401 ● (213) 451-3041

FIG. 1-27. Agreement to conduct a study.

* <u>Perform communication network performance analysis</u>, including system availability, response time, network monitoring capability, growth plans, and use of available hardware and software tools to enhance network performance.

* <u>Perform a systems and programming review</u>, encompass staff capability, performance, turnover, and compensation; project management processes, and workload management; use of standard system development methods; use of productivity tools; and the quality of installed applications.

* <u>Assess factors which are causing difficulties</u> in MIS's ability to support the business and perform to expectations. These may include:

    - Communication with senior management
    - Management of the MIS resource
    - Organization of the MIS function
    - Staff quality and quantity
    - Equipment

* <u>Identify short-term actions</u> which should be taken to improve communication between MIS and executive and user management, and improve the quality of direction given to MIS.

* <u>Develop a one year plan</u> to address network performance, organization, procedures, and management control issues.

* <u>Prepare and present a management report</u> of findings and recommendations.

<u>Study Plan and Cost</u>

Project activities and their duration are shown on the following chart. The estimated charge for professional services is $
There will be additional charges for any travel, living, and document preparation. Charges will be billed monthly.

FIG. 1-27. (**continued**) (Figure continued on p. 60.)

Page Three

We look forward to working with _____ on this assignment.

                              Sincerely,

                              Joseph E. Izzo
                              President

JEI/bi

Approved:_____

Date: _____

FIG. 1-27. (continued)

The JIA Management Group, Inc.

December 7, 1984

Dear

Based on previous discussions with you and _____ the following
outlines our approach for assisting the _____ Company in
migrating the computing activities of the _____ Corporation into
the _____ computer center. The JIA Management Group will
accomplish this in two phases:

    Phase I   - Review Current Environment and Migration Plan

    Phase II - Direction of the West Coast Computer Facility in
                 Achieving the Migration Goals

This letter proposal only addresses Phase I. The approach and
degree of involvement if JIA related to Phase II will be determined at the conclusion of the Phase I activity. The review of
the current environment and migration plan will be designed to
accomplish the following objectives:

    * Gain an understanding of existing environments at both
       _____ and _____ computer centers

    * Review the overall migration plan to determine the role
       that _____ can best perform in achieving migration
       objectives

    * Identify areas of vulnerability that may exist related
       to the _____ computer center close-down or the
       migration process

    * Develop an implementation for Phase II

The accomplishment of the above will require review of current
activities, plans, and computer centers in _____ and in
_____. The cost of Phase I will not exceed $_____ in
professional services, and will be billed per the attached rate
schedule. Additional costs for travel, living and report preparation will be billed as accrued.

1299 OCEAN AVENUE ● SUITE 333 ● SANTA MONICA, CALIFORNIA 90401 ● (213) 451-3041

FIG. 1-28. Two phase agreement. (*Figure continued on p. 62.*)

61

Page Two

We look forward to working with you and the _____ Company on this important endeavor.

                              Sincerely,

                              Joseph E. Izzo
                              President

JEI/bj
Attachment

cc:

Accepted:

_____

_____

Date

FIG. 1-28. *(continued)*

                    JIA PROFESSIONAL SERVICES

                         RATE SCHEDULE

        Managing Partner $ - $ per hour

        Managing Principal $ - $ per hour

        Principal Consultant $ - $ per hour

        Consultant $ - $ per hour

FIG. 1-29. Legal consultant's agreement.

HUGH W. HOLBERT
A Professional Corporation
171 E. Thousand Oaks Boulevard
Suite 205
Thousand Oaks, California 91360
(805) 497-7088

FEE AGREEMENT

I understand that your fee for professional services is $ per hour and that your minimum fee for any service rendered, including each telephone conversation, is $

I understand that I will be billed monthly for services rendered and costs advanced on my behalf during the month. I understand that your statement must be paid in full within thirty (30) days of your billing date. In the event that I fail to pay the balance of my account in full when due, I further understand that I will incur a monthly administrative charge of 2% of the unpaid balance or $ whichever is greater, and that you reserve the right to withhold rendering additional services until my account is current.

I understand that a retainer or security for payment of your fees will be required prior to commencement of services beyond the initial interview where the services to be rendered are estimated to exceed $

I understand that you may find it necessary to increase your hourly rates and that any such increase will apply to my case. I will, however, be notified at least sixty (60) days in advance of such change and will, at that time, have the option to retain other counsel.

I understand that by signing this Agreement I accept direct personal responsibility for all legal fees and costs billed to my account regardless of the fact that a third party may ultimately agree or be ordered to pay some portion of said fees and costs. I agree to pay reasonable attorney's fees and costs in the event that litigation becomes necessary to collect any amounts pursuant to this Agreement.

I am aware that you have the right to associate any other attorney of your choice in the handling of my legal matter at your discretion. I further understand that your firm does not render advice pertaining to state or federal taxation and that you recommend only that such advice be obtained from a Certified Public Accountant.

I understand that any modification of this Agreement must be in writing.

DATED: _____

                                      SIGNATURE

FIG. 1-30. Hugh W. Holbert fee agreement.

Zdonek ACCOUNTANCY CORPORATION

Date

Dear Mr. _____:

This letter is to confirm our understanding of the terms and objectives of our engagement and the nature and limitations of the services we will provide.

We will perform the following services:

1. We will compile, from information you provide, the annual balance sheet and related statements of income, retained earnings, and changes in financial position of Company for the year 19 __. We will not audit or review the financial statements. Our report on the annual financial statements of Company is presently expected to read as follows:

   We have compiled the accompanying balance sheet of Company as of December 31, 19 __, and the related statements of income, retained earnings, and changes in financial position for the year then ended, in accordance with standards established by the American Institute of Certified Public Accountants.

   A compilation is limited to presenting in the form of financial statements information that is the representation of management. We have not audited or reviewed the accompanying financial statements and, accordingly, do not express an opinion or any other form of assurance on them.

25500 Hawthorne Blvd., Suite 2120, Torrance, CA 90505-6828 • (213) 378-9911 • (714) 638-2430

FIG. 1-31. Second CPA consulting agreement.

Our engagement cannot be relied upon to disclose errors, irregularities, or illegal acts, including fraud or defalcations, that may exist; however, we will inform you of any such matters that come to our attention.

Our fees for these services will be computed at our standard hourly rates. Billings will be submitted monthly and are payable when due.

We would be pleased to discuss this letter with you at any time. If the foregoing is in accordance with your understanding, please sign the copy of this letter in the space provided and return it to us.

Sincerely,

H. Zdonek

HZ:bjp

APPROVED:

Company

_____
President

_____
Date

FIG. 1-31. (continued)

NEW CLIENT INFORMATION

Name of Client: _____

Home Address: (Street) _____

                    (City) _____ (Zip) _____ Own__ Rent__

Soc. Sec. # _____ Driver's License # _____

Phone: Residence (   ) _____ Business (   ) _____

Occupation: _____

Employer: _____

Work Address: (Street) _____

                    (City) _____ (Zip) _____

Name of Spouse: _____

Home Address: (Street) _____

                    (City) _____ (Zip) _____

Phone: Residence (   ) _____ Business (   ) _____

Occupation: _____

Employer: _____

Work Address: (Street) _____

                    (City) _____ (Zip) _____

For Dissolutions The Following Information Is Required:

Date of Marriage: _____ Date of Separation: _____

Place of Marriage: (City) _____ (State) _____

Children:

Name	Sex	Date of Birth
_____	_____	_____
_____	_____	_____
_____	_____	_____
_____	_____	_____

FIG. 1-32. New client information form.

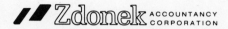
Zdonek ACCOUNTANCY CORPORATION

Date

Dear Mr._____ :

This letter will confirm our understanding of the nature and limitations of the accounting and review services we are to render to **The Corporation** with your needs as previously discussed.

Our engagement will consist of the following services:

1) We will review the balance sheet of **The Corporation** as of June 30, 19__ and the related statements of income, retained earnings, and changes in financial position for the year then ended, in accordance with standards established by the American Institute of Certified Public Accountants. We will not perform an audit of such financial statements, the objective of which is the expression of an opinion regarding the financial statements taken as a whole and, accordingly, we will not express such an opinion on them. Our report on the financial statements is presently expected to read as follows:

> We have reviewed the accompanying balance sheet of **The Corporation** as of June 30, 19__, and the related statements of income, retained earnings, and changes in

25500 Hawthorne Blvd., Suite 2120, Torrance, CA 90505-6828 • (213) 378-9911 • (714) 638-2430

FIG. 1-33. Third CPA consulting form. *(Figure continued on p. 68.)*

financial position for the year then ended,
in accordance with standards established
by the American Institute of Certified
Public Accountants. All information
included in these financial statements
is the representation of the management
of **The Corporation**

A review consists principally of inquiries
of company personnel and analytical
procedures applied to financial data. It
is substantially less in scope than an
examination in accordance with generally
accepted auditing standards, the objective
of which is the expression of an opinion
regarding the financial statements taken as
a whole. Accordingly, we do not express such
opinion.

Based on our review, we are not aware of any
material modifications that should be made
to the accompanying financial statements in
order for them to be in conformity with
generally accepted accounting principles.

If, for any reason, we are unable to complete our
review of your financial statements, we will not
issue a report on such statements as a result of
this engagement.

2. We will provide your chief accountant with such
consultation on accounting matters as he may require
in adjusting and closing the books of account and in
drafting financial statements for our review. Your
chief accountant also will provide us with a detailed
trial balance and any supporting schedules we require.

3. We will also prepare the federal and California
income tax returns for **The Corporation** for
the fiscal year ended June 30, 19___.

Our engagement cannot be relied upon to disclose errors,
irregularities, or illegal acts, including fraud or
defalcations, that may exist. However, we will inform you
of any such matters that come to our attention.

FIG. 1-33. *(continued)*

Our fees for these services will be based on our regular hourly rates and we will bill you monthly as work progresses. It is understood that the fee for our services will not exceed $0,000. Our invoices are due and payable upon presentation.

If these arrangements meet with your understanding and approval, please sign the duplicate copy of this letter in the space provided and return it to us.

Yours very truly,

H. Zdonek

HZ:lm

Encls. a/s

APPROVED:

THE CORPORATION

By:_____

Date:_____

FIG. 1-33. (continued)

CHAPTER 2

SETTING FEES AND BILLING TECHNIQUES

Consulting is an intangible service.

In contrast to a grocery store, parts house, or automobile dealer, when a customer purchases services from a consultant, he or she is buying a promise to deliver, not a tangible piece of goods.

The purchaser often pays a portion (or all) of the fee in advance for something he or she will not receive for months. Therefore, establishing prices, perceiving the value of your services, and collecting must take into account your desired profit, as well as the psychology of the customer.

Consumers have the ability to shop and compare when it comes to nonservice goods. For example, the price of a bag of C&H sugar can be easily compared by shoppers, and they know immediately if it is overpriced. There is no question when it comes to quality, either. The bag of C&H at one store has the same content as a bag of C&H at another store.

But what about the consultant? There is no guarantee of a fair price or quality service when the customer gives you the contract. That is why consulting involves psychology as well as performance when it comes to pricing, collecting, and selling.

It is a mistake to quote a fee to a prospective client without explaining how you came up with the figure. Remember, they are not buying a bag of corn, they are purchasing service—a bag of air. So, how do you justify the fee?

Let's say a client is leaning toward your services, but has a question: "What will it cost me?" Before answering, think of the things you should know about your costs and how to price. The pricing checklist which follows will give you some ideas.

Pricing Procedure Checklist

1. How long will the job take?
2. Can I do the job myself, or will it take additional help? If I do it myself, how many hours of my time will it take?

3. If it takes additional help, how many people will it take?

4. How much will I have to pay each person who assists on the job?

5. Will there be expenses? If so, should the client approve all of them, or just those expenses over a certain amount?

6. Should I allow extra hours for the unexpected? (Yes)

7. How will this job fit into my overhead calculations and profit-making goals? (In other words, make sure your pricing takes into account the overhead the job will incur, and the profit you want to make when it is completed.)

After considering the seven steps in the pricing checklist, you may come up with a total of 100 hours to do the job. If, for instance, it costs you $3000 in overhead and help, and you intend to make $3000, the fee would be $6000. Divided by 100 hours, you get $60 an hour.

It is advisable to outline the job for the client. Explain that you estimate it will take X amount of hours for interviewing and analyzing the results. X amount of hours may be needed for reinterviewing. You expect to spend X amount of hours compiling a summary of the problem, analyzing it, and proposing a solution. You may also require X amount of hours to implement the plan once the client accepts the proposal.

These areas should be broken down so the client does not believe everything "was simply pulled out of the air." The consultant should explain his or her past experience with similar clients and problems, and the time these problems took. Consulting is intangible, but the client should feel that the fees and costs were put together in a tangible, logical manner.

By breaking the total job into understandable units, the time and the fee becomes reasonable and acceptable (unless, of course, the client does not want to pay more than $30 an hour for consulting services!).

The mistake some consultants make when asked how much their fee will be, is to say, "Well, I estimate it will take 100 hours, and at $60 an hour that means $6000." This leaves the client uneasy. He or she has questions. How did you arrive at the 100 hours? How do you see tackling the job? Are you sure it is 100? Isn't that an inordinate amount of hours to complete a simple job such as this one? Is the $6000 a figure you had in your head all along, and you are using 100 hours to justify it?

Everyone has a difficult time seeing the entire picture. Imagine an audience viewing a motion picture before it was edited, or a play before it reached the dress rehearsal stage. People—clients—have a difficult time conceptualizing.

Without additional information, 100 hours of work does not give the client insight into what is involved. The burden rests with the consultant to provide that insight, and justify the hours and fees.

If the consultant does not carefully detail the reasons for the fee, the relationship may start on the wrong foot, and go downhill from there. Always make sure to explain your fee. Even if you are a consultant who works on a retainer basis ($2000 a month), make sure you break that down for the client so they can see approximately how many hours of your time they are getting and for what purpose.

If a client is sold on your service, he or she does not usually object to the price, unless it is unaffordable or the fee unexplained. Problems develop when consultants do a poor job of communicating what they are going to do, and how they are going to do it.

This brings us to another point—communicating the obvious. If you are an engineering consultant, the work you do is second nature to you, but it may be a mystery to the client. The client may lack an engineering background. Thus you should always explain the procedure. Do not take anything for granted, especially that the client knows how you are going to get the job done.

Another point: Do not make it seem simple!

Certainly, the job may be simple to you. After all, if you are doing a marketing job for a company, marketing is your business. Your experience is in that field. You know it backwards and forwards. It is easy for you because *you* know the steps. But it is not easy for the client. If it were, they would never have called you in to do it in the first place.

Whatever you do, never tell the client, "It's a piece of cake . . . it is simple." That type of statement will make the client question whether he should be paying you *any* fee. So do not comment on the ease of the job.

There is, of course, nothing wrong with your saying the job may be difficult, but you have confidence in your ability and background to see it through. You have worked on similar problems before. Clients want to feel they are getting their money's worth. If they believe the job too easy, they will question whether or not they should retain your services.

Psychology—an important part of business, and every consultant should keep this in mind. Remember, you must utilize these measures because of the intangible nature of consulting. This would not be the case if you were selling soup or sugar. The following checklist will assist you in communicating your services to your client.

Six Steps in Communicating Fees to Clients

1. Communicate the obvious. Do not assume the client knows anything about the job or what getting it done entails. Remember, the client has called you—the consultant—in for your skills.

2. Explain everything, regardless of how simple and mundane it may seem to you.

3. Never announce to the client that the job is easy. This may lead the client to believe the fee should be low, too.

4. Display confidence in your ability to do the job. Clients hire you for your expertise. If you do not appear confident, if you hold back, hesitate, and wonder about your ability to do the job, the client will detect the attitude and despite your ability, you may lose the contract. Attitude is critical.

5. Cite other similar jobs which you have done that have turned out well. Make the comparison whenever possible.

6. Explain your fees and rates carefully. Do not assume the client understands how you arrive at your rates. Take time to walk the client through your firm's procedures, so he or she understands how time consuming the project may be.

How much should a consultant make? Successful consultants generate fees which earn them gross profits of 10–50 percent (before taxes). In all of these cases, the profit is after the consultant has paid himself or herself a salary, and taken certain fringe benefits (i.e., auto, insurance, entertainment).

There are numerous ways to set fees in order to earn the desired gross profit. Initially you may make mistakes. You may under- or overestimate the number of hours it takes to complete a task. There are techniques, however, that make pricing easier.

MARKET AVERAGE BILLING PROCEDURE

With this procedure, you simply survey competitors, find out their fees, and ask your clients for the same.

1. To determine the going rate, make a few telephone calls. For example, if you are an attorney, call a few other attorneys and ask about their hourly rates. How much do they charge?

2. If you find the rates average $75 per hour, with a low of $60 and a high of $90, you can set your fees accordingly.

3. Hourly fees can be divided into minutes and minimums. Suppose you spend 60 seconds on the telephone with a client. Do you (if your billing rate is $60 an hour) charge him $1? Some consultants automatically charge a minimum, meaning they will charge 15 minutes—or $15—whether they spend 60 seconds or 5 minutes on the telephone. Make this decision.

Some consultants do not charge if the client calls and has a question they can answer in a minute or two. This involves judgment. The client may be calling you to clarify some work or instructions you left. Should you charge him for work he has already paid for? The answer is obvious. Judgment is essential when it comes to billing.

Some consultants have a practice of not charging if a client calls and questions them about a past issue, one that has already been billed. The breaking point, for these consultants, comes if the client brings up a new issue or problem. Then the meter starts ticking again.

If a current or potential client calls and asks about fees for a particular job (and outlines some of the job), do you charge the person? Obviously you cannot charge the questioner if he or she is not a client. If he or she becomes a client, the time you spent initially on the telephone can be built into the overall fee. However, it is not sound business practice to bill a potential client for business you have not been given, unless the prospect clearly understands you have an initial consultation fee for nonclients.

There is, of course, the problem of brain-picking. What do you do if a potential client calls and tries to get all the answers during the conversation? Once again, judgment is important. You can allow the client 5 or even 10 minutes, however, should it go beyond that period businesspeople understand the concept of "minimum compensation."

Many consultants avoid this by supplying clients with telephone or office consulting guidelines. The outline explains that your services (e.g., on the telephone) are free for the first 5 (or 10) minutes. After that there is a fee. The same rules apply to office visits.

Regardless of your policies, establishing a minimum is a good practice. It deters clients from engaging in frivolous telephone conversations, or wasted visits to your office. They know it costs when they call, and they will have their thoughts and questions organized when they make the call. This saves you time and the client money. Equally as important, it keeps a business relationship between you and the client, which is the foundation of a solid consulting practice. You must reinforce the fact that it is your skill, knowledge, and experience the client is paying for, and one way to do it is to show how valuable your time happens to be.

The following checklist can be used as a guide for determining fees—hourly, weekly, and monthly.

14-Point Market Average Checklist

1. Call competitors to determine hourly, daily rates

2. Make enough calls to get an accurate cross section

3. Determine where on the rate scale you want to be—high, low, or average

4. Break the rates into hourly fees

5. Break the rates into minutes

6. Develop a rough outline of potential rates

7. Multiply the hourly rates by the number of workable hours in a month (160)

8. Subtract a percentage of the workable hours to allow for marketing or sales activities which are not compensated by the client. Marketing hours for a new business can total 20 percent (32 hours) or more per month

9. Subtract the marketing and get new hourly base (128)

10. Determine your monthly gross with this method

11. Determine your monthly overhead (see Typical Overhead Items chart later in chapter)

12. Determine the profit (before taxes) you want to make

13. Does the monthly gross allow for the profit and overhead you desire?

14. If the monthly gross is too low, you must either readjust your salary, cut overhead, or look at the fee structure once again.

Another billing question is, "Do you charge for traveling time?" A good rule is charge for traveling when you have to travel out of town on behalf of the client. If there is out-of-town travel, make sure it is included in the cost of the consulting contract, and not presented to the client as a billing afterthought.

If a consultant drives from his or her office to the client, traveling time is usually not included. However, if you find yourself spending too many hours traveling, a portion of the traveling time should be included in the billing. Decisions about traveling time should be made before the contract is finalized.

You will not, of course, be able to charge by the hour or job in every consulting field. Some consultants (money managers, financial consultants) are compensated on the basis of the earnings they produce for clients. (See Figure 2-2 for an understanding of how money managers and some financial consultants derive their income.) There are sophisticated techniques that consultants should examine before deciding on how to set their rates.

OVERHEAD PLUS PROFIT BILLING TECHNIQUE

With this method, consultants determine their (yearly) overhead and desired profit. This is divided into (yearly) workable hours and hourly rates are established.

For example, if your overhead is $1500 per month, and you want to gross $2500 per month after overhead, your total needs are $4000 per month. If you want to *take home* $2500, the amount will be higher since you will have to include tax.

Overhead Item Checklist

1. Rent
2. Utilities (if not included in rent)
3. Cleaning service (if not included in rent)
4. Telephone
5. Postage
6. Equipment rental/leases
7. Insurance/worker's compensation
8. Auto (if company paying for it)
9. Letterhead/stationery
10. Secretary/other employees
11. Taxes (social security, disability, etc.)

DETERMINING HOURLY RATES THROUGH OVERHEAD/PROFIT METHOD

There are approximately four working weeks in a month, or 160 hours (40 hours per week). One hundred sixty divided into $4000 means your hourly rate should be $25 in order to cover overhead and attain the desired profit.

$$40 \times 4 = 160 \text{ (total working hours per month)}$$
$$160 \text{ divided into } \$4000 = \$25 \text{ per hour, your consulting rate}$$

There are, however, other considerations. Not *all* working time will produce income from clients. A portion may be spent on marketing (selling) services or bookkeeping. Some consultants subtract these hours from the 160, and increase their hourly rate to compensate for it. As an example, suppose you spend 10 percent of your time marketing your services. That means four hours a week (16 hours a month) will be nonincome producing. The 16 should come off of the 160. Now you have 144 hours available for clients. Your hourly rate (144 divided into $4000) should be closer to $28 to meet your goals.

$$40 \times 4 = 160 \text{ hours per month}$$
10 percent of hours (16) nonincome producing, used for marketing
144 hours to be billed during month
144 divided into $4000 = $28 per hour, your billing rate

With this method you would include employee salaries (as well as fringe benefits and taxes) as part of your overhead. Figure 2-1 will help you determine your fees using this method.

BILLING WITH HOURLY MULTIPLIER

Some consultants have found it profitable to use a multiplier for every hour of work they (or their employees) put in with a client.

1. Typically, one-third of the multiplier is designed to cover the employee's (or your) salary; one-third overhead and one-third profit.
2. If an employee makes $20,000 a year (or $9.60 per hour based on 2080 workable hours—52 × 40—per year), you would utilize a multiplier of about three to cover the salary, overhead, and profit. That means the employee's hourly billing rate would be $28.80.
   The multiplier is an excellent way to determine how much the consultant/ owner should be billing for his or her time. Frequently, consultants forget that their time should be marked up in order to cover overhead and profit. Even if the consultant is operating alone, the multiplier is an advantageous method.
3. Utilizing this formula, consulting firms will usually show a profit of around 20 percent (before taxes). Some consultants will increase the multiplier. However, if you use this method, the multiplier should not exceed four. If you find you need a higher multiplier, your costs and profit goals should be reexamined.

Hours Worked per month

	$25	$30	$40	$50	$60	$75	$100
160	$4000	$4800	$6400	$8000	$9600	$12000	$16000
150	$3750	$4500	$6000	$7500	$9000	$11250	$15000
140	$3500	$4200	$5600	$7000	$8400	$10500	$14000
130	$3250	$3900	$5200	$6000	$7800	$9750	$13000
120	$3000	$3600	$4800	$5500	$7200	$9000	$12000
110	$2750	$3300	$4200	$5000	$6600	$8250	$11000

Rate / Hour

FIG. 2-1. Overhead plus profit chart.

The differences in professions can be exhibited through this multiplier. A consultant seldom goes beyond a multiplier of four, but a manufacturing firm uses five when it determines the ultimate price of its product (to consumers or the ultimate buyer in the chain). At the same time, the manufacturer will not be as profitable as the consultant.

MULTIPLIER METHOD OF BILLING

The following multiplier chart gives you an idea of how an hourly wage and yearly wage relate to a billing rate.

Salary/Wage	Hourly Rate	×	Multiplier	Hourly Billing Rate
$20,000	9.60	×	3	28.80
$30,000	14.42	×	3	43.27
$40,000	19.23	×	3	57.69
$50,000	24.03	×	3	72.11
$60,000	28.85	×	3	86.54
$70,000	33.65	×	3	100.96
$80,000	38.46	×	3	115.38

It is easy to see why consultants usually charge no less than $75 an hour for their time, and a number charge between $100 and $300 an hour. In order to cover overhead and other expenses, and gross $50,000 a year, the typical consultant has to be in that range.

The consultant has to decide how much he or she wants to make. What are your financial goals?

PERCENTAGE COMPENSATION

Some consultants are compensated strictly on the basis of the growth they can show clients. This is particularly true of money managers, who earn their income by handling and investing portfolios.

Do not confuse money managers with financial consultants who generate their income from the commissions they earn when trading stocks, bonds, and so forth in a client's portfolio.

Money managers—and those who operate on a percentage compensation—must consider their overhead when determining if the percentage they are making is sufficient. Consult Figure 2-2 to determine how this type of compensation is structured.

PERFORMANCE BASED COMPENSATION

A relatively new type of nonfee structure is being used by marketing and other consultants who offer services that relate to increases in sales and/or productivity, or decreases in costs and/or overhead.

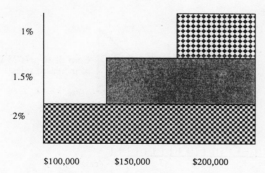

FIG. 2-2. Percentage compensation.

With this technique, the client does not pay any fee unless the company's sales (or savings) rise above a certain level. For example, let's say you are a marketing consultant hired by XYZ Company. XYZ's sales have grown annually at a rate of 10 percent. The company wants to accelerate that growth. The company hires your firm, and signs an agreement that stipulates you will not be paid any fees unless XYZ's growth *exceeds* 10 percent during the year. If, however, XYZ goes beyond that 10 percent (hopefully through your efforts), you will be compensated and given 25 percent of the *increased* profits.

In most cases, the companies pay the costs of the program (i.e., mailings, ad placements), but some consultants are even willing to pay these hard costs as part of the program. In return, they get anywhere from 50–70 percent of the increased profits.

This is an excellent arrangement for clients who may not have the capital required for a consultant's program. It could apply to consultants working in areas ranging from marketing (helping a company add a new product to its line, or increase the sales of an existing line) and personnel (reducing the cost of recruiting), to management (reducing costs of manufacturing or increasing productivity) to engineering (increase in productivity).

There are, however, risks for the consultant. If he or she puts in the effort but does not manage to exceed management's goals, there is no compensation. Time and energy have been expended with no profit.

From the company's standpoint, if a consultant is extremely successful and goes far beyond a firm's goals, management may begin to resent the huge percentage fees that are being paid.

VENTURE MARKETING/CONSULTING COMPENSATION

Before embarking on one of these ventures, a consultant must be sold on the potential of success. "Venture marketing" or "venture consulting" as it is called should not be taken lightly.

Figure 2-3 and the Venture Marketing Percentages Chart will give you an idea of the profit potential and structure of the arrangement.

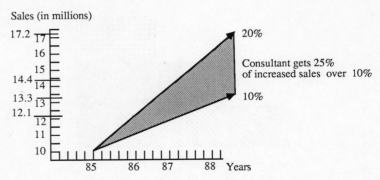

FIG. 2-3. Performance based compensation.

Venture Marketing Percentages

Current Sales (in $ millions)	Yearly Growth Average (%)	Expected Increase	Actual Increase	Increase Difference	25% Fee
100	10	10	14	4	$1 million
125	5	6.2	9	2.8	$700,000
125	3	3.75	4.75	1	$250,000
200	3	6	8	2	$500,000

Profitable? The venture marketing technique can be extremely rewarding to consulting firms willing to take the risk. Once again, this procedure does not just work with an increase in sales. It could be an increase in productivity; a decrease in absenteeism; a lowering of costs in the personnel area; or a more efficient operation in engineering. There are a host of possibilities.

There are, of course, many elements that go into setting fees. A consultant should carefully analyze costs and profit-making goals before deciding which fee structure he or she will use. The following checklist summarizes costs and billing methods.

Key Points in Setting Monthly Fees

1. Determine overhead
    a. Rent
    b. Telephone, utilities
    c. Office supplies
    d. Equipment leases
    e. Salaries, including your own
    f. Taxes
    g. Entertainment
    h. Automobile
    i. Insurance
    j. Uniforms, clothing

2. Call competitors and check rates

   a. Ascertain highs and lows

3. Determine desired profit

4. Decide on billing method

   a. Overhead plus profit

      i.   Decide on desired profit and add to overhead

      ii. Determine number of working hours in month

      iii. Subtract marketing hours from working hours

      iv. Divide net working hours into overhead and profit for hour rate

   b. Employee and hourly multiplier

      i.   Determine employee yearly wages, including your own

      ii. Determine employee hourly wages, including your own

      iii. Multiply by three to cover salary, overhead, profit

   c. Percentage compensation (for those in financial management)

      i.   Determine amount of portfolio over $200,000

      ii. Charge 1 percent management fee for amount over this figure

      iii. Charge 1.5 percent fee for funds between $150,000–200,000

      iv. Charge 2 percent fee for funds up to $150,000

   d. Performance based compensation

      i.   Determine annual growth rate of company sales

      ii. Determine if firm will pay costs of marketing program

          A. If company pays costs, compensation 25 percent of profits over annual growth rate

          B. If company does not pay costs, compensation of 50 percent of profits over annual growth rate

   e. Monthly retainer

      i.   Consultant should survey competition for fee range

      ii. Include overhead and desired profit

      iii. Set rates, and check to ensure they are competitive

5. Check competitive rates once more to ensure your rates are structured correctly

TIME SHEETS AND OTHER RECORDS

Relationships between clients and consultants change. Often, consultants find themselves taking on additional duties for the client, and spending more time than initially planned on the account. In some cases, consultants find themselves actually losing money on an account because they either expanded their services or underestimated the time involved.

For this reason, client time sheets are important. Every consultant should monitor the amount of time they and their staff spend on an account. Figures 2-4 and 2-5 are sample time sheets that will help.

```
                                    TIME SHEET
   Project Name:  _____      Dates From_____  To_____

   ****************************************************************************************
   |  Hours  |  Purpose  |  Hours  |  Purpose  |  Hours  |  Purpose  |  Total Hours  |
```

FIG. 2-4. Time sheet for tracking hours.

There are several other ways of tracking the time you put in for a client. One of the best tracking methods is shown in Figure 2-6, a time sheet which divides the time spent on a client into categories. This type of time sheet helps you determine if you are spending too much time in any one area. The code classifications, Figure 2-6, can be transferred to a master control sheet which summarizes both the purpose and time spent.

What can you do if you suddenly find yourself in a position where the account is not profitable? First, analyze why the account is no longer profitable. Is it the result of poor judgment when you bid the account? Is it the result of additional duties your firm has acquired? Is it the result of additional requirements the client has added since you started?

Determine the cause of the time problem. Examine the job and ask yourself, "Is there any way we can cut back without damaging the quality of the service we provide?" Are subordinates spending too much time at the client's place of business? Can some jobs be done on the telephone instead of with a personal visit?

Is it your fault or the client's that too much time is involved?

That is an important question. If it is the client who has put more demands on the firm, it is up to the consultant to document those additional requirements, and approach the client. The consultant should explain how the job started, what was initially promised, and how much additional time is being spent because of added responsibilities.

This is not a confrontation between client and consultant. It should be a businesslike discussion in which the consultant explains how things have

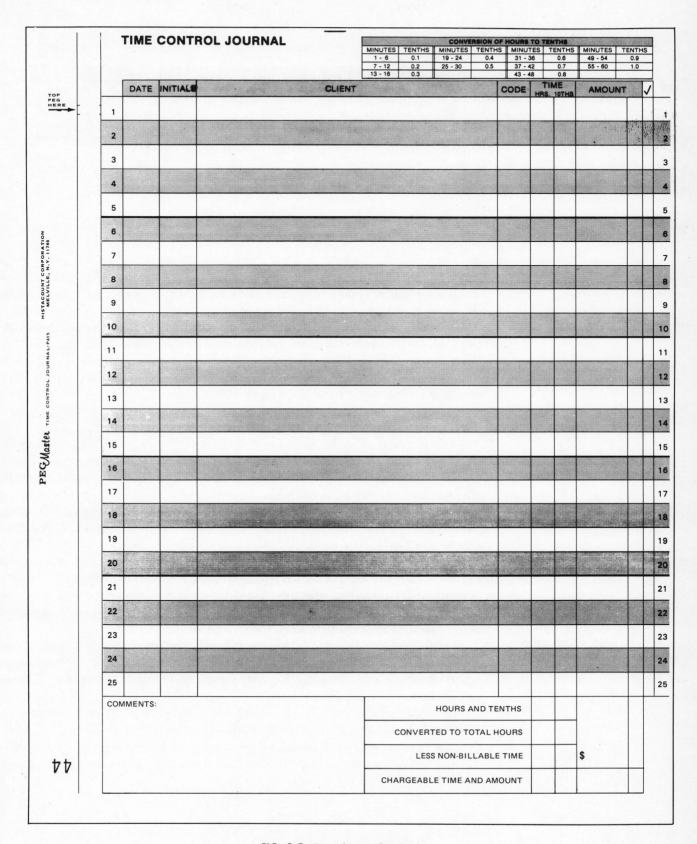

FIG. 2-5. Time sheet with activities.

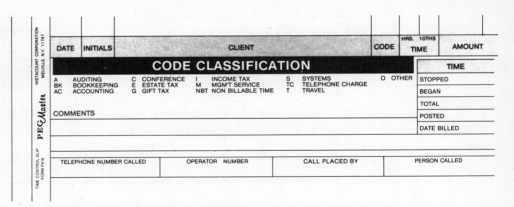

FIG. 2-6. Master time control sheet.

changed, and asks for a readjustment of the contract terms. If you have done a thorough job of researching, and have an accurate analysis which you can show the client, there will be little problem.

But if you approach the client without backup and ask for a raise, there can be problems. Consultants must justify a raise in their fees. If you are spending the time and doing the job, the client will know it (especially if you have communicated with him or her during the course of the job) and will usually consider an increased fee without any difficulty.

Aside from time sheets you should keep on accounts, there are numerous forms you will find helpful in running your business.

With International Revenue Service (IRS) rulings and tax laws changing almost daily, it is important to keep an accurate record of your expenses. There should be a business log similar to Figure 2-7. This enables you to separate client expenses from personal ones.

Itemize your expenses and keep receipts. File these logs monthly or more often if needed. Talk to your accountant about which items should be tracked and to what extent.

Car mileage and automotive-related expenses should be tracked as well (see Figure 2-7). If the auto is owned by the company, not all expenses may be 100 percent deductible. For example, the IRS presently asks businesspeople to subtract that portion of the auto's expense that was acquired from personal use. Thus it is important to keep the two separate.

The mileage logs shown in Figure 2-8 will give you an idea of how these forms should be structured and entered. Notice personal use of the auto is listed whenever applicable. Each month you should compile the mileage figures and enter them in the Recap form.

The next form, Figure 2-9, is for telephone tracking. It enables the consultant to accurately log long distance calls undertaken on behalf of the client. Later, this log is matched to the actual telephone bill and submitted to the client.

Chapter 12 provides a more in-depth analysis of record keeping.

SUMMARY OF EXPENSES

WEEK ENDING _____

ACCT. NO.	ACCOUNT	TOTAL THIS WEEK		TOTAL LAST WEEK		TOTAL TO DATE	
1	BREAKFAST						
2	LUNCH						
3	DINNER						
4	HOTEL OR MOTEL						
5	TRANSPORTATION: PLANE						
6	RAILROAD						
7	TAXI OR BUS						
8	AUTO RENTAL, ETC.						
9	BAGGAGE CHARGES						
10	ENTERTAINMENT						
11	GIFTS						
12	TIPS						
13	TELEPHONE						
14	TOLLS						
15	POSTAGE						
16	AUTO EXPENSES: GAS, OIL, LUBRICATION, ETC.						
17	REPAIRS						
18	TIRES, SUPPLIES, ETC.						
19	PARKING						
20	WASHING						
21	INSURANCE						
22	.................MILES @ c						
23	OFFICE EXPENSE						
24	TRADE SHOWS						
25	MISCELLANEOUS						
26							
27							
28							
29							
30							
	TOTALS						
	LESS CREDIT CARD (EMPLOYER)						
	BALANCE						

FIG. 2-7. Monthly recap for log. (*Figure continued on p. 86.*)

RECORD OF SUBSTANTIATION

ELEMENTS REQUIRED BY LAW: (a) date; (b) item; (c) place; (d) business purpose; (e) name and business relationship of persons entertained; (f) amount.

(a) DATE	(b) ITEM	(c) PLACE	(d) and (e)	ACCT. NO.	(f) AMOUNT	
	Optional (Miles — End of week					
	Mileage { Miles — Beginning of week					
	Method (Miles traveled	at	¢			
				TOTAL		

FIG. 2.7. (continued)

How to Complete the Monthly Car

The 1985 Business Expense Log contains two basic sets of records for substantiation purposes. These records are to be completed on a monthly basis and are for (1) car mileage and operating expenses and (2) other business expenses. Entries are to be made in these records at or near the time of the event or usage of the car occurred. Two yearly recap sheets are provided at the back of the Log to post totals from the monthly records. A reimbursement record and a chart for computing the tax basis of a car are also located at the back of the Log.

Entries concerning the use of a car are made in the "Destination—Purpose of Trip—Contact" column. A single entry generally must be made for each use of a car in this column. Round trips can be accounted

Month: ___Jan___, 19

Date	Destination—Purpose of Trip—Contact	Odometer Begin	Odometer End
1/3	Home to office	8,653	8,660
1/3	ABC Corp. – Sales call to Mr. Smith, V. P.	8,660	8,693
1/3	Brooks & Bell Stock Brokers investment consultation	8,693	8,703
1/3	Home	8,703	8,707
1/29	Dr. Smith appointment	9,405	9,414
TOTALS	(Post to Car Recap at back)		

Note: Retain receipts for all lodging. Retain receipts for transportation and single expenditures of $25 or more.

19 RECAP OF CAR MILEAGE & EXPENSES

Mo.	Mileage Breakdown Business	Invest.	Personal	Expenses Gas, Oil, Lube	Parking —Tolls	Other
JAN						
FEB						
MAR						
APR						
MAY						
JUN						
JUL						
AUG						
SEP						
OCT						
NOV						
DEC						
Totals						

Total car expenses $ _____

FIG. 2-8. Car mileage operating expense log.

Car Mileage & Operating Expenses

Date	Destination—Purpose of Trip—Contact	Odometer Begin	Odometer End	Business	Investment	Personal	Gas, Oil, Lube	Parking—Tolls	Other	Describe
1/17	OFFICE to HOME	37842	37847			5				
1/18	HOME TO OFFICE	37847	37852			5				
1/18	OFFICE TO HOME	37852	37857			5				
1/21	HOME to OFFICE	-857	-862			5				
1/21	OFFICE TO PARK del ANO (WMA- newsletter/Back	37862	37921							
1/21	YMCA for MKTG meeting	37921	37940							
1/21	OFFICE to Home	37940	37945			5				
1/22	Home To OFFICE	37945	37950			5				
1/22	OFFICE TO PACIFIC Biz BANK	37950	37965							
1/22	OFFICE To Home	37965	37970			5				
1/23	Home to OFFICE	37970	37975			5				
1/23	Entrepreneur - meeting w/ Wellington-PR plan	37975	38041							
1/23	OFFICE - Home	38041	38046			5				
1/24	Anaheim - NATURAL FOOD EXPO Booth	38046	38126							
1/24	Anaheim - office	38126	38166							
1/25	Anaheim Con. Center - EXPO	38166	38204							
1/25	Anaheim - SAN Diego Darryl Chettayar- G-1	38204	38450							
1/26	SAN Diego - Anaheim - EXPO	38450	38550							
1/28	Home To WORK	38550	38555			5				
1/28	WORK To Home	38555	38560			5				
1/29	Home To WORK	38560	38565			5				
1/29	WORK TO Home	38565	38570			5				
1/30	Home TO WORK	38570	38575			5				
TOTALS	(Post to Car Recap at back)									

Note: Retain receipts for all lodging. Retain receipts for transportation and single expenditures of $25 or more.

Total reimbursements for month $_____

FIG. 2-9. Sample telephone record.

TELEPHONE CALL

_____
            Place Called

_____
(Area Code)   Telephone No.

_____
          Person Called

CHARGE TO:

_____
            Company

_____   _____
      Date   Initials

TELEPHONE CALL

_____
            Place Called

_____
(Area Code)   Telephone No.

_____
          Person Called

CHARGE TO:

_____
            Company

_____   _____
      Date   Initials

TELEPHONE CALL

_____
            Place Called

_____
(Area Code)   Telephone No.

_____
          Person Called

CHARGE TO:

_____
            Company

_____   _____
      Date   Initials

TELEPHONE CALL

_____
            Place Called

_____
(Area Code)   Telephone No.

_____
          Person Called

CHARGE TO:

_____
            Company

_____   _____
      Date   Initials

FIG. 2-9. (continued)

CHAPTER 3

STRUCTURING BROCHURES

A brochure alone does not close sales, but it portrays a definite image of the consultant's company. Usually, it is the first impression a prospective client gets. Thus the way it looks is as important as what it says.

Brochures can take many shapes. They may be 8½ inches × 11 inches, 11 inches × 14 inches, and so on. The configuration is not nearly as critical as the "appearance" and "appeal." Appearance refers to the type of stock, color, and quality of the brochure. Appeal refers to the message—it should always address the client's *needs*. (People buy things because they have needs, and the products and services that are sold promise to answer those needs.)

Although written content should focus on a client's needs, it should also give the prospective client:

1. An idea as to how your company operates
2. The type of problems, situations, and so forth you are prepared to handle
3. Any specialties you might offer
4. Your background/qualifications

Avoid stating fees in your brochure. Fees allow prospects to prejudge services and make a decision before they ever meet you. In addition, listing fees will outdate your brochure within a short time.

INITIAL STEPS

There are two ways to put together a brochure. One requires a large budget, the other allows the consultant to do most of the work, negotiate prices, and save money.

In the former case, you contract services, and you may deal with as many as five people (artist/designer, printer, writer, photographer, and lithographer). In the latter, you may only have to deal with a printer.

In both situations, price negotiation is critical. Negotiating with printers, photographers, and designers can save you up to 60 percent on the price of a brochure. When you get a quote from a printer, photographer, or designer, that price is not embedded in stone. Those three fields are competitive and negotiation is a rule.

Now, if you are starting out, how do you go about putting together the elements that go into a brochure? The following checklist will help.

Four Key Requirements

1. Someone has to provide the content or written material. You must first decide what audience you are trying to reach with the brochure. In other words, who are your present and potential customers? What are their needs? What will they buy? The brochure should be directed toward them.

2. Someone has to design the brochure and decide if photographs are to be utilized. The design takes into consideration the type style, headlines, paper stock, the amount of color that will be used in the brochure. For example, is it going to be two, three, or four (or more) colors?

3. Someone has to take the photographs for the brochure. This comes about after the design has been decided on. You (or the designer) will decide where and how many photos should be used, and who will take the photos.

4. Someone has to print the brochure and quantities must be decided on.

KEY REQUIREMENTS FOR A BROCHURE

Step One: Writing and Content

Before writing the brochure, you must analyze the needs of your present and potential clients. Then address those needs. For example, suppose you are a money manager consultant. Your clients are going to be interested (their needs) in seeing their portfolios grow in value. Some will favor short-term rapid growth; others long term. They will want to know your capabilities. What gives you the ability to handle thousands of dollars of their money? Do you have the background, a history of success stories? These are questions that must be answered by a brochure.

To determine a prospect's needs, put yourself in his or her place. What would you want to know before you hired a money manager, CPA, personnel, management, electrical, data processing, or any consultant?

When you can answer those questions you will know the direction the brochure should take. If you hire a writer, he or she should ask those questions (of you) in order to determine the direction. If you are the writer, ask those questions of yourself.

There are several ways to find a writer. Select brochures you admire that have been produced for others. Ask the principals within those companies who did the writing, and how you might contact them. Usually, they will be happy to give you the name of the writer.

You can also call local ad agencies and ask for the names of freelance writers. Or talk to the local chamber of commerce and ask if they have any writers. Another technique is to consult the English and/or journalism department of the local university. Find a junior or senior who can write. If you hire a writer, ask for samples of his or her work. Ask for references as well.

Step Two: Design

The brochure has to be designed. You can hire a designer in a number of ways. You can go to the *Yellow Pages* (under artist/designer) or approach local ad agencies and/or the local chamber of commerce, who may have members in the design profession. University art departments are another possibility. Obviously, the experience factor of someone in college is going to be vastly different from someone already working at an agency.

Another option is go to a printer, explain that you are putting together a brochure, and ask if they can recommend any designers. Most will be able to give you several names, and in many instances you will find the printer has an in-house designer. Do not, incidentally, approach an instant printer for this type of information. Typically, instant printers deal primarily in one (perhaps two) color printing, and they seldom get involved in designing the complex, quality brochure a consultant needs.

Before hiring a designer, examine his or her portfolio. Look closely at the type of brochures they have produced. Ask for references.

If you find a printer that does design work, you can save by not having to hire an outside artist/designer. You not only save with the designer's fees, but the markup that usually goes along with it. (Many designers automatically tack on 10–15 percent to the printing and photography bills to compensate for their time. This is in addition to their design fee.)

Remember, if you utilize a printer for design, you will have to provide direction. A printer's business is printing, and most do not have full service design departments. If your brochure is one or two color, you can bypass a designer. However, if you are producing three, four, or more colors you may need the designer's expertise.

Step Three: Photography

There are several ways to find good photographers. Try selecting brochures that have photos that you admire. If you obtained the brochure from a company, ask who did the photography work.

Printers are another source for finding photographers, as are ad agencies, and local chambers of commerce. If you hire a designer, he or she will usually take responsibility for finding a photographer.

Photographers often specialize. Thus, if you see a brochure that has exceptional food shots, do not hire the photographer unless you are planning a brochure with food in it. You will find that a photographer who is good at shooting food, may not be any good when it comes to photographing people and vice versa.

Because of the diverse skills of photographers, studying their portfolios is a necessity. Make sure they are capable of shooting the pictures you need.

Step Four: Printing

If you are going to have a four-color brochure, make sure the printer has experience in four-color production work. Look at his or her portfolio, ask for references. And do not forget, printing rates, prices, and so forth are negotiable.

Postprinting Tips

When the brochure is printed make sure you regain possession of the original art (often called mechanical boards). If you have utilized a designer, he or she may keep the boards. Or if you went directly to a printer, he or she may want to retain the boards as well.

Insist that the boards be returned to you. After all, you paid for it. In fact, do not pay the printing (or design) bills until the boards are in your hands. Additionally, a printer makes a negative from the boards. Ask for the negative as well. Make it a policy.

The reason—suppose you need the brochure reprinted or revised. Months may have passed and you may have lost touch with the printer and/or designer. You may have had a falling out with one or the other or you may have found a printer who will do the job for less money. If the boards are not in your possession and you have paid the bills, you will have a difficult time obtaining them. Some designers and printers will not want to give them up. If you do not have any leverage (i.e., an unpaid bill), it may become difficult and time consuming. Legally they belong to you. However, it is best to avoid courtrooms, and the way to do that is make sure the art is in your hands when the job is done.

At the same time, if you have used a photographer, make sure he or she has your negatives. Occasionally, they will give the negatives to the designer. If so, you should get them back before accounts are settled. It is acceptable for the photographer to retain the negatives, but make sure they are not in the designer's hands. If you want to obtain negatives from the photographer, state your intentions—and get the photographer to agree—before you hire him or her.

21 KEY TERMS AND DEFINITIONS

Artist/Designer

They design and layout brochures. They can plan photos and supervise the photo session. They can also hire a photographer, select a printer, and supervise the printing of the brochure.

Artist/designers may charge fees for services other than design work. For example, if they select and supervise the photo session, some may tack on a percentage to the photographer's bill as their supervision fee. If you want the designer to hire and supervise both the photographer and printer, be prepared to pay this fee.

This markup may even be buried in the printing and photography bills, and neither vendor will say anything about it when they present you with their invoices. You pay the markup and the printer and photographer then pay the percentage to the designer. This issue should be discussed with the designer beforehand. The markup percentage is in the area of 15 percent.

Naturally, if you bypass a designer and go directly to a printer, you will not have this additional expense. You must, however, weigh the expense against the services an outside designer can offer.

Printers

Printing is a competitive field. Negotiate the price. Make sure you examine previous work to determine if the printer can handle your job. For example, you do not want an instant printer (who does primarily one- and two-color work) tackling your four-color brochure. Talk to the printer's previous clients. Ask them about promptness, billing accuracy in comparison to bid, and any difficulties they encountered.

Some printers may give you one estimate and then tack on additional charges when it comes to the actual job. Make sure the bid spells out the total costs for the job. If there are to be exceptions, they should be spelled out and amounts estimated.

Writing/Writer

A fee for a writer is negotiable. Some will charge by the hour, others by the job. If you have a budget, ask for a written estimate to determine if the brochure can be produced within it. If the bid is high (compared to your budget), negotiate. Ask for samples of previous work. Examine the writer's style. Does it fit with your proposed brochure? The writer should spend time with you determining who your market is and what the thrust of the brochure should be.

Photographers

They usually have day and hourly rates. Watch out for the cost of film, processing, and prints. At times those three items can add up to more than the shooting itself. If you are using black-and-white photos, ask for a contact sheet. A contact sheet is much cheaper to produce than the actual photos, and from the sheet you can pick the shots you like and have them produced.

Lithographers

If your brochure has color photos, your designer may go to a lithographer. A lithographer makes color separations. These separations then go to the printer. Often the printer can supply this service.

Cover Copy

This should be short and to the point. It should be designed and written to pique the curiosity of the reader. If possible, it should address the potential client's needs. For example, if you are a management consultant trying to appeal to a company, cover copy that says, "Hire a Management Consultant" or "Hire a Top Management Consultant" falls flat. It does not address the client's needs. On the other hand, a brochure with cover copy that says, "How to Increase Your Company's Productivity 100%" is enticing.

Inside Copy

Once again, focus on the prospective client's needs. Of course, your firm's capabilities, advantages, and so on cannot be ignored, but the thrust of the copy should be to appeal to whatever the client needs.

Size

Brochures come in every shape and configuration. Remember one of the most cost-efficient is 8½ inches × 11 inches, when folded, fits neatly into a #10 (business) envelope.

Stock

Printers will have samples of stock. They are more than happy to show you everything.

By utilizing a colored stock (nonwhite), you can give your brochure a color look even if you are only using black ink on the color stock. Be careful when selecting an ink color. Make sure you utilize one that will stand out, not blend in with the stock. Once again, the printer can be of help.

Glossy stock usually works best with black-and-white photos. If you are going four-color, virtually any quality paper will work. Keep in mind, however, that if you are going to use one or two colors with black-and-white photos, glossy stock will look best.

Lead-Ins

In a brochure, the first few words of the paragraph are known as lead-ins and a designer may choose to italicize or utilize a bold face on the lead-in to make it stand out.

Type Styles

Times Roman and Garamond are conservative styles that are easily readable. They work well in headlines/heads. Helvetica type styles are also easily read and should be utilized in body copy. Boldface type styles can be used for titles or lead-ins. Italics can be used for emphasis in the body copy.

Be careful—do not use all caps in too many consecutive words. It is difficult to read.

Photos

If you are using black-and-white, have a metal plate (instead of plastic) made. It will cost a few dollars more but the quality of the photo when printed will be significantly better.

Color Photos

When shooting color for a brochure, photographers utilize 35 mm color or a film which may have a large (2 inch or more) negative. The 35 mm film is mounted as slides and can be viewed through a projector. The large negatives can be placed and viewed on a light box (a box that has light underneath it).

Duotone

Essentially, this is a black-and-white photo, but with more depth and feel. It almost gives the look of a color shot—without the added cost. Duotone photos usually look better on a glossy stock. Ask the printer (or designer) to show you samples.

Screens

This is another way to give your brochure variation without adding an additional color. This is really a shading effect. If you were using blue for the color of your type, the printer could provide various shades of blue throughout the brochure. Be careful not to overdo screens. Ask the printer for samples of screens in other brochures to give you an idea of what they look like.

Color Hints

Blues, grays, and reds have more stature. Earth tones (browns) can go either way. For consulting brochures, stay away from greens and oranges. These are too flashy and may make the potential client uncomfortable.

Mechanical Art

When type is set and photos are selected, the designer will paste the type in position on a board, and indicate where the photos should be placed. Any type or design alterations should be done before the type is pasted down. This board is then given to the printer who shoots it and makes a negative (for printing) from it.

Blueline

Just before the brochure goes to press, you are presented with a proof—a blueline (sometimes called a brownline). The blueline usually serves as a final check for typographical errors. This is not the time to change the design of the brochure. Bluelines are primarily to check accuracy.

Color Key

If your brochure is going to be in color, ask for this before you go to press. It is similar to a color proof and gives you an idea of the variations of the colors. If you are using a designer, he or she will usually ask for one before the job is printed.

Quantities

Do not go overboard. Things change and so do businesses. You may be adding a service, partner, and so forth. Think about how many brochures (and how) you would be handing out. Usually quantities ranging from 1000 to 3000 are more than sufficient.

Logo

A logo is an identifying symbol, like a trademark. It may be a combination of letters (e.g., ABC) or a design. If you do not have one, this is one of the first things you should have done.

To produce a logo, you need a designer. The designer will talk to you and get your ideas. He or she will then come up with three or four rough ideas. The one or two you like best would be refined.

When selecting a logo, do not use more than two colors. If you use a three- or four-color logo, it can increase your printing bills significantly when putting a brochure, letterhead, or business card together. Stay away from screens as well. Stay with solids if possible, and have the designer avoid fine lines. They do not show up well in advertising (in newsprint) or in photocopying.

Bold logos work the best. The designer will ask you how you want to use the logo—letterhead, business card, t-shirt, and the like.

Figure 3-1 will give you an idea of who handles what, in terms of duties and responsibilities.

The following checklist details the steps that should be taken when putting together a brochure.

Step-by-Step Checklist

1. Determine need for brochure
2. Determine budget
3. Find writer/through ad agencies, newspapers, public relations firms, local chamber of commerce, or business brochure that you admire
4. Talk to writers/examine past work
5. Select writer
   a. *Negotiate writing fee*
6. Sign letter of agreement detailing rates and terms
7. Writer interviews consultant for brochure information
8. Write brochure
9. Begin designer selection
   a. Ask writer for suggestions
   b. Ask printer for help/suggestions in finding designer

	Layout	Copy	Type/photos	Printing	Photo choice	Type Style	Ink/Stock/Choice
Artist* Designer	X		X	X	X	X	X
Printer				X			
Writer		X					
Photog**			X				
Lithographer					X		
Consultant ***	X	X	X	X	X	X	X

FIG. 3-1. Brochure responsibility chart.

X = Responsibility.

*If you are not using a designer, the responsibilities then fall into the printer's area.

**Photographers should be working with designers in order to stage the correct photos.

***Regardless of whether you use a printer or five people to help you put the brochure together, the ultimate responsibility belongs to you. You should have input and overall supervision of the entire project.

    c. Call local ad agencies

    d. Ask other businesses who designed brochures you prefer

10. Interview designers

    a. Examine previous work

    b. Check references

    c. Get designer's thoughts on your brochure.

    d. Determine and *negotiate* fees

11. Select designer

    a. Set groundrules; your involvement

    b. Sign letter of agreement

12. Design logo

13. Design brochure

    a. Look at direction, stock, photo possibilities, total cost

    c. Decide on type of photos needed

    d. Decide on stock

    d. See rough layout

14. Find photographer

    a. Consult printer, designer, ad agency, public relations agency, other businesses that have brochure photos you admire

    b. Interview photographer

    c. Look at portfolio

15. Hire photographer

    a. *Negotiate the fee*

    b. Sign letter of agreement

16. Shoot photos

    a. See contact sheet unless in color, then see either negatives or 35 mm transparencies

    b. Select photos

17. Finalize brochure layout

    a. See and approve comprehensive brochure layout

    b. Produce mechanical boards

    c. Check mechanical boards for accuracy

18. Find printer

    a. Consult designer

    b. Consult photographer

    c. Talk to other businesses

19. Select printer

    a. Decide on printed quantities

    b. Get three written competitive bids

    c. *Negotiate the cost*

    d. Determine time that printer will need to produce brochure once art is in his or her hands

    e. Get definite finalization from printer on brochure data

    f. Put in writing, as part of agreement, that mechanical boards be returned to consultant when the rest of the job is delivered

20. Select lithographer (if needed)
    a. Ask printer and designer for recommendations

21. Send art boards to printer
    (If printer is acting as designer, he or she will set type and produce mechanical art)

22. Approve printer's proofs (designer and/or client)

23. See blueline and approve

24. See color key (if brochure in color) and approve

25. Print brochure

26. Deliver brochure
    a. Returned artboards with brochure

27. Pay bills

The cover of a brochure is like the headline of a newspaper, or the lead sentence in a sales letter.

In other words, it must grab *your* potential customer/client. If you cannot attract them with the cover, you will never get them to open and read it. A good cover line is 70 percent of the appeal of a brochure. The cover line should address your prospect's needs. Or, it may reiterate your *Unique Selling* (USP) Proposition. (A USP is present in every product and/or service. It is the one thing that sets your practice apart from your competitors. It may be faster service, a money back guarantee, 25 years of service, and so forth. The USP is covered in Chapter 7. Before writing the copy for your brochure, refer to Chapter 7 and the section on USP.

Finally...

... A Benefit for
Employers

...a working partnership

HIRE
THRU
PIC

CARSON — LOMITA — TORRANCE
PRIVATE INDUSTRY COUNCIL

FIG. 3-2. Brochure covers.

SAMPLE BROCHURES

In Figure 3-2 you will find the cover of two brochures, each going after the same market. One promises a benefit, the other just asks to buy mine without offering any benefit. Both brochures were produced by the Private Industry Council (PIC). The PIC seeks employers who will hire the unemployed. For the employers who work with them, there are significant benefits.

Brochure 1 promises those benefits with its cover line:

"Finally . . . a Benefit for Employers"

Compare that with the cover line on brochure 2:

"Hire Through PIC"

The second cover line does not offer any benefits. In fact, if the employer is not familiar with PIC, he or she would be baffled by it. The first, of course, promises something to the employer, and has enough mystique so the employer will want to open it and find out what the benefit happens to be.

Opening the first brochure (Figure 3-3), the employer is drawn in with the tantalizing head, "Can Your Company Use One (or all) of the Following Benefits When Hiring?"

It offers the employer six possible benefits, not one. On the other hand, the second brochure (Figure 3-4) promises nothing even when it is opened. It explains the PIC, and a few other things. Then it finally states what some of the hiring advantages are. By this time, the brochure would have lost the prospect.

Can Your Company Use One (or all) of the Following Benefits When Hiring?

- Salary reimbursement for a portion of an employee's wage?

- Tax advantages and credits.

- Free training of an employee paid for by Job Training Partnership Act Funds prior to the employee officially joining your company.

- No fees or costs to you or your employees when hiring.

- No red tape.

- And when you hire, you will not only get a competent employee, but a willing, enthusiastic worker who has come to our offices, and spent countless additional hours in testing, counseling and training in order to be prepared for employment.

Those are only some of the benefits available to companies when hiring through the Private Industry Council.

FIG. 3-3. Brochure 1 interior.

WHAT IS THE PRIVATE INDUSTRY COUNCIL?

THE PIC is a locally-based organization comprised primarily of representatives of large and small business.
Operating in partnership with local government, the PIC plans, establishes policy and maintains oversight for local job training programs funded under the JOB TRAINING PARTNERSHIP ACT (JTPA) of 1982.

WHAT IS JOB TRAINING PARTNERSHIP ACT?

The Job Training Partnership Act (JTPA) is a Federal law designed to develop employment potential through training programs and other services to assist those who have obstacles gaining employment.

The Job Training Partnership Act is different from past employment programs because it gives to business people the responsibility for selecting and developing training programs that local businesses want and need.

WHAT ARE THE ADVANTAGES OF HIRING EMPLOYEES THRU PIC?

Employers may receive:

1. Salary reimbursement for a portion of an employee's wage.

2. Free training of an unskilled employee paid by Job Training Partnership Act Funds prior to the employee officially joining your company.

3. Tax advantages.

4. No fees to employees or employers.

5. No red tape.

FIG. 3-4. Brochure 2 interior.

THE EFFECTIVE BROCHURE

Benefits should be stressed immediately. That is how you appeal to the client. Keep in mind, however, that what you promise on the cover should be inside. If you promise a benefit, and do not deliver it inside, you not only lose a prospect but you alienate them as well. The prospect feels as if they have been tricked. They will resent you for it, so do not use trick headlines or copy simply to get the prospect to read.

Actually both these brochures contain the same information. Brochure 1 was a follow-up to 2 and increased the PIC's inquiries by 34 percent.

THE BEST COVER LINES

The coverline on the next brochure (Figure 3-5), "Why Do People Lose Hair?," has two elements that are desirable on any cover. Most important, it promises a benefit. It is going to explain why people lose hair. And if it can explain why they lose hair there is a good chance that explanation will provide a way in which they can avoid losing hair—certainly a plus for anyone who wants to keep their hair.

Second, the brochure poses a question. This is an excellent way to attract and hold someone's attention, whether the copy is for the cover of a brochure, the lead sentence in a sales letter, or the headline for an ad.

Notice, too, that this brochure is targeted directly at a particular segment of the market. The head is specific, not general. It does not say, "Find out how you can have a healthy head of hair," which might appeal to a broader market but does not have the urgency of, "Why Do People Lose Hair?" When you see that line there is no question. It is meant for anyone who is experiencing a hair loss. The answer (the benefit) is provided inside (Figure 3-6, "Because they secrete too much oil"). Remember, when posing a question, or promising the benefit, you must deliver.

The next brochure (Figure 3-7) promises a benefit, also. It offers the reader (this brochure was given to unemployed workers) not one benefit, but two— a job and a job with a future.

The following three checklists contain questions that the consultant should answer before putting together a brochure's coverline, copy, and graphics.

How to Put Together Brochure Coverlines

1. Think about the audience—who will read it?
2. What needs does this audience (prospects) have?
3. How do those needs tie into my services?
4. Can I answer those needs and translate them into benefits?
5. Can I offer them any of those benefits?
6. Can I offer those benefits on the cover of a brochure?
7. Can I fit that cover benefit into five to seven words?
8. Will they understand the benefit on the cover?
9. If they understand it, is it misleading?
10. Can I supply the follow-up inside the brochure?

Putting Together Brochure Copy Checklist

1. Does the body copy go along with the cover copy?
2. Is it easy to understand?
3. Is it easy to follow?
4. Is it written on a one-to-one basis?
5. Is it factual?
6. Will it interest the reader (prospect)?
7. Does it have a USP?

Q:
WHY DO PEOPLE LOSE HAIR?

FIG. 3-5. Brochure cover.

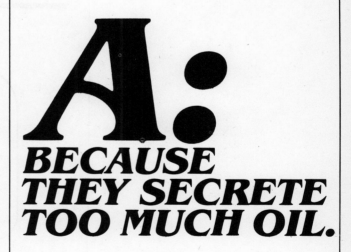

A:
BECAUSE THEY SECRETE TOO MUCH OIL.

FIG. 3-6. Brochure interior.

More Than a Job...
...It's Your Future

FIG. 3-7. Brochure cover.

8. Does it explain my service?

9. Does it address his or her needs?

10. Does it contain information on my firm?

11. Does it promise enough to spark curiosity?

12. Can I deliver on those promises?

13. Would I buy this service if given the brochure?

Graphics Checklist

1. Is the cover copy no more than five to seven words?

2. Is the cover copy legible?

3. Is it in a typeface that can be read without squinting?

4. Is the body copy legible?

5. Are there too many screens in the body copy?

6. Are there too many boldface sentences in the copy?

7. Are there too many sentences or sections reversed out which will make the brochure hard to read?

8. Is the body copy helvetica or similar typeface?

9. Are there too many sentences in all capital letters?

10. Are the photographs crisp and clear?

11. Is there enough contrast between copy and color. In other words, does the type punch out and not blend-in with the background? Is it easy to read?

CHAPTER 4

WRITING PROPOSALS AND DESIGNING PRESENTATIONS

Appearance is everything in a presentation.

Ask Joe X (we will leave his last name out to remain discreet). Several years ago, Joe was hired by the personnel department of one of the largest companies in the country to head its marketing department.

Joe was one of the most knowledgeable marketing men in the country. He had more than 15 years experience in the field, and knew the ins and outs of the business and industry.

While Joe's knowledge was a plus, his appearance was a minus. He smoked cigars, wore loud, plaid sportscoats, his shoes were never shined, and he always needed a haircut. He would have fit perfectly as a carnival huckster—but not as a corporate consultant.

Appearance, however, did not phase his immediate supervisor. But the day Joe met the president of the company things began to change. In his position, Joe had frequent contact with the president. The president was cognizant of his company's image. He also knew that Joe met with the press daily, and would, at year's end, play an important role at the annual stockholders meeting.

Joe did an excellent job for the firm. In two months, his competency was the talk of the company. Unfortunately, they were also talking about the way he looked.

At the end of the third month—the conclusion of his probationary period— Joe was called into his supervisor's office and fired. Joe never understood what happened. He drifted from job to job, always the victim of the same deficiency.

You have probably heard similar stories. The important lesson in this true story is not just to shine your shoes but to be aware of prejudices and preconceived notions that exist within every potential client's company. Study the company's image. You will find, with few exceptions, the best way to dress when you make a presentation is conservatively. That is, wear a dark blue or even a black suit. Keep your shirt and ties simple. If you are wearing dark blue keep the shirt color white or light blue, the tie a solid blue.

Blue (and black) are colors which command authority and attention. Reds and oranges are flashy. In some companies you will be dealing with presidents, vice presidents, and department heads who are conservative. Bright colors will turn them off . . . as will smoke. So do not light up. The executives to whom you make a presentation will more readily identify with (and accept) businesslike clothing.

Although most companies were started by entrepreneurs who might accept the flashy dress and cigars of a Joe X, the management team they eventually bring in is generally more conservative. A great many established company chief executive officers (CEOs) have accounting or financial backgrounds. They are excellent CEOs because of their meticulous nature, and their numbers background.

Even companies that have executives with marketing backgrounds may be turned off by a flashy dresser. Once someone assumes a position of high responsibility, they become conservative. Always keep this in mind when making a presentation—you can lose before you utter a word.

Think of yourself as a new car on a dealer's lot. You might have the most reliable, economic engine under your hood, but if you have not been washed or polished, your chances of selling against inferior automobiles with a better appearance are not great. Never forget that aside from your capabilities as a consultant you are also selling an image—your image.

Appearance, however, goes beyond your personal dress and looks. It also has enormous impact with your presentation materials. If you are coming in with a flip chart, make sure the chart has not been frayed or beaten by past presentations. If need be, do it over.

If you have an audio/visual, make sure your slides drop and do not get jammed. Run through the show beforehand. If you are using graphs on slides (or on a flip chart or presentation board), be sure the graphs appear professional. Carry a spare lamp for the projector.

If you have flip charts or presentation boards, make sure you bring in a stand. Do not rely on the client to supply one. The same is true of an audiovisual—bring your own screen. There is nothing more detracting than having to show a slide show on a bare or paneled wall. You lose much of the impact.

Sloppiness. If your charts and graphs look that way, those you are talking to in the room will automatically get one thought in their heads—"if his (or her) presentation is that sloppy, what is his work like? It is probably just as bad."

You might have the best ideas and information in the world, a winning presentation, a presentation that any company would buy, but if it looks sloppy, you will suffer. Examine your brochure, too. Does it reflect a neat, competent, positive image? If you are going for a $100,000 data processing contract, your brochure should not appear to be something that came off an instant printer's press. Be sure and study chapter 3 in this workbook. This does not mean you have to spend tens of thousands of dollars on a brochure. On the contrary, good brochures are the result of careful planning and design—not money.

One other thing—your presentation case, or portfolio—examine it before the meeting. Is it neat, clean? Will it portray the kind of image you want?

Appearance. In consulting, and any business for that matter, the customer buys image. He or she is emotionally moved to a decision. Logic enters later when the buyer has to rationalize his or her decision. Once you have an appointment with a potential client, you should gear your presentation to do one thing—answer the client's needs.

A presentation should have background and information about your firm. It is called a company or individual profile. You do not have to be a creative writer to put one of these together, however, if you completely lack writing skills you should consult someone who has writing ability. The following checklist will give you an idea of what a biography is and what it should contain.

Biographical Checklist

1. The biography should contain all the facts about you and your firm— who, what, when, where, and why.
2. It should contain a history, when you started, where.
3. It should mention any awards, honors given to your firm.
4. It should mention any special expertise.
5. It should refer to previous campaigns, accomplishments.
6. It should not mention clients who prefer to remain anonymous.
7. It should be updated at least once a year.
8. It should run no longer than three pages.
9. It should contain your operating philosophy.
10. It should not contain names other than principals, since they may change.
11. It should not contain terms that praise your firm to the sky, since clients know your firm is writing about itself. However, it may contain praise from other clients or infer your expertise by citing challenges you have met.

SAMPLE BIOGRAPHY

Figure 4-1 is a typical biography of a sole practitioner who owns a design firm. His name is Carlton Wagner. Notice how the profile, although factual, sparks the reader's interest in the subject without being subjective.

SAMPLE COMPANY PROFILE

A second type of biography is one on a company, often called a company profile. The elements contained in a company profile differ in several respects from a biography as indicated by the following checklist.

Elements in a Company Profile

1. Company name
2. Year founded
3. Products manufactured (distributed, sold, etc.)
4. How products are distributed (if applicable)

(This should be on letterhead and should be double-spaced)

Profile: Carlton Wagner

Have you ever seen a green fast-food restaurant, a blue lightbulb in a refrigerator, or the President giving his State of the Union message in a brown, plaid blazer?

The answer to all three questions is, of course, no--and for good reason. That reason is...color.

Green is a turnoff when it comes to food; a blue bulb can help you diet and cut your appetite; and the President wears dark blue because it is a color that connotes authority.

Color plays a critical role in virtually every decision we make. In fact, 60% of an item's appeal (durable or non-durable) is predicated upon its color. Color has impact on our selection process when it comes to dating, marriage, and our opinion of others.

Color is an indicator of the health of the economy. It can help a company succeed (or fail), and it can make--or break--a romance.

Theories? Far from it. In fact, all of the above (and many more) statements are the product of more than 15 years of scientific and empirical research conducted by psychologist/designer Carlton Wagner, one of the leading authorities on color in the world.

-More-

FIG. 4-1. Profile: Carlton Wagner.

Wagner, who heads the Wagner Institute for Color Research, is also head of the Color Marketing Group's (CMG) research committee. CMG has 800 members who represent virtually every major company and manufacturer in the U.S. They meet periodically to forecast and select "future colors" that will be used on products ranging from autos to clothing.

He received his degree in psychology from California State University, and went on to study at the prestigious Carl Jung Institute in Zurich, Switzerland, where he did graduate work.

Following his tenure at the the Jung Institute, he taught psychology and became involved in a graduate study program that concentrated on the influences of color on behavior, and the psychological and physiological responses to color.

Wagner became fascinated with color, and glandular responses to various hues. To further his insight, he returned to school and studied interior design and received a degree from the Fashion Institute of Design and Merchandising (Los Angeles).

His knowledge of color and its impact has led hundreds of companies in a variety of industries to his Santa Barbara offices where he specializes in advising and suggesting color schemes for products ranging from fast food franchise restaurants (Der Weinerschnitzel) to universities, hospitals and even prisons.

-2-

FIG. 4-1. (continued) (Figure continued on p. 114.)

He spends nearly six months out of the year on the road lecturing
to such groups as designers, economists, kitchen planners, and
professional associations on color. He is also a member of the
Decorative Arts Council of the Los Angeles County Museum of Art,
and member of the International Society of Interior Designers
where he served as a board member for three years.

Recently, Wagner produced the "Wagner Color Response Report,"
a lengthy study which details consumer responses to colors.

To Wagner, the study of color is as scientific as the study of
physics. And as is the case with physics, color effects every
phase of human life.

"Color," he says, "effects us in ways we do not realize. It
impacts our appetite, sexual behavior, business life, and leisure
time.

"Interestingly, it also reflects our nation's economic health, and
is a forecaster of its future. It can influence our foreign trade
as well as our foreign relations.

"When you combine psychology and color, you can immediately see
the possibilities for all of us to live fuller, happier, more
productive lives."

###

-3-

FIG. 4-1. (*continued*)

5. Yearly sales

6. Address (is this headquarters?)

7. Length of time at location

8. Number of employees

9. Is the company publicly held?

10. President of company

11. Officers

Figure 4-2 is a typical company profile. It is similar to the biography of the individual in that it remains factual and stays away from subjective statements.

If you need help writing the profile, there are places to go. Contact a local publicity firm. Publicists are writers and can be retained to do a profile. The cost will run anywhere from $60 an hour (for writing and interviewing time) to a flat rate of $300–$400.

Some firms may be more expensive, depending on the city in which you live. For example, expect to pay more in New York than in New Orleans. A city with a higher cost of living will usually be more expensive when hiring free-lancers, writers, and similar craftspeople.

If you want to watch your budget, contact the local newspaper. Look for the writer's name on a story that you think is well-written. Call him or her and ask if they would consider doing some extra work (after hours) for you. Tell them you need a company profile or biography. If they decline, they may have a suggestion. You can usually hire the newswriter at a lower cost than the publicity firm.

Another source would be the local college English and/or journalism department. Contact the department head, tell him or her you are a local businessperson who needs a student with some writing ability who may want to earn a few extra dollars by writing a profile/biography. Do they have anyone they would recommend?

Of course, a presentation should have background and information about your firm, but the client wants more than background; he or she will buy what you can do for them. Presentations are sales tools, and effective selling is not arm-twisting but answering a client's needs, helping them solve their problems.

Thus it is important to understand—before you ever make the presentation—what needs and concerns the client company may have. This is where research comes into play. Before you make your appointment for a formal presentation, learn about the client's industry as well as his or her company. Understand where the company is going, and where it has been.

Before interviewing any of the principals at the company, find out about the industry. Call a trade association (every company belongs to an industry, and every industry has a trade association), go to the library, talk to some of the people you may know at the firm. Call the company and ask for an annual report, 10K, and whatever other information they may have. If it is publicly held, call a broker and ask for some information.

When gathering information, be discreet. During a presentation it is impressive (to the prospective client) when you drop a piece of information about his or her company, or the industry that he or she deems important. It gives them the feeling that you do know the business. (Do not, however, drop a piece

Profile: Entrepreneur Group, Inc.

> "How much profit does Joe's business make (exactly)?
> Any small business? Case history, details including
> how to start one."

That was the beginning. The year was 1973 and with that one-inch
ad in the <u>Wall Street Journal</u>, Entrepreneur Group, Inc. (it was incorporated in 1975 as Chase Revel, Inc., went public in 1981, OTC;
and changed its name to Entrepreneur Group, Inc. in 1985), the most
unique small business organization in the country was launched.

Today, EGI has developed into one of the fastest growing companies
in the country through the unusual services it provides to present
(and future) small business entrepreneurs: it produces in-depth
research reports on new and unique small businesses and in-depth
reporting on up-and-coming small business trends.

Through its monthly publication <u>Entrepreneur Magazine,</u> it was the
first to predict the antique and bicycle crazes; the emergence of
such fad businesses as skateboard parks; and other businesses such
as tune-up shops, computer stores and lo-cal bakeries long before
they became known throughout the country.

Its products include more than 200 "how to" start-up manuals,
detailing exactly how someone can start and succeed in a small
business. The 200 manuals cover businesses ranging from retail
and service to manufacturing. Each was individually researched
and compiled by EGI's staff of editors and researchers.

-More-

25550 hawthorne blvd.   •   suite 100   •   torrance, california 90505   •   (213) 373-9335

FIG. 4-2. Profile: Entrepreneur Group, Inc.

With its manuals and monthly magazine (which reaches more than 250,000 present and potential small business owners each month), EGI will gross more than $10 million in 1985. The Company, which is also benefitting from the increased desire of millions of Americans who want to "do their own thing," is growing at a rate of more than 30%.

None of this, however, would have been possible without the efforts of Chase Revel, a young, aggressive entrepreneur who was born in Tennessee, raised in Chicago and became EGI's founder.

It was Revel who first placed that ad in the Journal--and with good reason. At the time, Revel had more experience and background in small business than anyone in the country. He had started and run enterprises ranging from service and manufacturing to retail and wholesale. He knew the "ins-and-outs" of virtually every small business.

He also realized there were millions of present (more than 13 million small businesses exist today) and potential (a Gallup Poll showed that the "great American Dream" for more than 65% of all Americans is "owning their own business") small business owners who wanted that information.

Since that time, EGI's accurate forecasting has made it a nationally-known and respected voice in the small business field.

Under its President and Publisher, Wellington Ewen, that respect

-2-

FIG. 4-2. (continued) (Figure continued on p. 118.)

has grown internationally. At present, the Government of China is

evaluating the possibilities of translating EGI's business

information and disseminating it in China.

Still, the basic thrust of EGI has not changed since its founding.

"It is and always will be," says Ewen, "an organization dedicated

to giving everyone a chance at not only pursuing that Great

American Dream but making it a reality as well."

FIG. 4-2. (continued)

of information that has been given to you in confidence. This can kill the presentation.)

What you want to display is your knowledge and understanding of the company and its industry. Aside from information gathering sessions outside the company, you should also gather internal information from the prospective client or other executives within the firm.

During these information gathering sessions, come prepared. Have your questions ready. Do not waste time. Have questions such as those listed in the following checklist.

Prospect Questions for Presentations

1. How has the economy affected your business, if at all?
2. Are there cycles involved?
3. What are some of the problems (in your data processing, engineering, management, or whatever consulting area is involved) you see?
4. What do you think is causing them?
5. Has anything been done?
6. If so, what kind of results have you had?
7. What do you think should be done?
8. Are there any specific solutions you are after? (This is akin to a money or financial manager asking do you have any specific goals for your financial future?)
9. Who buys your products or services? How do you reach them?
10. How often do you introduce new products, services?
11. What is the outlook for your industry? The company? (Listen to the prospect, and what their concerns may be. Do not try to sell them service if their prime need is speed or some other factor. Listen.)

Sometimes these sessions can be done on the telephone. Whether you do it on the telephone or in person, be sure you have gathered all possible data from other sources (i.e., annual reports, associations, chamber of commerce) *before* you set an appointment with officials within the company. You will save your time and theirs.

Interviewing and information gathering is a skill, but it can be learned, even if you have never done it before. The best interviewers are prepared. They have questions written beforehand (on a pad or on a sheet of paper). They have thought about the information they need, and are ready. Think about the information you would need for a presentation. Think about the information you would need in order to do a thorough consulting job. Now, structure your questions so you can get answers.

Do not schedule interviews with someone from the company and fly by the seat of your pants. Disorganization comes through loud and clear. No one wants their time wasted. Write down the questions you definitely want answered. You will find, during the course of the interview, the person will supply other information that may stimulate additional questions.

Take notes or tape the interview. Do not rely on your memory. And above all, *listen*. You may have prepared questions; however, the client may say something that opens an entirely new line of questioning. He or she may, during the course of an interview, say something (or hint at it) that may be the underlying cause of the company's problems.

What makes an impression during a presentation? There are a number of elements, and the following checklist will give you examples.

Presentation Checklist One

1. *Organization.*   Be prepared and rehearsed. Do not ramble. Time yourself. Do not take more than 30 minutes. If you can make a presentation in a shorter time frame, do so. Businesspeople are busy. Their time is valuable. They will respect you if you realize the importance of their time. Structure your presentation. It should have a beginning, middle, and end.

2. *Use Visuals.*   This may involve slides, graphs, or other aids. It is difficult for any potential client to listen to you for 30 minutes if you do not have any visual aids. (See chapter 11 for details.)

3. *Build in Credibility.*   Structure your presentation so that you can mention other clients or similar situations. You must show the client you have experience or can handle his or her problem. The best way to do this is though past experience and/or clients you have handled. If you are approaching your first client, utilize your background (perhaps you were employed by a company that handled a similar situation) to show you can handle the job.

4. *End on a High, Positive Note.*   Do not sell negativity. Do not criticize competitors. There is a tendency on the part of many in business (especially in the advertising field) to put down the competitor's product in an effort to make their's look better. These agencies underestimate today's consumer. Today's businessperson is usually even more astute. He or she will recognize your attempt to look bigger and better by using someone else as a stepping stone. Equally as important as what you say is how you say it. Practice your presentation. Use emphasis in your voice when it comes to key points. Speak loud, but do not shout. Remember, in a room with people you not only want to be heard, but you want to command attention. You can do this through your voice and mannerisms.

5. *Use Gestures.*   Make eye contact consistently with everyone in the room. Do not read from prepared notes. Memorize the presentation.

If you are unsure about your ability as a speaker or if you want additional practice, enroll in a local Toastmaster's Club. This inexpensive (less than $75 a year) club will provide you with a multitude of speaking hints. You will also get used to speaking before groups, and the more you speak the better you will become.

The following checklist lists the steps in a good oral presentation.

Oral Presentation Checklist

1. Introduction
   Brief background, your capabilities
   Relate your background to the client's business
   (Do not forget eye contact)

2. Statement of problem
   This is the client's problem as you understand it
   Based on your information gathering sessions
   (Make sure you use gestures to emphasize points)

3. Possible solutions
   Alternatives and consequences of each
   (Speak in a clear tone and project your voice)

4. Your solution
   Rationale
   Timetable
   (Memorize your presentation)

5. Open for questions

6. Wrap-up
   Thank you
   Leave brochure/outline/business card

How much do you give away in a presentation? And isn't it possible if you give too much, the client will simply take it and run or give it to another firm to utilize?

Certainly stealing ideas is a possibility, but most consultants do not give the entire idea away. In a presentation, you outline the solutions and how you would proceed. Do not go into detail. There is nothing wrong with revealing your solution—the key. The area you do not detail is the *execution* of the solution.

For example, a marketing consultant might propose an ad in a particular trade journal or other publication in order to reach a specific audience. Or, he or she might propose a direct mail piece structured to sell a certain product. The actual content of the ad, direct mail piece, and so on is not spelled out in the presentation.

A money manager may discuss a particular industry that represents an excellent investment for the client—without revealing the companies within that industry that would be the most advantageous for investing.

A management consultant might talk about increasing productivity in a certain area without outlining the specific steps.

An engineer could talk about redesigning a particular operation or piece of equipment without going into detail on the exact redesign.

This is what is often called the sizzle in a sales presentation. You drop ideas and potential results. You do not go in-depth and explain how the idea would be executed. This type of approach piques the interest of the potential client. It gets his or her imagination going.

There are not, incidentally, an infinite number of solutions to a problem. There is a good chance your competitors may have come up with a similar solution. Each consultant, however, may have a different way in which he or she goes about executing the solution. Thus it is important for you to convince the client that your firm has the ability to execute the solution. That is why you should always outline the skills of your company and its experience with similar problems.

THE WRITTEN PRESENTATION

Potential clients may ask for a written presentation or you may find it is advantageous to provide one. The written and oral presentations contain the same elements. There should be information on your firm, its abilities, the problem (as you see it), and solutions. You can do things within the written presentation that you cannot do orally.

For example, you can include an in-depth biographical sketch (or profile) of your company and its abilities. You can insert reprints of newspaper articles that were written about your firm or articles you wrote pertaining to certain problems. Reprints—from the media—give you credibility, and will impress a potential client. Written presentations should be thorough, but not verbose. They can also contain references.

The following lists the steps in preparing a presentation for a prospective client.

Presentation Checklist Two

1. Determine needs
   a. Interview client
   b. Get idea of client's true needs
2. Research industry
   a. Call industry trade associations
   b. Research competitors in industry
   c. Check library for industry information
3. Research company
   a. Annual reports/10K/clippings
   b. Trade journals
   c. Newspaper articles/morgue in newspaper
   d. Check library
   e. Check chamber of commerce
   f. Check company vendors

4. Research presentation area
   a. Determine how many will be in room
   b. Where room will be
   c. What type of equipment will be available during presentation
5. Begin presentation preparation
6. Divide presentation
   a. Your company's expertise
   b. Your background in field
   c. Your knowledge of potential client and industry
   d. Some creative ideas
   e. A time frame (if feasible)
   f. Design questions to bring out client involvement
7. Prepare approach
   a. Find your USP to present to client
8. Prepare visuals
   a. Use slides, reprints, other visuals
9. Prepare portfolio
10. Prepare presentation kit to leave with client
    a. Insert your company brochure and background

TWO TYPES OF PRESENTATIONS

There are two types of presentations. First, the in-depth document that lays out ideas. The second is more of a conceptual document. It does not go into detail. It may only cover one or two pages. There is an example of it later in this chapter.

The in-depth document is usually presented by the consultant to a prospective client who has spoken to several different consultants and wants to see what kinds of ideas each has to offer. When presentations of this type are given to a client, they should not be stapled. They should be put in three-hole presentation books. The danger of this presentation is that the client may give the account to a competitor, as well as your proposal, which contains a great many ideas.

(Note: The following is an actual presentation given to a client by a marketing consulting firm. The company seeking the marketing help was an organization—The PIC—that specialized in placing unemployed workers in permanent private industry positions. The PIC's marketing needs are threefold: (1) they must appeal to employers to come to them with job openings for PIC applicants; (2) they must attract the applicants to fill the jobs, and (3) they must make the community aware that they exist.)

The PIC was mentioned earlier in this workbook. This proposal was in response to a Request for Proposal (RFP), that city, county, and federal officials usually put out before they award a contract. An RFP (Figure 4-3) is the government's way of asking for a proposal, and for those consultants interested in submitting bids to the government, this is the type of document you will be answering. The proposal is preceded by the RFP.

REQUEST FOR PROPOSAL
FOR

MARKETING

THE PRIVATE INDUSTRY COUNCIL

DIVISION OF EMPLOYMENT AND TRAINING

OF

(NAME OF CITY)

is inviting

PUBLIC RELATIONS AGENCIES, MARKETING SPECIALISTS, ADVERTISING
AGENCIES AND COUNSELORS, AND OTHER SIMILAR ORGANIZATIONS OR ENTITIES
to submit proposals for
MARKETING CAMPAIGN FOR PROGRAMS
under Title II-A and Title III
of the Job Training Partnership Act

PRIVATE INDUSTRY COUUNCIL
DIVISION OF EMPLOYMENT AND TRAINING

FIG. 4-3. Sample request for proposal. (*Figure continued on p. 124.*)

1.0 SOLICITATION

1.1 BACKGROUND ON THE PRIVATE INDUSTRY COUNCIL

The Private Industry Council/Division of Employment and
Training of (name of city) (PIC/DET) is an agency of the (name
of city) governed by the County Board of Supervisors.
PIC/DET was established to administer programs funded through
the federal Job Training Partnership Act (JTPA). The (name of
city) Private Industry Council (PIC), appointed by the Board of
Supervisors is charged with principal responsibility for
program planning, development and oversight. The Private
Industry Council/Division of Employment and Training administers
and manages a wide variety of employment and training programs.

The Private Industry Council has established the following
objectives in the administration of the employment and training
programs in (name of city):

O Provide occupational skills training in demand/stable
   occupations which will result in permanent unsubsidized
   employment;

O Provide on-the-job training in occupations that will lead to
   permanent unsubsidized employment;

O Place emphasis on private sector employment;

O Stimulate economic development in coordination with the private
   sector to promote business information and expansion to increase
   job opportunities to eligible participants;

O Increase private sector involvment through participation in the
   development of employment and training programs;

O Provide for the coordination of programs under JTPA with other
   employment and training related and social services programs,
   including economic development agencies, vocational education
   agencies, rahabilitation agencies, public assistance agenies and
   community based organizations to insure that programs are
   coordinated and non-duplicative;

O Utilize public facilities and services, provided in-kind, to the
   highest degree possible;

O Operate quality, cost effective programs;

O Give priority consideration to short term training programs
   which will allow participants to move quickly through training
   and employers to obtain qualified workers rapidly;

FIG. 4-3. (*continued*)

O   Reduce welfare dependency through the development of employment and training programs and services for welfare recipients;

O   Provide programs which will lead to employment opportunities for youth;

O   Serve clients who are the most disadvantaged and who are most likely to succeed considering available services, resources, and timeframes.

O   Provide supportive services, through the JTPA system or in coordination with other agencies, which are necessary to eliminate barriers to employment; and

O   Aggressively market the program and services available.

1.2   SOLICITATION

The PURPOSE of this Request for Proposal (RFP) is TO SOLICIT PROPOSALS FOR A STRATEGIC MARKETING CAMPAIGN ON ACITIVITES, PROGRAMS AND SERVICES OFFERED BY THE PRIVATE INDUSTRY COUNCIL WHICH WILL INCREASE AND EXPAND PARTICIPANT OUTREACH AND INCREASE EMPLOYMENT OPPORTUNITIES (JOBS) FOR TRAINEES.

In summary, the marketing campaign is designed to:

o   attract new participants (youth and adults)
o   attract more employers from (name of city) (to use PIC services and hire more participants)
o   attract businesses to locate in (name of city)
o   make the PIC programs common knowledge in the communities of (name of city)

The major parts of the marketing campaign are:

1.   Participant Outreach
2.   Employer Outreach
3.   Industry Attraction
4.   Program Marketing

Proposals may be submitted by public relation agencies, marketing specialists, advertising agencies and counselors, and other similar organizations or entities. Proposers may submit a proposal on one, two, three or all four of the major parts (as described above) the marketing campaign.

1.3   FACTS AND PROGRAM HIGHLIGHTS

The total budget for programs, activities and services offered by the PIC/DET for the period July 1, 1986 through June 30, 1987 is

FIG. 4-3. (*continued*) (*Figure continued on p. 126.*)

$10.5 million dollars. The expenditure of funds are directly related to the achievemnt of certain enrollment and job placement goals for youth and adults who receive employment and training services. For the period of July 1, 1986 through June 30, 1987, the following enrollment and job placement goals have been established for youth and adults:

	#to be enrolled in Training Programs	#to obtain emploment after completion of Training
YOUTH:	2,800	485
ADULTS:	2,350	1.037
TOTAL	5,150	1,522

Significant program activities for the period July 1, 1986 through June 30, 1987 include the following:

ADULTS:

O Enrollments for the on-the-job training (OJT) program is planned for 930 individuals.

O Enrollments for classroom training is planned for 500 individuals.

O Enrollments for job search training is planned for 524 individuals.

YOUTH:

O Enrollmentes for youth programs (in-school and out-of-school programs) are planned for 2,800 individuals.

NEW PROGRAMS:

O Enrollments for Limited Work Experience is planned for 200 individuals.

O Remediation and basic skills training may be offered (program option are currently being reviewed).

O English-As-A-Second-Language (ESL)training may be offered (program options are currently being reviewed).

1.4 PROGRAMS AND SERVICES OFFERED BY PIC/DET

Examples of programs and services funded by the PIC/DET include the following brief descriptions:

FIG. 4-3. (continued)

126

o   Education for Employment: provides eligible high school
    dropout youth, ages 18-21, with basic skills remediation
    designed to result in the attainment of basic education
    competencies and/or general education diploma.

o   Project School Training Alternatives for Youth (S-T-A-Y):
    provides pre-employment skills training, try-out employment and
    work experience to eligible youth who are at risk of dropping
    out of school.

o   Project SUCCESS: provides eligible handicapped youth with
    assessment, pre-employment skills training, try-out employment
    and job placement services.

o   Senior Jobs Program: provides eligible graduating
    seniors with pre-employment skills training, try-out employment
    and job placement.

o   Older Workers: provides county-wide job search (job
    finding techniques) and job development services to eligible
    participants who are 55 years of age or older.

o   Dislocated Workers Training: Provides job search or
    on-the-job training or occupational skills training in classroom
    setting to participants who have been laid off from their jobs a
    are unlikely to return to those jobs.

o   Occupational Skills Classroom Training: Provides eligible
    participants with skills needed for a specific occupation (i.e.
    clerk typist, data entry clerk, welder, etc.)

o   On-the-Job Training (OJT): Provides participants an
    opportunity to acquire new skills while performing "on-the-job".
    Employers who use the OJT program to meet their employment needs
    are reimbursed for up to 50% of the wages paid to the participan

o   Job Search Training: Provides participants with job
    seeking skills and techniques to assist them in locating
    employment.

o   Limited Work Experience: Provides participants an
    opportunity to acquire work experience in a work setting on a
    short-term assignment with a public agency or private non-profit
    agency. During the work experience activity participants are
    also concurrently receiving basic and remedial education,
    pre-employment skills training and occupational skills training.

o   Industry Specific Training: Is customized training
    designed to meet a company's employment needs. Companies who
    are expanding or relocating in (name if city) may use this

FIG. 4-3. (continued) (Figure continued on p. 128.)

type or training as a means of obtaining a ready and qualified work force which has been tained to meet the specific needs of the company.

O <u>Loan Packaging Services:</u> Is available to assist in the securing of capital through a business loan such as the SBA lend participation guaranteed loan programs. No fees are charged for this service, however, the loan must result in the creation of new jobs and employment opportunities for (name of city) residents (more specifically) for applicants or participants who are registered with PIC/DET for employment or training).

O <u>Business Seminars:</u> are offered to provide technical assistance and information to individuals who are interested in going into business or who currently have an existing business in (name of city).

2.4 INSPECTION

As part of the proposal review process, PIC/DET reserves the right to obtain any or all information associated with this RFP, including, but not limited to: reviewing the specific qualifications of staff designated to perform marketing tasks including the staff of any subcontractor; contacting any individuals of agencies listed in the proposal with knowledge of the proposer's performance and qualifications.

2.5 CONTRACT

PIC/DET will execute a negotiated cost reimbursement contract with successful proposer(s). Agencies who are unable to comply with this procedure should indentify and substantiate the use of a different method of contracting.

The initial contract period can be up to 12 months duration with a negotiated start date between the period July 1, 1986 through June 30, 1987. Extension options may be exercized at the discretion of PIC/DET.

2.6 SUBCONTRACTING

Subcontracting is not prohibited, but is subject to approval by PIC/DET. If any portion of the marketing proposal is to be subcontracted, the proposer must identify the subcontractor(s), define the specific scope of work to be subcontracted and describe the management controls which the proposer will install to ensure subcontractor(s) performance.

FIG. 4-3. (continued)

2.7 NEGOTIATION

PIC/DET reserves the right to negotiate the final terms of
all contract(s) with the selected service provider(s). Items
that may be negotiated include, but are not limited to; type and
scope of services an activities, implementation schedule, taget
group, geographic goal, and price and conditions of payment.

2.8 LIMITS

Costs incurred by the proposer in anticipation of funding
under this RFP are solely the responsibility of the proposer.

This RFP does not commit PIC/DET to award a contract, to pay
any costs incurred in responding to this RFP, or to procure or to
contract for services.

PIC/DET reserves the right to accept or reject any or all proposals
received in responce to this RFP. PIC/DET may fund part of the
proposed program or negotiate to fund smaller units of larger
programs.

2.9 RESTRICTIONS ON DISCLOSURE

Proposals received will become the property of PIC/DET and
become public record.

2.10 COMPLIANCE REQUIREMENTS

Contractor(s) must comply with the Job Taining Partnership
Act, as amended; Family Economic Security Act, as amended;
Section 504 of the Rehabilitaiton Act of 1973; policies and
operating requirements of PIC/DET; the California Public Records
Act; and all applicable Federal, State, and Local laws and
regulations.

2.11 RULES AND REGULATIONS

It is the policy of the Private Industry Council/Division of
Employment and Training to comply with the provisions of the Job
Training Partnership Act (JTPA) , the Family Economic Security Act
(FESA) and all other applicable Federal, State, and Local laws and
regulations. Agencies or individuals claiming violation of
applicable laws and regulations may file a grievance, pursuant to
JTPA and FESA, with PIC/DET. A copy of the required grievance
procedure at the PIC/DET office. PIC/DET is committed to Equal
Opportunity and Affirmative Action.

FIG. 4-3. (continued) (Figure continued on p. 130.)

2.12 INSURANCE

All contractors must, prior to signing contract, provide
proof of insurance. Such insurance shall be in an amount of not
less that $ 1,000,000 for public liability and not less than
$500,000 for property damage insurance. These policies shall
inclue the County as an additional insured and coverage shall
be made primary with respect to any other coverage. Public
institutions may meet these insurance requirements with self
insurance, provided adequate reserves are maintained.

2.13 ADMINISTRATIVE RESPONSIBILITY

All contractors will be required to maintain adequate
financial records. Records must be maintained and available for
audit upon reasonable notice. Records must be maintained and
auditable for a period of three years from the end of the
program funded, or until all audits affecting the program are
resolved. Record retention must be in compliance with applicable
laws and regulations.

3.0 EVALUATION PROCESS

3.1 COMPLIANCE REVIEW

The first step in the evaluation process is conducted by
staff. Staff will review the proposals for completeness and
compliance with applicable laws, regulations and the RFP.
Proposals not in compliance with this RFP are subject to
elimination from consideration.

3.2 PROPOSAL REVIEW

Proposals accepted for consideration will be rated by a PIC
Review Panel. The rating will be based on the following
evaluation catagories:

1. Marketing Campaign Design

2. Marketing Performance Outcomes (Expected
    Results)

3. Qualifications of Agency and Staff (including
    staff of any subcontractors) Providing
    Marketing Services

4. Proposed Cost

PIC/DET reserves the right to use a different but uniform
evaluation and rating methodology.

FIG. 4-3. (continued)

Proposers may be requested to make an oral presentation to the Review Panel. The Review Panel will provide funding recommendations to the full Private Industry Council.

Proposals selected by the Private Indstry Council will be submitted to the County Board of Supervisors for consideration. In order to be funded proposals must be approved by both the Private Industry Council and the Board of Supervisors.

4.0 TARGET GROUP GOALS FOR PARTICIPANTS

4.1 <u>JTPA ELIGIBLE POPULATION</u>

PIC/DET training programs are for individuals who met JTPA eligibility criteria.

Participants eligibility criteria for Title II-A programs include:

O Persons whose income during the immediate past six months which is at or below the poverty level established by the Federal Government;

O Persons whose income during the immediate past six months was at or below 70% of the lower living standard income level;

O Persons who receive, or is a member of a family which receivs cash welfare payments under a Federal, State or local welfare program;

O Persons receivimg food stamps pursuant to the Food Stamp Act of 1977;

O Foster child status on behalf of whom State and local government payments are made;

O Handicapped adults whose own income meets economically disadvantaged criteria but whose family income does not

Participants eligibility criteria for Title III programs include:

O Persons who have been terminated or laidoff or who have received notice of termination or layoff from employment, are eligible for or have exhausted their entitlement to unemployment compensation, and are unlikely to return to their previous industry or occupation;

O Persons who have been terminated, or who have received

FIG. 4-3. (*continued*) (*Figure continued on p. 132.*)

notice of termination of employment, as a result of
any permanent closure of a plant or facility; or

o Persons unemployed for long terms and having limited
   opportunities for employment or reemployment in the same
   or similar occupation in the area in which they reside,
   including older individuals who have had substantial barriers
   to employment by reason of their age.

4.2 GEOGRAPHIC GOALS

PIC/DET is mandated to serve targeted participants on a county
wide basis. Marketing efforts to attract applicants for employment
training programs must include a county wide approach.

4.3 DEMOGRAPHIC AND TARGET GOALS

Demographic and target group goals for adults are as follows:

                                    % of Clients to be Served

S   Male   42 %
E   Female   58 %
X

A   %
G   22-54   83.52 %
E   55 and over   16.48 %

E   White   49.9 %
T   Black   10.7 %
H   Hispanic   30.4 %
N   Asian/Pacific Islander   6.2 %
I   Filipino   1.5 %
C   American Idian/Alaskan Native   1.4 %
I
T
Y

T G   School Dropouts   44.2 %
A R   AFDC/WIN Work Registrants   18.3 %
R O   Veterans   9.1 %
G U   Handicapped   10.6 %
E P
T S

Title III - Characteristics of Title III participants vary
according to individual plant closures etc. As such, no

FIG. 4-3. (continued)

notice of termination of employment, as a result of
any permanent closure of a plant or facility; or

O Persons unemployed for long terms and having limited
   opportunities for employment or reemployment in the same
   or similar occupation in the area in which they reside,
   including older individuals who have had substantial barriers
   to employment by reason of their age.

4.2 GEOGRAPHIC GOALS

PIC/DET is mandated to serve targeted participants on a county
wide basis. Marketing efforts to attract applicants for employment
training programs must include a county wide approach.

4.3 DEMOGRAPHIC AND TARGET GOALS

Demographic and target group goals for adults are as follows:

                                            % of Clients to be Served

S   Male   42   %
E   Female   58   %
X

A   %
G   22-54   83.52 %
E   55 and over   16.48 %

E   White   49.9 %
T   Black   10.7 %
H   Hispanic   30.4 %
N   Asian/Pacific Islander   6.2 %
I   Filipino   1.5 %
C   American Indian/Alaskan Native   1.4 %
I
T
Y

T G   School Dropouts   44.2 %
A R   AFDC/WIN Work Registrants   18.3 %
R O   Veterans   9.1 %
G U   Handicapped   10.6 %
E P
T S

Title III - Characteristics of Title III participants vary
according to individual plant closures etc. As such, no

FIG. 4-3. (*continued*) (*Figure continued on p. 134.*)

5.2 RELEVANT CONSIDERATIONS

The objective of having a marketing plan is to attract employers to hire trainees and to encourage and motivate eligible individuals to participate in PIC/DET sponsored training programs.

O   The marketing campaign may be written for a one-year period (July 1, 1986 to June 30, 1987).

O   The marketing plan may include either: participant outreach, employer outreach, industry attraction or program marketing.

O   The PIC/DET will retain sole ownership of the completed marketing plan with discretionary rights to use it as deemed appropriate.

O   The selected contractor(s) will be responsible for securing any required licenses to use original or copyrighted materials.

O   The selected contractor (s) must agree to the unencumbered transfer of all use rights, licenses, releases, etc., to the PIC/DET or its assignees and to hold harmless the (name of city) to be contained in the contract language.

5.3   ELEMENTS AND TIMETABLES

The proposal must identify and describe each element in the marketing campaign. The campaign must include a timetable for the elements proposed and the associated elements:

a.   Printed materials (brochures) to attract inividuals (youth and adults for enrollemnt into the various training programs sponsored by PIC/DET.

b.   Printed materials (brochures) (to the business community employers) on training programs availble to assist them in meeting their work force needs and on available services such as loan packaging and business seminars which offer technical assistance.

c.   Audio visual presentation on training programs suitable to potential participants.

d.   Audio visual presentation on training programs and services suitable to employers or business groups.

e.   Advertising including newspaper ads, radio, television specialty advertising and public service announcements.

FIG. 4-3. (continued)

f.   Industrial marketing package which could be used to attract new industry in (name of city).

g.   Joint venture marketing which would entail linkages and coordination with other local economic development agencies.

Proposers must develop a detailed work schedule to outline the sequence of events and activities for the development of any product or materials proposed. Time frames for media distribution and other media coordination activities (i.e., the publication of ads, air time arrangements for PSAs and the production of printed material) must be included.

6.0   PROPOSAL STANDARDS

Each proposal shall include at a minimum the following:

1.   Completion and submittal of the Proposal Cover Sheet (Attachment A).

2.   The name of the author(s), their relationship of position with the applicant organization, and a telephone number where they may be reached.

3.   The name and telephone number of the person who is authorized to represent the applicant organization for contract negotiations.

4.   Statements or resumes concering the qualifying experience and other background of personnel, including personnel of any subcontractor) who will work on the proposed marketing plan.

5.   A statement of the number of personnel who will work on the proposed project.

6.   A list of commercial and public agency clients for whom services were performed with the name and telephone number of a person with whom work/services can be verified quantitatively and qualitatively (a minimum of 3).

7.   Sample marketing plans that show work performed including most recent examples.

8.   A concept outline which describes the applicant organization's proposed design and execution of this project (including time frames).

9.   The proposed cost of the development of a marketing campaign including a breakdown of all expenses.

FIG. 4-3. (*continued*)

THE PROPOSAL: NEEDS AND OBJECTIVES

The Private Industry Council has three needs and objectives: the recruitment of employers with jobs for applicants, the recruitment of applicants, and a greater awareness of and higher profile for the PIC. That higher profile will enable PIC not only to reach employers, but make them aware of what PIC is, what it does, and the benefits that are available to companies that work with it.

Our goal (the marketing company) is not only to reach every employer and recruit every possible candidate, but also to make the PIC a recognizable word to every businessperson and applicant. When people think of placement and jobs, they will think of the PIC.

Many of these goals will be accomplished through publicity and promotion, and other low-cost or free marketing techniques. Publicity and promotion carry the credibility that the PIC needs. People believe what they read, see, and hear in the media.

(A general description of the problem is standard for the opening of the proposal. The consultant wants the client to be aware that there is an understanding of the problem.)

MARKETING CAMPAIGN DESIGN

Marketing is sales, and an effective sales program communicates and educates the potential buyer. In the _____ County PIC's case, we have three buyers: applicants, employers, and consumers. Each product, whether it be the PIC or a bar of soap, has a USP (unique selling proposition) that appeals to each buyer—applicants, employers, and consumers.

The one thing all three of the PIC's buyers have in common is they buy quality. In other words, whatever elements are put into a marketing program should be quality oriented. The PIC should be sold as a quality, caring organization; its literature should reflect this image; and everything that is done from a marketing standpoint should be uniform and quality oriented.

In appealing to those markets, we recognize that _____ County has an irregular, seasonal, high unemployment rate. It is also rapidly growing and changing. In the future, it will be a county that will have a more balanced economic base. We believe light manufacturing, high tech, and an expanding port employment base, will one day offset the agricultural ups and downs of the county.

(The preceding paragraph is an example of what research can do for a presentation. This company studied the market area and its characteristics, just as any consulting firm would study a prospect's company. By displaying knowledge but not revealing confidential information, a consulting firm can make a definite impression on the prospect.)

The marketing campaign we designed involves two phases. Phase one enhances the image of the PIC, and brings in additional employers. Phase two recruits applicants. Effective marketing in these areas will spill over into a third phase—greater awareness of the PIC by the entire county.

Although the plan is designed to appeal to two different segments, employers and applicants, that does not mean they are totally separate. Each benefits from the other—and most important—they will be conducted simultaneously. Once again, it is impossible to reach these two segments without affecting the third—the consumer.

For example, a story in the _____ *Record* or _____ *Sentinel* may be seen by potential employers as well as applicants. The same is true of an interview that might be done with the PIC Chairperson on KJOY, a local radio station.

(Although the PIC is seeking a marketing consultant, that does not mean it has knowledge of marketing or how a marketing campaign functions. Thus there is reference in the preceding section to the impact certain marketing procedures would have, meaning the spillover. Consultants should keep this important point in mind—although a company needs your services, that does not mean they understand what you do or how you accomplish your goals.)

TARGETING EMPLOYERS

What, if anything, does the employer think of the PIC and its candidates? Do they realize there are highly skilled, cooperative workers being turned out by the program? And are they aware of the tax and other benefits?

Our marketing approach to employers would address these questions. Incidentally, all of these techniques have been utilized and perfected during the past 16 months in our association with the _____ PIC.

(The consulting firm is referring to a client with similar problems. If they could handle the problem with this client, they can also do it for the prospective one. This is an important selling point for any consultant; if you have done it before for companies with similar problems, you can do it again by duplicating some of the same programs.)

Our initial thoughts and how we would proceed:

Speaker's Bureau

A program would be developed where someone from the PIC would be scheduled to address service clubs, chamber of commerce groups, civic organizations, and the like. We recommend the speaker always be accompanied by a staff person in the event questions become technical or involved. We would set the engagements. An audio/visual would be written and produced to accompany this part of the program. An audio/visual is important for two reasons. First, it makes the job of the volunteer PIC speaker easier. Second, it would be self-contained and entertaining. The audio/visual would run about 10 minutes—any longer and you can lose the audience—and it would explain, in basic terms, what the PIC is, how it operates, the benefits, and so forth. It would not go into detail. That would be left for the Q&A period. This approach has been effective for the _____ PIC. There is at least one engagement a month, sometimes more, depending on potential outlets.

Audio/Visual Production

We propose producing an audio/visual (A/V) geared to employers. This A/V could be utilized by speakers who go out to meet clubs and other organizations.

It could also be used by staff when meeting with personnel of various companies to give them a quick overview of the PIC, what it is, how it operates.

Newsletter

Communication between employers and the PIC is critical. The newsletter would be produced four times a year with the fourth issue an annual report as well as newsletter.

The newsletter would go to personnel departments and key executives within companies. It would focus on what the PIC has to offer to their company. It would detail some of the PIC's unique programs and benefits, the skills of applicants, and success stories. The idea is to make the employer aware that they can get highly skilled, qualified, exceptional employees and significant benefits as well.

Business Publications

Aside from chamber of commerce publications, there are numerous business magazines that would take a PIC story—if the story had the proper hook or angle. A story geared to these publications would have to emphasize employer benefits, new training programs available, and so forth. Those are the kind of features that these magazines utilize. We would write and service these features on a regular basis. It would be our responsibility to develop the material, just as we would develop and supervise the newsletter. Once again, the stories are important for two reasons: first, they attract employers, and second, they make them aware of the PIC.

News Releases

New programs, contracts, and contractors would be publicized via news releases. These releases not only attract the attention of potential employers, but they also help develop the PIC's profile in the community.

Feature Stories

These differ from news releases. In this kind of editorial, someone from the publication comes out and interviews the PIC. When it comes to radio, we would arrange guest spots, and the same for TV. Once again, feature coverage in this area is designed to increase the profile of the PIC among potential employers. The kind of material that makes news revolves around such topics as the success ratio of the PIC to the growth in the number of companies involved in the various PIC programs. This material would be developed by our firm following interviews with members of the PIC.

Employer of the Year

Once a year, there would be a reception held to recognize both the small and large employers of the year. Small refers to the number of employees in the company. This reception would also bring together new employers. During the reception the PIC A/V would be shown. This gives new employers some insight into the PIC. It would be hosted by the PIC and well-known civic officials.

We originated this concept for _____ PIC, and last year during our first ceremony, more than 100 new employers were recruited by the staff and board via this program. Appointments by staff are generated through this reception. A third award should also be considered—summer or youth employer of the year. The critical aspect of this reception is the personal contact generated between the marketing firm, PIC, and employers.

DBAs

Hundreds of DBAs (doing business as) new businesses are filed weekly. There would be a regular mailing to these people to inform them about the PIC, and its benefits to employers.

Employer Brochure

We would write and design an employer-oriented brochure. This brochure would explain to potential employers the benefits of the PIC, who was on its board, how it ran, and what it offered. It would be used as a handout at the employer reception, speaking engagements, and appointments that staff or others had with potential employers.

Employer Letters

One of the best ways to sell employers on the PIC is through continuous communication. That is, whenever there is a new program, benefit, news, and so forth, the employers throughout the county would be informed via letter. Do not wait for a newsletter to be produced. Tell them immediately. These letters, which would all be personalized, would be designed to keep the lines of communication open between PIC and employers. They would be designed as informative/education pieces—the best way to sell.

There are two keys to developing a relationship with employers: communicating and answering their needs. The newsletter, employer of the year awards, and employer letters are examples of good communication. Employers must become familiar with the PIC; it should become part of their everyday vocabulary. This can only be done through adequate communication. Also, employers are not going to respond to the PIC simply because it is the PIC. Like all of us, employers are motivated by benefits offered to them and their companies. These benefits must be spelled out and constantly communicated to the employer. Our marketing program is designed to accomplish both these goals.

(Note how this firm has outlined every idea. There is, of course, the possibility that the potential client could give this proposal to a rival firm; that happens. This marketing firm, however, believes that there still is a significant challenge in the execution of the program—and there certainly is one. Note how the firm also spells out each program in the remainder of the presentation.)

TARGETING APPLICANTS

The PIC's applicants are not reading the *Wall Street Journal*, nor are they listening to all-news stations—although employers may be. Typical, unemployed, unskilled or semiskilled workers or candidates for youth positions watch TV, frequent parks, playgrounds, and fast-food restaurants; they shop in malls and may have language barriers. Some of the techniques we would use in attracting this segment of the market:

(Note the understanding the firm has for another segment of the client's market. Apparently, it has researched this element in the program equally as well as it did the first segment, the employers.)

PIC a Job Week.

This would be a special week and promotion set aside throughout the service delivery area (SDA). We would tie-in retail locations—such as McDonald's, Burger King, and other such chains. Each would have counter merchandisers or posters pushing the PIC and the opportunities for the unemployed. There would be civic tie-ins as well (proclamations, etc.). The idea is to make the week a major event and make potential applicants aware.

Supplement

We would be putting together a newspaper supplement for the *Record, News Sentinel, Bulletin,* and one or two other county newspapers that would focus on "PIC a Job Week." It would focus on Job Training Partnership Act (JTPA) applicants, the seniors, youth, dislocated, and other success stories. It would show the opportunities that are available to applicants. This supplement, which would hit countywide, would have enormous impact on both potential applicants and employers as well.

   Previously, we made the point that applicants do not read the newspaper to any great extent. Why, then, have a newspaper supplement (or success stories listed below)? The reason is while the applicant may not read, many others (friends, family, etc.) they know do read and they will pass the word on to them. This technique enabled us to increase applicants by 500% in _____ PIC. The supplement, as with the success stories, have to be put together a certain way. We have included samples for your perusal.

Merchandisers

A key part of any campaign to generate applicants. As we said previously, applicants frequent fast-food restaurants, bowling alleys, the post office, the unemployment office, and so on. Our counter merchandisers would be designed and placed in each of these outlets. We would fabricate and design the merchandiser, as well as place it. It would have a "take one" pocket so the message could be changed frequently. This is one of the most effective ways of reaching the applicant. Once again, this is also a technique that reaches the general public and employer.

Success Stories

We would approach one or two key local newspapers (i.e., *Record, Bulletin*) and attempt to sell them on the concept of running regular success stories about PIC applicants who have been placed on the job. These are applicants who have come in, qualified, and gone on to become successful employees. This type of story can show applicants the positive things that are out there when they come to PIC. We would find the applicants, interview them, write the story, and set the photography with the newspaper.

This proposal has a two-fold approach. First, it can reach applicants either directly (they read) or indirectly (one of their family or friends reads). Second, employers and the community see and read it as well, and they become more familiar with the PIC.

Publicity

News releases would back each event. News releases pertain to timely events. Suppose, for instance, one of the PIC's contractors was opening a new training class for cable TV technicians, mechanics, or computer repair specialists—this is the type of event that presents opportunities for news releases and features as well.

Public Service Announcements

An important tool, both for radio and TV. We would write and place them for all programs, and also design a special public service announcement (PSA) campaign for youth. We also envision a PSA that would be directed toward theaters, which have a large, youthful audience. Recently, we recruited Bruce Jenner for PSAs, and we would attempt to do the same for _____ PIC. Another positive effect of PSAs is making the general public and employers aware of the PIC.

Audio/Visual

Another important tool. Applicants, particularly those in the youth category, are video oriented. A good A/V, talking about the benefits (to the applicant) of the PIC can be a potent sales tool. In _____ PIC we have sold a local television station on the concept of doing a 10-minute applicant film. They are providing the film and crew at no cost. We are scripting and editing. When we are finished we will have a film worth $30,000 that can be used commercially (on TV) as well as in schools.

Brochure

A brochure, appealing to all applicants and written in plain, easy-to-understand terms, would be written.

Display for Fairs

There are, of course, job fairs and shows, where applicants and employers pass through. Our idea is to put together a quality display that can be folded, packed, and used over and over again. It could be set up and dismantled by one person. It would be an attractive, image-building display.

Matching Funds

A critical area, especially concerning an ambitious program with employer of the year and PIC A Job. In the past 12 months, we have generated $72,920 in matching which has enabled us to conduct an expanded marketing program.

School Tie-Ins

Applicants for youth (and other) programs can be reached through schools. For example, grammar school kids will carry home literature to make parents, friends, and relatives aware of the PIC programs and opportunities. At the same time, youngsters can be reached via A/V showings, posters, and other materials before they drop out. And they can also tell other dropouts about the program, if they know about it.

Bus Placards

Countywide, we would design and fabricate placards for display inside and outside buses. This is another area where there are an abundance of applicants.

(In this next section, the marketing firm outlines what results it expects from this program.)

MARKETING PERFORMANCE OUTCOMES

Without question, we expect to help the County PIC to reach 100% of its goals, and possibly exceed them. To do this, a marketing plan has to be creative— and flexible. Thus, with any plan, it is important to monitor results. For example, we need the cooperation of in-take to determine where applicants are coming from (once the plan is underway). Are they coming from PSAs on radio? TV? The newspaper supplement? Merchandisers?

We will find certain marketing techniques are more effective than others. When we do, we should readjust the marketing plan and concentrate on those areas that are most productive.

On the basis of the plan we have formulated, we expect that within 12 months, the _____ County PIC will be well known to consumers throughout the county.

We also expect that employers will not only be familiar with the PIC, but that their involvement will be increased tremendously. This will be accomplished through such employer-oriented events as a speaker's bureau, employer of the year awards, and constant communication. We expect a significant number of new contracts opened with employers through these efforts. In the case of applicants, we expect the PIC to easily surpass its goals and the number of qualified candidates it expects to recruit.

Why? Because we are going to the applicants—merchandisers, in-store signage, schools, and the like—and not waiting for the applicants to come to us. We are reaching out for them.

We would recommend a quarterly plan in which applicant results are monitored. We would develop a monitoring plan along with PIC, especially with in-take, which is a key to the success of any plan.

QUALIFICATIONS OF AGENCY AND STAFF

The project will be managed by _____ . In addition, there will be two staff persons assisting.

_____ has spent 20 years in the marketing field. He was a writer for the _____ *Times* and learned the ins and outs of working with the media and generating features and media coverage during that period. He opened his own firm in 1967 and has done campaigns for a variety of companies ranging from the Marriott Corporation to GW Electronics.

In 1974, he developed a private/public sector work program in which Host International provided training and employment opportunities for L.A. city youths who were in need of jobs. The program, which lasted three months, resulted in the training and employment of more than 30 students. It became a page one story in the local newspaper.

In 1978, he worked with the University of Southern California and a half-dozen universities throughout the country, to set up a private/public sector program for young men and women who were interested in going into business. His job was to bring the educational and private sector together to train people for business opportunities.

As a result, the city of Los Angeles, Mayor Tom Bradley, as well as 15 other cities across the country, presented his client with proclamations praising its work. Media coverage ranged from local radio and TV to major metropolitan newspapers.

(This portion of the proposal is similar to a company profile. It gives the consultant the chance to blow his or her horn in an objective, factual manner.)

PIC EXPERIENCE

(Here the consultant expands on his or her experience with similar clientele. If you are competing against other consultants for a contract and have a background that they do not have, let the prospect know about it. It could mean the difference between gaining or losing a potential client.)

In 1985, our firm embarked on the first marketing program for the _____ PIC. We originated the concept of a "PIC A Job Week," "Employer of the Year" awards, and success stories which run in two of the local newspapers.

These monthly success stories give the PIC high local visibility. In addition, we have arranged for tie-ins with two of the local malls in the SDA. Our contract has been renewed with the PIC on two occasions.

STAFF ASSISTANTS

(Under this section, the marketing firm or consultant, gives an overview of the abilities of the people handling the project. This is particularly important if you are not going to be involved at all times.)

CONCEPT OUTLINE

(This phase of the plan outlines exactly how the firm would proceed with the ideas it has outlined; what steps would be taken first.)

Employer outreach is critical. Therefore, within the first three months we would start and complete an employer-oriented A/V, brochure, and newsletter. A fourth element produced within this period would be a computerized PIC paper, so we could customize letters and other materials to employers. These are the first basic communication devices in the program portion that involves employers.

At the same time, we would be generating news releases to publicize the PIC's programs to the community and employers. These releases could range from PIC Board appointees to special tax benefit programs for JTPA training programs.

During this first quarter we would hope to develop and sell the _____ *Record* on a feature revolving around the PIC. This would be a positive story, which we would utilize later as a mailing and information piece to employers.

During the following quarters, we would attempt to sell other dailies on the same approach. Our first business stories would also be developed and placed during this period. The DBA mailings would begin in the second quarter, and the speaker's bureau would be launched during this period as well.

Our "Employer of the Year" award ceremonies would take place in the third quarter. Our fourth employer newsletter would be an annual report, and employer of the year recap, mailed following the awards. Along the way we would monitor, with staff's help, the enrollment of employers and new programs.

When we had something special to offer, something of interest to employers, we would supplement newsletters and news releases with personalized letters.

During the first quarter we would be producing a program brochure and merchandiser for in-store placement to lure applicants. During this first three month period, we would also prepare stuffers for the merchandisers, contact retail outlets, as well as such places as Employment Development Department (EDD), and place the merchandisers.

We would approach the local media with our idea of a success story to be run on a regular basis. We would also be working extensively with the staff in developing people (applicants) to be used in stories. News releases pertaining to programs and training opportunities would be written and placed. Our first

PSAs would be cut and placed during this quarter as well. We anticipate utilizing a celebrity in this phase of the program.

In the second quarter, we would complete the applicant A/V and begin our school outreach program to reach applicants. Additional PSAs would be cut for both radio and TV and there would be an ongoing series of news releases on PIC programs being offered to applicants. The type of releases we envision would range from special youth programs to senior citizen opportunities and schooling availability.

During the third and fourth quarter, bus placards would be designed and placed. Merchandisers would be replenished each quarter.

"PIC a Job Week" would take place in the third quarter and there would be civic recognition to go along with it. At the same time, we would prepare and insert our four-page supplement in all print media.

It is important to recognize two other things in this timetable. First, we would be reaching consumers with elements in both these programs. Second, as we become more familiar with the operations of the PIC, there will be other publicity and promotion opportunities that arise during the course of the contract.

(This can be looked on as a timetable. This timetable could also have been done in chart and/or graph form.)

MARKETING BUDGET

Employer Portion of Program

Audio visual

Newsletter (4)

Brochure

DBA mailings

Sheet-fed paper/envelopes

Speaker's bureau

News releases

Employer of the year awards/reception

Employer of the year trophies

Employer mailings (not including newsletters)

Newsletter mailing

Participant Portion of Program

Merchandisers

Success stories

PSAs

Merchandiser inserts

Brochures

Audio visuals

School program

Newspaper supplement

Bus placards

Display booth

Water bill stuffer

(The budget portion is divided into two parts, for the separate parts of the program. This particular budget includes costs plus the marketing company's fees. In some budgets, the potential client would just pay the cost of the particular item and compensate the consultant on a cost-plus, retainer, and/or set-fee basis.)

In addition to the aforementioned items, an in-depth proposal should also contain references. Before submitting an in-depth proposal, you must determine whether you want to give away ideas.

The second proposal, which is less detailed, usually follows after several oral presentations between you and the client. The client is sold on your services and he or she wants to hire you. The document you submit is an outline of what you will perform.

Figure 4-4 is an example of this proposal. Notice that although the ideas are there, the execution is still not detailed. When a client ultimately makes a decision, he or she will not only take into consideration the ideas, but the ability of that firm to carry them out.

(This should be on your letterhead)

Date

Name
Title (if any)
Company
Address
City, State, Zip

Dear

After spending time going through the notes and comments we
garnered from the last meeting, Jay, Wil (the partner you have
not met, as yet), and I came up with several initial programs
that I think you will find quite fascinating.

Before embarking on any, we would go into detail with you and
the other committee members to determine if there were any
potential problems you foresaw.

These are not necessarily in the order, but they represent our
initial thoughts.

(1) Personalized letters and customer follow-up. We would put
all names on computer, and schedule a four-time a year mailing.
When someone comes in and rents, they automatically "kick-in"
a chain of letters. The first would be a thank you, however,
each mailing would offer something specific to the customer, and
would be designed to pay for itself.

That's the key...this program would not only be designed to
thank the customers, but get them to come back in and "buy"
something.

We would suggest the "offerings" and consult you and the other
owners to see about feasibility.

We would supervise the letters and mailings, and if it works we
would put the system in place at each agency.

(2) Rent a (name) and it does not cost you anything. When someone
rents a (name), they would receive a package that paid for the
(name) because of the package's value. We are not talking about
coupons. For example, we might have tie-ins with a (name of
compay). Rent from us and you get a half-hour message on the
house. (Name of company) would have merchandisers/signage that
plug (name).

-More-

FIG. 4-4. Sample letter proposal. *(Figure continued on p. 148.)*

While the solo businessman, might get the health spa, the husband and wife might get tickets to the Mann Theater, the Music Center, or something similar. Packages would be customized, personalized.

We would work the tie-ins, displays, literature, and design the letters that would go to both companies and prospects. This program could work with industrial/commercial companies with out of town VIPs, and with neighborhood renters as well.

(3) Hotel tie-in. Instead of trying to wrap-up the concierge, we suggest tieing in with hotels that do not have transportation to and from the airport. If feasible, we would offer them a shuttle service. In return, as part of the confirmation, guests get our material. It becomes a joint venture beween (name of company) and the hotel. The hotel also gets a cut of the rental. In each hotel room, (name of company) has signage and is plugged. There might also be something in the lobby as well.

We could add to this package by putting in things (name of company) has rights to such as (name things).

Other programs...

--Renting van owner mailing lists, and sending personalized letters that would make them aware of the renting benefits (if they needed a rental durng a breakdown, etc.), and some of the special things that (name of compay) does that others do not.

--Taking the "8 hours" free rental, and designing variations that would appeal to business people who have VIPs coming in; people who have visiting relatives, and those who may have cars in the shop.

--A visitor and convention bureau program in which we offer them "up front" commission--that is a commission before the rental is made, in-turn for promotional help with all incoming exhibitors, conventions, meetings, etc.

--Val Pak or neighborhood mailing that would tie into our package of "it won't cost you to rent" for the weekend, etc.

...and a (name of product) sale in which we would design the approach with your approval.

There are other ideas we have developed, such as "canned" features and news releases for local media, however, the above will give you some insight into how we would proceed.

I'll give you a call to see what you think.

Best Regards

(Your Name)

YN/si

FIG. 4-4. (continued)

CHAPTER 5

HOW TO GET FREE PUBLICITY

How would you like to make $10,000 during the next three days?

LETTERS

If you are a consultant in the right field, it can be done. Alec Stevens, an insurance consultant, did it with a simple promotion technique that can be duplicated by others in a variety of fields.

Alec belongs to the local visitors and convention bureau. Virtually every city in the country has one. These bureaus keep track of incoming conventions, exhibits, and meetings. They distribute lists of events to convention bureau members.

The list contains the convention name, place, the convention coordinator (the person in charge of making all arrangements for the conventioneers), and the coordinator's address and telephone number.

Alec scanned the list. He determined that nearly every listed convention could use his services. Why? Because every major convention hall requires its users to provide liability insurance—usually in the amount of $1 million or more. Since conventioneers generally have no idea how to go about providing the policy, the convention center buys it, and supplies it to the conventioneers—at a premium price.

From his past experience, Alec knew this happened all the time. He scanned the list and picked out several conventions. He then wrote a personalized note to each of the convention coordinators. He introduced himself, told them he was an insurance consultant, and had contacts that would enable him to offer the conventioneers a liability policy at favorable rates.

He mailed the letters about three months prior to the convention opening. Giving the letters a week to arrive, he then called each of the coordinators, asked if they had received his letter, if they had any questions, and would they be interested in a liability policy that met the convention center's needs, but could also be purchased at a lower cost.

Every one of the coordinators said they needed a policy and wanted to see his rates and coverage. Alec followed with a brochure that outlined the coverage, benefits, and rates. At the same time, the brochure also covered some of Alec's other services. He called the coordinators once again to close the sale.

As a result, Alec not only made $10,000 from a handful of conventions, but he developed a new flow of income at the same time.

The question usually asked is, "Well, what about the other insurance firms? Where are they? Didn't Alec have competition?"

Interestingly, he did not because people in business seldom think about conventions as a source of business. Even businesspeople who are members of convention bureaus fail to approach the incoming meetings and conventions in the proper manner. Most, if they are after business, send a form letter to the coordinator. The letter usually suggests that, if he needs help, the coordinator should call (the businessperson) upon arrival.

This is the wrong approach. Coordinators make arrangements in advance. They do not wait until the last minute. If they arrive in town and find they have forgotten something or are in need of some particular service, they will look in the *Yellow Pages* or ask the center for a vendor. They will not hold onto form written notes—and form letters are the weakest selling tool for a service business. Yet, that is the way most businesspeople approach coordinators. Leaving the response up to the prospect is a mistake. How many times do you respond when you get written, form letter solicitations for insurance, investments, or other significant purchases? Seldom.

Successful consultants do not leave the response in the hands of the prospect. If they send direct mail to a prospect, they may close with a line that says something like, "I'll give you a call to see if we can get together . . . " or "I will give you a call to see what you think."

The following is a well-structured letter from a service company to a potential client. Notice where the burden of contact lies.

Sample Letter to Potential Client

Ms. Joan _____
California Veterinary Medical Association
1024 Country Club Drive
Moraga, CA 94556

Dear Ms. _____ :

Many thanks for the time you took discussing the possibilities of utilizing Dr. _____ as a lecturer for your "Practice Management Session."

As I mentioned, Dr. _____ is a colorful, articulate, and fascinating economist/tax authority who practices in San Francisco. He is also a contributor to the CBS affiliate, KCBS, where he handles economic and tax issues from the (call-in) audience. He speaks in "plain, easy-to-understand, how-to" terms so that anyone can grasp what he is saying.

Dr. _____ offers a subject (and approach) that few can match. His lecture, which ranges from one to three hours, is, "How to make money in the 1980s."

It is a combination tax and investment lecture and is geared specifically to veterinarians.

Dr. _____ starts with the most common mistakes people make when investing—and why. He categorizes investments in 10 areas, ranks them from high to low risk, explains why, and has some fascinating opinions as to which investments are the best—and worst.

For example, he says (and proves), "You are guaranteed to lose money if you have funds in a bank, Savings & Loan (S&L), or money market fund." He also answers, "Can anyone beat the stock market?" and has a 10 year game plan for financial well being. He also has interesting and original opinions on tax shelters/investments and why most tax shelters lose money. He will also show those in the audience how to evaluate investments through five (simple) different dimensions.

A good portion of the lecture is devoted to little-known tax savings techniques that have been developed specifically for the veterinarian market. And most important, Dr. _____ does not sell securities, investments, or the like, so he does not tout anything—he weighs everything objectively.

A native of _____ , he was one of the youngest PhD graduates from the prestigious University of California at Berkeley School of Economics. He was a practicing economist for five years and then turned to tax consulting. He has lectured throughout the country and for groups as diverse as the National Ice _____ to the National Realtors.

I think he could be a real eye-opener at your session. I've enclosed some additional material and will give you a call to see what you think. In the meantime, many thanks for your time and interest.

Sincerely,

This letter was sent on behalf of a CPA who was trying to generate clientele from a veterinarian association's meeting.

Notice how the writer appealed to the needs of the audience ("How to make money in the 1980s"). The writer spent a good portion of the letter addressing those needs. He also established the speaker as someone who knows how to talk to a group. This was indicated by dropping the name of a radio station ("he is a contributor to it") and several other groups which the speaker addressed.

Convention coordinators have a number of things to worry about when it comes to speakers. However, their one great fear—they will put a dud behind the podium who has no speaking experience and may put the audience to sleep. A second fear is putting someone on who had nothing of value to contribute to the audience. The writer of this letter understood those fears and did a good job of alleviating them. He also did a good job of establishing his speaker as someone who was experienced and knowledgeable.

Notice that a telephone conversation preceded this letter. The following is a guide for those seeking speaking engagements, contracts, or anything else from convention coordinators.

Convention Coordinator/Business Checklist

1. Plan your calls at least three months before the convention comes to town. Speakers and arrangements are finalized about this time and, in many cases, before.

2. Note the time difference, if there is one.

3. When you call, ask for the coordinator by name. The person answering may ask you what the call is about. This is common practice, especially if you are dealing with a large convention. Tell them you would like to talk to the coordinator about a speaker (policy, etc.) for their upcoming meeting. Remember to mention the city and date. Many coordinators spend all their time putting together three, four, or more meetings a year, so specify which one you are calling about.

4. With some conventions, the coordinator has appointed an assistant or someone else to make arrangements for speakers, and so on. If that is the case, you may be referred to them.

5. If they are busy, call back. You can leave your name but do not leave your number. You should make the return call—after all, you are the person doing the selling.

6. When you get the proper party on the line, introduce yourself, outline your service, your background, and ask if they are in the market for something of that nature. This portion of the conversation (i.e., your portion) should not take more than 60 seconds. Impossible? Not at all. Practice. You will find you can cover the subject and capsulize your abilities within that time frame. The person you are talking to will appreciate your brevity and ability to get to the point. There is nothing more nerve-wracking than picking up the telephone and listening to a voice on the other end of the line that refuses to get to the point.

7. If there is interest, offer to send the details in writing. Coordinators will not want to make an instantaneous decision, even if they are interested. By putting it in writing, you give them a chance to look and study it. Give the coordinator about eight days from the time you mail the proposal letter, then call back. Ask if they have read it. If they have not, offer to call again. Suggest calling the following week. You do not want to put it off indefinitely. A one week delay says to the coordinator that he or she has to get down to business and read it.

8. If they have read it, ask if they have any questions or thoughts about it. If so, answer them. Once you have done this, go for the close.

9. There is, of course, no guarantee you will get the business. However, if you have presented your case in a timely manner, have a service the convention can use, have done the proper follow-up, have written the letter so that it addressed the needs of the conventioneers, and have listened to the comments of the coordinator so you come up with the right answers—you have a good shot.

Another key to getting business is personalization. Do not send form letters. They are anathema, especially in the consulting field.

Just look at your own habits. Do you respond to form letters? Do you tend to buy from the person who offers personalization and service or the person who offers the fast-food, impersonal approach.

Consulting is personal, more than any other business. If you go into a Sears, Penney's, or mass-merchandised store you do not expect personalized service. Usually it is self-serve and you carry your goods to a counter. That, however, is not how successful service or consulting businesses are run. When you deal with a CPA, insurance person, engineer, or anyone in the service field, you expect service—personalized attention. After all, you are dealing in a competitive field and could easily go elsewhere if the service lacks.

Alec Stevens remembered that.

There is a catch. Belonging to convention bureaus is not free. Some bureaus charge $300 and more for a year's membership. There is a way to reduce the fee. Contact three or four other consultants in noncompetitive fields. Tell them about the bureau, suggest you split the fee, and each of you can use the list.

Working with conventions is not restricted to insurance consultants, either. Look at all the other services that are needed—everything from computers to seminars. That's right seminars. Numerous conventions offer seminars as part of their meetings. In many cases, those seminars are given by outsiders who are authorities in the area.

The following case study can be adapted by consultants in almost any field.

CPA Case Study

A few years ago a struggling, west-coast-based accountant was trying to build his practice. Like most CPAs he relied primarily on references and acquaintances. Most consultants are in the same boat.

This CPA became restless. He thought there had to be a quicker, better way. And he thought of one. He called the local convention center and asked for a list of upcoming conventions. They told him they would be happy to supply one if he sent a stamped, self-addressed envelope, which he did.

When he got the list, he scanned it for incoming conventions. He found one—a major company that sold high priced, high-tech equipment to businesses in the $5 to $10 million sales category. Businesses in this range seldom have full-time accountants on staff. They rely on outsiders, and our consultant was aware of that fact.

He called the convention coordinator, introduced himself, and explained that he gave seminars to groups on how they could use tax benefits to *sell* equipment.

The coordinator was fascinated. Each year the salespeople in attendance were given motivation and sales-oriented seminars, but they had never attended one on how to use tax to sell.

The CPA followed up with an informational kit. It contained some background on the CPA, references, and a 15-minute cassette tape sampler in which the CPA outlined one or two tax-oriented sales techniques—in a practical, how-to fashion that anyone could understand. He took technical information and translated it into a language that the salespeople could understand and use. A week later he called the coordinator back and was hired to do the seminar.

The CPA did not make much on the seminar. He was, in fact, willing to do the session free of charge if he could make contact with the salespeople. Why? Because those salespeople make contact with companies; companies that are potential customers for the CPA. During his session, the CPA told each of the 300 salespeople that if they had any question or any problem, he would be happy to answer it. He passed out his business card at the close of the session along with a brochure on his services.

From that one seminar, the CPA wound up with three clients. Two were companies that the salespeople worked with and the third was a company, referred by one of the salespeople, that was in the market for a good accountant.

Why did the CPA wind up with the business? Because he did something that every consultant should be doing—supplying information, educating, and helping others. Sales are made by educating prospective clients, not twisting arms.

If the CPA had structured a seminar in which he told the salespeople about the tax environment or the economic outlook for selling their products, it is possible he would not have succeeded.

CPAs who discuss tax laws and the economy are abundant. CPAs who tell people how to increase sales and make more money are in short supply. Outlining tax breaks may help some salespeople, but not all. The appeal of the CPA's seminar was his session offered to help everyone; both the superior and average salesperson.

This approach does not just apply to CPAs. Suppose you are an engineering consultant who deals with governmental agencies and construction contractors. You could put together a seminar on development and how to deal with government officials for builders.

Or perhaps you are a management consultant specializing in productivity or a data processing consultant who specializes in redesigning computer systems. You, too, have the same seminar opportunities.

The management consultant could suggest new and innovative productivity techniques, and how companies can save money and increase output through them.

The data processing consultant could discuss when and why systems should be redesigned, the pros and cons, new innovations in design, how to avoid redesign and save money, and the dollars involved.

In each of these cases, the consultant is not directly selling his or her services. He or she is offering information and educating the potential buyer. He or she is not up on the podium pounding their chest and saying, "I'm a great consultant . . . hire me."

Remember, buyers make decisions when they believe they have sufficient information. If you give a seminar that supplies information instead of touting yourself, they may buy.

By educating and informing the prospect in the seminar audience, you also enhance your image in his or her eyes. They begin to think, "Well, if this consultant is so open, so willing to give me this kind of insight and information, perhaps I should be talking to him or her about doing the work for us."

Seminars do not guarantee you will get the business, but handled correctly they can be enormous business builders. Seminars are not limited to conventions. You can give them for local groups (civic or social), associations, clubs, and chamber of commerce organizations.

The key—do not make the sessions self-serving. Too many believe that once they get the podium, they should spend the time selling their services. That is the wrong approach. Concentrate on educating and informing the audience—and the business will come.

ARTICLES

Another effective free business builder for consultants is the article. That is, a consultant talks to a publication, writes an article, gets a byline, and benefits from the credibility being published brings. That credibility can be used to sell the consultant's services.

Articles, like seminars, should not be self-serving. The only mention of the consultant might be the byline and a small credit the publication inserts that identifies the consultant and his or her business. If the article becomes self-serving, chances are the publication will not use it.

Articles must educate, inform, and entertain the publication's audience. If you are a consultant involved in money or finance who writes an article for the local suburban newspaper, the theme should relate to the local economy, and how oil prices, unemployment, or some other newsworthy issue will affect the area. To make an article particularly effective, make sure it ties into a newsworthy topic—meaning, for example, the local economy and how it will be affected by the new tax law (if there is one), increased or decreased trade, and so on.

If you are a management or personnel consultant a publication may be interested in an article that centers on drugs (or some other contemporary topic) and the dangers, how it will affect on-the-job performance, and how companies should handle the problem.

Every consultant has a field and expertise. Study publications that reach your market, your potential customers, and write for them.

If you work with personnel managers (they are your customers), write for personnel journals. If purchasing agents buy your services, write for purchasing journals. If you are an engineering consultant catering to aerospace, write for aerospace publications.

Even if you are not a professional writer, when you structure an article about something you know, you may find that writing is not as difficult as you believe. Remember, you are not trying to be Hemingway. Look at the following checklist for structuring an article.

How to Get Articles Published—20 Key Points

1. Select your industry—the area in which you are trying to market your services (i.e., personal, purchasing, aerospace, engineering specialties, etc.)

2. Examine the trade publications that cater to that industry.

3. Select one or two of the leading trades within the industry. Discover leading industry publications by talking to or observing what your potential clients are reading.

4. Examine the editorial approach of these trades. Look at the table of contents for themes/angles. Read the headlines in each story for themes/angles.

5. Look at the bylines on the articles. (Are they staff writers, freelance, or a combination? This can be determined by matching names to those listed by the magazine near the table of contents.)

6. Think of topics that would be of interest to the readers. (If you are selling to those in the personnel field, think of something that would interest them—new personnel techniques; new ways to evaluate candidates; new ways to discipline employees; new ways to deal with labor unions; new ways to increase worker productivity.)

7. All topics must be something you know about; something related to your field; something on which you have specialized knowledge.

8. Write down the topic.

9. Write other points that relate to the topic directly underneath.

10. Try to write at least 10 other points beneath the main topic.

11. Go back to the main topic and write a general description of it.
    a. Make the description no more than 50–75 words, perhaps two paragraphs at most.
    b. Make sure the description is written in easily understood terms.
    c. Avoid the use of acronyms and trade names.

12. Do the same for the 10 other points you have listed.

13. Try to tie the main theme together with the 10 other points you have listed.
    a. Separate each by paragraphs.
    b. Remember to write in easy-to-understand terms.

14. Organize the 10. That is, following the introduction, put them in order from beginning to end.

15. Structure the 10, plus the lead, in a beginning, middle, and end configuration.

16. You have just created the rough of an article. (Each article should have a beginning, middle, and end.)

17. Read the article to yourself.
    a. Does it proceed logically from beginning to end? If not, rearrange.
    b. Can it be easily understood? If not, rewrite the areas that are unclear. Translate or break down complex terms into simple language.

18. Read the article once more.
    a. If it makes sense, have it typed neatly, double spaced, without erasures or misspelled words.

19. Put your name—byline—at the top.

20. Structure a 25-word explanation of what you do, that is, what kind of service you offer, the business you are in, and so on. This usually goes into the credit box the publication gives to authors.

You have created an article for an industry trade publication. All you did was take what you know, put it down on paper in the proper order, and make sure it was readable.

If you have information but feel you cannot write and no one you know does, contact the local college or university. Talk to the journalism or English departments. Find a student who wants to make a few extra dollars; a student who will ghost write the article for you.

Once you come up with the topic and decide on the publication, call the editor. Briefly explain who you are, and ask if they ever utilize articles from outsiders (meaning freelance writers). Follow the Checklist for Placing Articles when approaching editors.

Most publications—even *Time* magazine—will publish articles from outside sources. But the articles have to be newsworthy and must relate to the readership.

The following are copies of articles that have been written by freelancers for magazines and/or newspapers. The first (Figure 5-1) is for *Success* magazine. The author is Nancy Austin, coauthor of two books. Notice the publication gives Austin credit and mentions her two books. *Success* is a magazine that goes to Austin's potential market, salespeople and corporate executives who might benefit from the author's books.

The key to *Success* magazine's utilization of the article is that it is not self-serving. The article does not try to plug Austin's books. It gives the readers of *Success* valuable, usable information—that's what the editors of every magazine want for their readers.

The second article (Figure 5-2) was written by the author (this author) of a book on consulting. It was placed in a magazine (*Entrepreneur*) that caters to consultants and others interested in starting their own business. It benefits the readers of the magazine with its how-to approach, and the author by plugging his book.

The third article (Figure 5-3) was written by Darlene Phillips, a freelance writer for *Newsweek* magazine. Although Phillips is not selling any products or services, it is an example of how canned features (or features written by freelancers) are utilized in major newsmagazines.

The fourth article (Figure 5-4) should hit home with many consultants. It is written by the vice president of an economic consulting firm, Richard Rapp, and was accepted by one of the largest, most prestigious newspapers in the U.S.—the *Los Angeles Times*.

Rapp is not writing about his consulting business. He is writing about a subject that the *Times* feels would be of interest to their readers. This type of exposure enhances the stature of Rapp and his firm and will certainly garner his company credibility in the eyes of his present and prospective clients.

How does this type of article come about? It usually starts with a call. Follow the next checklist.

How to Place Articles Checklist

1. What is your consulting field?
2. What trade and/or consumer publications does your potential client read?

GET NICHE QUICK

How a Unique Service Can Set Your Company Apart from the Crowd

It's early evening in Latham, N.Y. Party guests clad in everything from jeans to mink coats are nibbling hot hors d'oeuvres as the host and hostess greet newcomers at the door. From one corner of the room, a local DJ is broadcasting a live radio show. Guests mingle. A young man catches a glance from a woman across the room. Encouraged, he makes his move and maneuvers his shopping cart alongside hers.

Shopping cart?

Welcome to "singles night," a new promotional event at Price Chopper Supermarkets. The company operates 58 stores in New York, Massachusetts, Vermont, and Pennsylvania, and industry sources estimate last year's sales to be $700 million. Although business at Price Chopper is good, the supermarket inaugurated singles night last year as a solution to a problem that could affect sales in the near future: How can Price Chopper distinguish itself from the plethora of other food store chains?

Changing the types of products the store sells was out of the question, executives decided, because all supermarkets by their very nature must offer the same basic products. So Price Chopper focused on services. Robert Wishnoff, the supermarket's consulting psychologist, proposed singles nights. The event would set Price Chopper apart from the crowd, he figured, and give unattached adults a chance to shop for meals and mates at the same time.

So far only a handful of supermarkets have hosted the event, but early ap-

Gage (right) looks on as two Syracusians meet for the first time over cake samples.

praisals deem it a success. "On that first evening in Latham we held our breath and hoped for the best," recalls Joanne Gage, the supermarket's manager of consumer affairs and the organizer of the singles night. As it turned out, guests began arriving early, and by 11 P.M. 1,000 singles were on hand. Many were not regular Price Chopper customers; they had come, they said, "just for the fun of it."

Encouraging Feedback

Gage and other Price Chopper executives didn't analyze the sales that night. Instead, they judged its success by customer feedback. The response was so overwhelmingly positive that two other New York stores — one in Syracuse, one in Schenectady — scheduled singles soirees. Gage promoted these events with the same media kits she used in Latham: tiny shopping bags packed with candy, cookies, and cheese. But she made these festivities even more elaborate than Latham's: free carnations to the

first 50 men and women to arrive; abundant food samples; expensive "sweepstakes" prizes, including three "escape weekends" at nearby luxury hotels. "When shoppers taste and rate the food samples," explains Gage, "we enter them in the sweepstakes."

Again the events were a hit. And again they attracted more than Price Chopper regulars. As the evenings in each of the stores drew to a close, many guests asked when Gage would hold the next singles night. Price Chopper was well on its way to carving out a special niche in the local supermarket trade.

Just as important as customer response was the reaction of suppliers. Typically, supermarkets have to drag suppliers into promotions at the stores. When they *do* agree to participate, they send product samples only. It's up to the supermarket to hire people to staff the promotions. Not so on singles nights: Vendors were *more* than happy to showcase their products to the growing singles market. In fact, so many vendors wanted to participate that Price Chopper had to turn some away for lack of room. Many companies chose to unveil new products so they could get feedback from the shoppers. Borden used the events to show off a new version of Elsie the Cow, the animated character that appears in its advertising. "Many vendors actually came to the store just to see how their products were doing in the taste tests," says Gage.

Price Chopper's success with the singles market is a study in how so-called "ordinary" businesses can distinguish themselves from competitors by offering imaginative services. All it takes is a little ingenuity. ◆

Nancy K. Austin is coauthor of A Passion for Excellence *and* The Assertive Woman.

FIG. 5-1. Nancy Austin article from *Success!* magazine.

Acquiring Consulting Expertise:
A How-To Approach

by Ron Tepper

How would you like to build a multimillion-dollar consulting business and never spend a dime on advertising in the process?

Believe it or not, it is possible. In my new book, *Become a Top Consultant—How the Experts Do It*, 10 of the most successful consultants in the country tell exactly how they built their businesses—without spending any money on advertising.

All 10—who are in such fields as data processing, money management, civil engineering, management and government consulting—outline the steps in a practical, how-to fashion. Each used different techniques; however, every method outlined is adaptable by any consultant looking for a way to build a business with a minimal expenditure.

Take, for instance, data processing/information systems consultant Joseph Izzo. He worked for various firms for 25 years. He was a highly paid consultant, but for as long as he could remember, he always wanted his own business. One day he took the plunge. He decided the best way to build a business was to 1) make a list of everyone he knew that could possibly give him any business and 2) make sure he communicated with them on a quarterly basis.

"You would be amazed," Izzo says in the book, "at the number of people you know who are in a position to give you business. When I started, my first list had 300 people on it. Today that list has grown to 1,500." Izzo sent an announcement card to those 300 people. A week later he began following up with telephone calls.

Once he got the prospect on the telephone, he did not try to "sell" the person. "That's a mistake many consultants make. They immediately try to sell without knowing the potential client's needs. I simply told them what I was doing and asked how things were going. They would often bring up a problem. Sometimes I solved the problem for them—right on the telephone. At other

INDUSTRY EXPERT—*Ron Tepper has compiled 10 success stories to show you how to excel as a consultant.*

times, it led to a meeting." On several occasions he found himself giving free advice. "Don't let that bother you. You cannot solve complex problems on the telephone. A call merely serves as a door opener," he says.

The key to building a consulting business, from Izzo's standpoint, is regular communication. "If someone only hears from you when you open, there is little chance they will keep you in mind unless you keep your name in front of them. I advise quarterly mailings."

Those mailings worked well. In less than seven years, his company has grossed nearly $20 million, and he has 40 employees. Today his list has grown to 1,500, and although he cannot possibly call each one, he finds he will get at least one client from each mailing.

Hank Zdonek was a struggling CPA until one day he "accidentally" found a unique way to sell his services. The discovery occurred shortly after he opened his one-man office. An insurance salesman walked

in and tried to sell Zdonek a policy.

Instead, Zdonek wound up showing this salesman how he could use tax benefits to sell more policies. The salesman was so impressed he rushed back to his office and told his supervisor about the session. The supervisor called Zdonek and asked if he would be willing to put on a seminar for the rest of the sales force. "I agreed," recalls Zdonek. "After all, it was a chance to meet people and perhaps bring in business."

Zdonek gave the seminar. He showed each salesman in the room how he could more effectively market his insurance products if he informed potential customers about taxes and how they related to the policy. Salesmen took Zdonek's material and began to increase their business. Several started referring clients to him.

"It taught me a valuable lesson," Zdonek says. "Most people who give seminars only try to sell you something. But if you give a seminar and help people, the favor is returned ten-fold. "I began to look at other industries and examined the tax consequences. I found ways that tax issues could help them increase their businesses as well. Then I would call the group (or business) and offer to do a free seminar, a seminar that would help everyone increase sales. No one turned me down. Find a group you can help. You would be amazed at the potential business."

Today, Zdonek has one of the fastest-growing CPA firms in the country. In fact, his staff is only slightly smaller than those of most "Big 8" accounting firms. Recently he moved everyone into his own newly constructed two-story office building.

Most of the business-building techniques used by the 10 consultants in this book are so logical and simple that they are seldom utilized. "There's no magic way to build a business," says management consultant Dr. Larry Senn. "The most important thing is getting out of your office

---

FIG. 5-2. Ron Tepper article from *Entrepreneur* magazine. (*Figure continued on p. 160.*)

and meeting people. You don't meet people if you are stuck away in an office."

Senn knows. When he opened, he focused on small businesses in the area. He mailed a letter to 1,000— and waited. "I got six returns. Four came back because of a lack of postage, and two others were addressed wrong. I learned quickly that mailing and waiting for people to pound on the door does not work."

What did work was a concept Senn developed that he calls "centers of influence." He explains: "There are certain groups and organizations in which important people gather. For example, I am a management consultant, and bankers and CPAs can refer business to me.

"After my mailing disaster I asked myself how I could reach bankers and CPAs. The answer was easy. All I had to do was join the same organizations (community groups, etc.) that they belonged to. In doing so, I met the bankers and CPAs, the people who could refer business. These organizations, such as the Rotary, Exchange Clubs, the Chamber of Commerce, all have 'centers of influence,' " Senn continues.

He points out, however, that just joining does not get you business. "That's a mistake many consultants make. They join a group and wait for business to come knocking. It does not just happen. You have to get involved, volunteer and spend time working for the group. That's how you meet people and find the centers."

Interestingly, Senn's first client came as a referral from one of those centers. Today, his firm occupies several thousand square feet of luxurious office space in a Southern California high-rise. None of it would have been possible without joining a group that had a "center of influence."

Similar, easy-to-duplicate methods were utilized by the other seven consultants discussed in this book. One of them summed it up this way: "Building a consulting business is work, but it is something anyone with the right skills can do. And you certainly do not need to spend a fortune on marketing in order to be a success."

Ron Tepper is a former Entrepreneur, Inc. vice president and director. His new book is published by John Wiley & Sons. ■

FIG. 5-2. (continued)

An American's Fear of Fallout

BY DARLENE M. PHILLIPS

Strontium 90 and iodine 131 have been detected in the local milk supply. I cancel the dairy, get my neighbors to do the same, and buy powdered milk. "You are overreacting," two men from the dairy say when they call on me. "All contaminated supplies have been dumped." I hold my ground. I have five small children—and children, I hear, are especially vulnerable. My kids need calcium, but there is a rumor circulating in town that the contaminated milk has somehow been "reconstituted," not dumped at all. So I compromise: I buy dried, powdered milk processed elsewhere, and then mix it, half and half, with whole milk.

The local newspaper reports that cesium 137 is beginning to show up in meat products. Government scientists assure us we have no cause to worry. My family will eat fish anyway. Then I learn that the same radioactive isotopes have been found in the mountains east of us; that they fall with snow and rain, gather in rivulets, concentrate in streams, pool in our reservoirs. They are in the very water I mix with the powdered milk. So I surrender. We will drink whole milk, and live and work and play as if nothing had happened.

Chernobyl, the Soviet Union, 1986? Actually, it is Salt Lake City, Utah, in 1962, a year after the Soviet Union broke a test-ban moratorium. Until 1958, nuclear tests had been conducted aboveground in the Nevada desert nearby, but news about atmospheric tests in the United States now frightened me. I no longer applauded the atomic tests to my west—or felt that watching them was the patriotic thing to do. It had been different in 1951 when I tended the soda fountain at Utah's Bryce Canyon National Park. Those of us who worked and lived there were told the time of a test so we could watch the predawn sky light up red, as if the sun were rising in the west.

Geiger counter: Now my family's health is my major concern. Prospecting in Nevada during the early '50s, my husband's uncles were stopped at a roadblock by federal employees and tested with a geiger counter. They were told to go home and hose down their car, wash their clothes and take a good shower. Assured they were in no danger, they received no follow-up care. One died of leukemia. The other from "idiopathic" hemorrhaging; by the time we buried him, I was losing my hair—an uncommon occurrence for a woman in her mid-20s.

My symptoms were a mystery to every doctor who examined me. I had an enlarged spleen, low platelet count, low white count, no free-iron stores and serious gastrointestinal problems. After multiple injections of intramuscular iron, my platelet count stabilized at a low, but survivable amount. My white count never returned to normal; I fought one infection after another. In 1973 I got very lucky. Scientists at the National Institutes of Health had sent a letter to physicians asking them to look for patients with unexplained immune failure. Isolated in a critical-care unit, I was just what they were looking for. Weekly injections of gamma globulin were prescribed to sustain my immune system. The research program I was assigned to is monitored by the National Cancer Institute. I was put in it not because I had been exposed to fallout or because I had witnessed nuclear blasts while living in southern Utah. I was there because of the novel theory at the time that the immune system recognizes malignant cells as foreign and destroys them.

Only one thing is certain: because our government funded a research program on human immunity, my life was saved and my family was rescued from certain financial ruin. To this day, a great deal of my medical care, several experimental medicines and my weekly gamma globulin come courtesy of the NCI.

Because of my immune disorder, I am careful about chemicals, steroids, X-rays, even exposure to ultraviolet rays from the sun.

Why my immune system collapsed is still an unanswered question. But I think now about the children and women and men downwind from Chernobyl. Like everyone else, I am appalled that the Soviets did not immediately warn their neighbors of the accident. I am frustrated by the piecemeal reports about the damage and more than angry about their ambiguous assurance that "measures are being taken to eliminate the consequences of the accident."

Continued exposure: Unfortunately, such language is painfully familiar to me. In the 1950s the Atomic Energy Commission assured those of us who live near the Nevada test site that "there is no danger." I suspect governments will always find it easier to say that fallout is not dangerous, or cumulative, especially since long-term health effects manifest themselves as diseases we already know—cancer, leukemia, melanoma, birth defects, even heart attacks.

While many Americans are worried that the Chernobyl fallout has reached the United States, I watch the sky to the west of me with different eyes. My government now explodes nuclear devices underground in the Nevada desert. As Utah's former Gov. Scott Matheson told a U.S. Senate subcommittee in 1979, "There is at least the possibility" of continued exposure to radiation.

"The Utah-Nevada-Arizona area presents one of the largest populations ever exposed to low-level radiation for a long period of time," Matheson told the senators. "There can be no doubt," he charged, that the federal government "has continually worked to suppress information about the true extent of the fallout and to undermine any attempt to study the problem." As it is, I will never know how much radiation I received, or what part isotopes in milk, water and meat played in an immune disorder now labeled "idiopathic acute variegated hypogammaglobulinemia." Was fallout the cause, a contributory factor or a coincidence?

I will never know if atomic tests caused my disease

Phillips, 52, is a free-lance writer in Salt Lake City, Utah.

FIG. 5-3. Darlene M. Phillips article from *Newsweek* magazine.

Courts Could End Predatory Trade

By RICHARD T. RAPP

The United States now runs a trade deficit of about $140 billion a year. We pay it by borrowing annually $50 billion from Japan, $35 billion from Western Europe, $20 billion from Canada, $14 billion from Taiwan, $14 billion from the OPEC nations and $7 billion from other trading partners.

For the first time since 1914, we owe more to foreign countries than they owe us. The United States, the world's richest country, has become the world's biggest borrower.

This troubles the American peo-

Richard T. Rapp is a senior vice president of National Economic Research Associates, an economics consulting firm based in White Plains, N.Y.

---

ple, including many who never before gave a hoot about international trade and capital flows. They view our unfavorable trade balance and net debtor role as portents of economic decline, and they worry about our ability to pay for imports and compete in international markets.

Paradoxically, if it's any comfort, it is the relative power and security of the American economy that put us in the present predicament. In recent years, real rates of return in the United States have been extraordinarily high, compared to both our own past performance and recent rates of return in other countries.

In 1984, the 12% average yield on U.S. government bonds, minus a 4% inflation rate, provided an 8% real return, with virtually no risk. In the same year, in Britain, West Germany and Japan, the return on long-term debt was about 5%. In the United States during the high

inflation of the 1970s and the low-interest period preceding them, it was about 2%.

The high yields in the United States created a relentless demand for dollars to lend and invest here and sharply raised the dollar's value relative to other major currencies. The strong dollar weakened exports and strengthened imports. As bargains from abroad poured onto our shores, trade deficits washed ashore with them.

Happily, the recent decline in the value of the dollar against the Japanese yen and other major currencies is producing a healthier competitive climate for American exports and the prospect of an improving trade balance.

Though not the fundamental cause of our trade woes, unfair competition is a significant factor. How to deal with it poses a conflict between economic theory and history.

Theory underpins our bias for free trade and tells us that it is efficient and beneficial. But history warns that trade often degenerates into economic warfare and that mature economies such as ours are particularly vulnerable.

This is the American dilemma: Must we give way to protectionism or can we find some middle ground that will enable us to hold fast to our free-trade ideals?

Protectionism is not the solution, nor would all the trade-impeding measures floating around Congress help. Protectionism would only transfer income from consumers and exporters to import-competing industries such as shoes and textiles.

Consumers would pay higher prices once the foreign competition was eliminated. Exporters would pay, because higher domestic prices mean higher domestic labor costs.

What's more, trading partners respond to trade barriers with barriers of their own, which would make it doubly hard for exporters to get by.

Also, tariffs and quotas offer little hope for boosting employment.

Import-competing industries such as automobiles, steel and electronics have a higher-than-average capital intensity. On the other hand, American export industries such as business and scientific equipment manufacturers tend to be more labor-intensive. As a result, curbing exports costs jobs.

Fortunately, there is a middle ground. The best defense against predatory invasion of U.S. markets is selective enforcement of our trade laws by government and by private-sector targets of unfair competition.

The Trade Act of 1974 gives the President substantial authority to interdict unfair trade practices.

He can enforce U.S. rights in response to any foreign policy or practice that "unreasonably restricts or discriminates against" U.S. commerce. To expedite responses to unfair import competition, the act provides that an investigation can be triggered by petition from any interested party, without proof of injury.

The U.S. semiconductor industry has recently invoked these provisions in its defense against dumping of computer chips by Japanese producers.

Under the law, the President can also act in defense of American intellectual and industrial property.

The protection of patents and trademarks encourages research and provides an incentive to invest in productivity-increasing innovations. The unauthorized importa-

FIG. 5-4. Richard Rapp article from the *Los Angeles Times*.

tion of an unpatented product made by a patented process may be deemed unfair competition.

No damages may be claimed, but the further import of the offending products can be blocked. This is important because much of the international trade litigation in the United States concerns patent infringement.

The Trade Tariff Act of 1984 increased the effectiveness of our anti-dumping and countervailing duty codes.

Also, the International Trade Commission, in determining causation and damages, must take into account imports from all countries into the United States in a particular industry.

In addition, countervailing duty provisions now take into account subsidies on components of the product exported.

A major legislative initiative now in Congress would put still more muscle in our trade laws. The bill would allow cases involving dumping, subsidies and customs fraud to be considered by federal district courts.

In addition to expanding plaintiffs' options, it would open the door to retroactive damage claims. Foreign producers who dump their products into the U.S. market now pay no compensation to U.S. manufacturers for goods already entered.

Now more than ever, trade litigation can be the bulwark against international economic warfare.

Gone are the days of junk economics and amateur-act petitions that used to circulate in ITC hearing rooms.

The same economic reasoning and carefully marshaled evidence customary in complex antitrust and commercial cases have become the norm in trade matters as well.

If we continue to sharpen our trade litigation into a more effective tool and learn to rely on it more when called for, we will be able to defend ourselves against unfair practices without threatening the gains from free trade that have contributed so much to our standard of living.

FIG. 5-4. (*continued*)

3. Select a publication that reaches your audience. For example, if you want to reach auto dealers, look at *Automotive News*. If you do consulting in the restaurant industry, pick up a copy of *Nation's Restaurant News*. The important thing is to pick the publication that reaches your market.

4. Study the publication. Does it use freelance features, that is, articles by people other than staff writers?

5. If so, study the thrust of the articles. What type of themes are present? How long are most articles?

6. Start thinking about themes that relate to the readership. The themes, however, must be on subjects that the magazine (or newspaper) is interested in printing.

7. Select a theme. Outline it.

8. Place a call to the editor of the magazine.

9. Identify yourself. Give him or her a brief background on your skills. Tell the editor you have an idea for an interesting story for the magazine, a story you think his or her readers would find fascinating. Outline it briefly. Ask if it sounds interesting. If it does, he or she will probably not commit immediately. The editor does not know if you are a good writer. He or she will want to see a sample first. Suggest submitting the article to see if it meets the publication's criteria.

10. If the editor likes the idea, he or she will agree to you submitting it for perusal.

11. Write the article and submit it—double-spaced. Keep it neat. Make it look professional.

12. Give him or her a week to 10 days to read it, then call to find out the response.

Does it work? Will the editors permit you to write a story? Let's look at an actual case, and how a consultant generated space in an important publication.

Data Processing Case Study

Joseph Izzo is one of the most successful data processing/information systems consultants in the country. His firm does a volume in the millions of dollars. Izzo's offices occupy nearly an entire floor of a high-rise building on the west coast.

Still, even with the business, Izzo does not forget that he has to market his wares to his customers, and that there are many free ways he can reach and influence potential clients.

Izzo's market is huge and there are numerous industry and consumer publications that can reach his audience—any company that has computerized systems and is in need of help.

One way to reach that audience is through some of the business magazines such as *Nation's Business*. Several years ago, Izzo examined *Nation's Business*, studied its format, the stories, the themes, and angles that the publication utilized. From this examination he developed an idea. Although computers were sweeping the country, many companies were having a difficult time with them. Once they were installed, communication gaps developed between the data processing (usually the accounting department) area and the rest of the company. In many cases, this was costing companies millions of dollars of lost time and sales. In more serious cases, there was a split between the data processing people and other areas. Thus, top management—the readers of *Nation's Business*—could certainly use some help in closing those gaps.

Like every consultant, Izzo knew his field, and he knew about the problems. In fact, his company had developed a solution (a seven-step program) designed to eliminate those gaps and open communications. If some of those companies became aware of his seven steps, they just might become clients.

He called the editor of the magazine, introduced himself, and said, "I have an idea for a story that I think all your subscribers would find fascinating. It revolves around computers, the communication problem that is rapidly developing in business because of them, and how companies can eliminate those problems and open lines of communication once again.

"We've developed seven simple steps that any company can utilize in order to overcome those gaps, and I wondered if you might be interested in a story revolving around those seven steps?"

The editor went for the story. Izzo wrote and submitted a draft that was accepted. As a result, his firm and his skills were exposed to hundreds of thousands of potential clients—and his cost was a telephone call and some writing time.

Naturally, not every one of your clients is going to see the article if it is published. Some may be out of town, others may simply miss it. But editorial coverage has a great advantage. Even if someone missed it, you can cut it out, paste it up, reprint it, and send it to all your past, present, and potential clients. This is called merchandising. Merchandising simply entails reprinting articles about your products and/or services and distributing them to present and potential clients on an ongoing basis.

One of the most astounding success stories in the reprint field belongs to a company called International Entrepreneur's Association.

Case Study: International Entrepreneur's Association

In the mid-1970s, International Entrepreneur's Association (IEA) was a company doing under $550,000 in sales. Most of the sales were generated through mail order. The company sent out nearly one million brochures a month with a fairly good return. In August 1977, the *Los Angeles Times* did a story on the company's founder, Chase Revel.

It was a highly positive story and appeared on the front page of the financial section. International Entrepreneur's Association clipped it, reduced it, and asked permission from the *Times* to reprint it for customers. The *Times* granted permission and by November 1977, the story was included in every one of IEA's mailing pieces.

The results were astounding. Although IEA continued to use the same mailing lists, the returns changed radically. With nearly one million pieces going out, the return percentage increased a full percentage point—a substantial jump in mail order. Even more significant, the average order which had been approximately $18, jumped to $44.

Within two years, IEA was a $3 million a year company; within three years, nearly $5 million. Although the company was using other marketing strategies and the reprint does not deserve all the credit, the initial impetus and sales jump came from that reprint about Chase Revel.

Even today—years after that story was printed—people come up to Revel and say, "Hey, I saw that story about you in the *Los Angeles Times* the other day." Of course, they did not see the story in the *Times*, they saw the reprint.

SAMPLE NEWS ANGLES

Reprints, however, can have a lasting effect. People are not only influenced by them, they remember them. They can do wonders for sales and every businessperson should utilize them.

If you obtain a feature of this type, be sure you reprint it and it becomes part of every one of your presentations and letters to potential clients.

Why should consultants reprint articles? What could a piece of paper with a story on it have to do with increasing sales? Those stories represent something that every business needs—credibility. They add credibility to your service. It (the media coverage) is an independent, third-party testimonial that says your products are good.

Everyone, of course, recognizes an ad and that someone paid for it. But what about an editorial? Most assume that the media pursued the person or company for the story. They seldom consider that it might have been the other way around. When it comes to feature coverage, it usually is a case of the company or personality suggesting the story to the media.

There can, however, be problems with reprints. You should get permission from the publication to reprint the article. In many cases, particularly if you want to reprint an entire article, the publication may charge a fee. Most of the time they will request that you do not use their logo. For example, you could say, "From the *Los Angeles Times*" and then have the story reprinted, but you could not actually reprint the *Times'* logo. This will not diminish the effect of the reprint.

The media can be helpful in other ways besides publishing your article. They may write about your business or service. Typically, there are two types of news—hard news and feature news.

Hard news is represented by the front page of tonight's paper; the lead story on the 6 and 11 o'clock news; the burglary that has to be reported tonight. In other words, hard news has to be reported immediately or it becomes old news—and no one buys old news.

As a consultant, you will not be involved in that type of news. You will be involved in feature news. Feature news is timeless. It can be written about today, tomorrow, or next month.

If you are a management consultant, a story on your business would be just as timely next month as it would next week. This feature news category offers a tremendous opportunity for consultants if they handle it correctly.

Newspapers, radio, and TV stations use feature materials on consultants (and other types of businesses) all the time, as does television. Did you ever watch the Johnny Carson Show? His guests are feature guests. That is, they could be on tonight, tomorrow, or next week. It does not matter. Usually their material (and subject) is timeless. Carson schedules guests six to eight weeks in advance. Some newspapers may spend a few days, three or four months, or longer working on a feature story. Radio shows may take one to four weeks to schedule guests.

How do they get these guests? Usually someone (a professional PR person) sells the media on the guest.

How do they sell them? The same way any good salesperson does. He or she finds the right news angle or hook. To do this, the salesperson has to know what type of news hook the media wants. Just as a salesperson must know what the prospective customer is interested in buying, so must the PR person who sells the media. By studying different shows and publications, PR people learn what the media wants. You can do the same.

For example, you know Johnny Carson is usually interested in guests or subjects with a celebrity angle. Study the media. Pick up the Sunday newspaper and carefully look through it. Notice all the feature (timeless) stories. Notice that most have the hook or angle right in the headline.

In Figure 5-5, you will find five headlines. All are feature stories taken from a local newspaper. Notice how the angles are spelled out in the headlines.

Before outlining different hooks, let's look at how the media is sold once the hook and/or angle is developed.

One of the easiest and most effective media selling methods is the news release. Some consultants send out releases and they never get printed. They wonder why. Usually it has nothing to do with the angle. Most of the time it is because the consultant failed to follow one of the structural rules involved in putting news releases together.

The structural rules are as important as the hook or angle that will eventually be the theme of the release. Figure 5-6 is a news release with structural rules. It is followed by a checklist which explains the rules.

Hughes Aims to Change 'Cadillac' Image

THE KIROV GOES MODERN, AFTER ITS OWN FASHION

Whole Earth Access Stores Are 'Bargain Basement' for Yuppies

UCLA's Mellinkoff Is in Medical Spotlight

Neil Diamond: "I realized I had to take a deep breath and get back to work."

DIAMOND OUT OF THE ROUGH

FIG. 5-5. Headlines.

10-Point News Release Structural Checklist

1. *Double-space*. Whenever you send your release out, make sure it is double-spaced. Remember, editors read all day long and their eyes get tired. Double-spacing is easier to read.

2. *Typographical Errors.* These are one of the leading causes of news releases being tossed in the round file. More than half of all releases that reach the editor's desk have a typo, erasure, or crossed-out word. This says to the editor that since the writer did not care enough to spell it correctly, it must not be important enough to look at or print. You would never send a business letter out with a typo and you should never send a news release out with one, either. That type has the same effect on the editor as the business letter typo does on the prospective client.

3. *Black-on-White.* News releases are best presented when they are typed on white paper with black or dark ink. Do not get fancy colors. They are difficult to read. Remember, the editor reads all day. Make his job easier.

NEWS

ron tepper & associates

*public relations
advertising
marketing*

For Immediate Release   For Further Information:
                                                          Ron Tepper, (213) 373-9335

SPORTS EXPO SET ⬅ heading (optional)   contact source ⬅

dateline   double space ⬅

Santa Monica, Oct. 12 -- "Exotic Sports Expo," the first consumer

show to feature every new and exotic sport in existence has been

set for the Los Angeles Convention Center, Nov. 5-9.

                            no typographical errors

The five-day Expo will have both exhibits and demonstrations of

the world's most unique sports. 25,000 square feet of exhibit

space has been set aside for demonstrations that will be held

every half-hour during the show's run.

                            most important things first

Among the sports to be exhibited and demonstrated are Hacky-Sack,

a game played on a volleyball court in which the contestants kick

a three-ounce sack over a net; and Hwarang-Do, a Korean form of

martial arts.

                            "who, what, when, where, why"

Show hours are noon until 10 p.m., Wednesday-Friday; and 10 a.m.

until 10 p.m. Saturday and Sunday. Admission is $3.50, with

children under 12 free.

                            price always last

plain white paper   always on letterhead

                                    ###

25550 hawthorne blvd. • suite 100 • torrance, california 90505 • (213) 373-9335

FIG. 5-6. Sample news release.

---

4. *Dateline.* Notice the date near the top of the release. This is important.
   The dateline should be the city of origin and the date on which the
   release is mailed. If it has no date, how does the editor know it has not
   been in the mail for six months?

5. *Contact.* Notice in the top right-hand corner there is a name and telephone
   number. This should be your name and number. If the editor has a
   question, he or she must have someone who can answer it.

6. *Letterhead.* Send your releases out on your letterhead. It does not have
   to be a fancy sheet of paper with NEWS RELEASE set in type. You can
   type the words News Release at the top. It should, however, be on your

letterhead. Why? Did you ever get a business letter on plain white paper? What does that say to you? Usually it means that the person is operating out of a shoebox. They probably do not have an office. Non-letterhead says you might not be in business.

7. *Duplicated Professionally.* Once your release is typed (either on a type-writer or a letter quality printer from a computer), you should have it duplicated professionally. That is, if you are sending out 25 releases to the local radio and TV stations, run down to the instant printer and have them run off copies (on an offset press). The quality of the last copy will equal the original. Do not run them through a copy machine that produces fuzzy, inferior copies.

8. *Pyramid.* The most important items in the release (the hook or angle) are first, and the least important are last. Why? Because of space limitations. Suppose the editor likes your release and wants to run it. Suppose again he or she only has 5 inches of space and your release runs 8 inches. The editor needs to trim 3 inches. Editors like to trim from the bottom, therefore put the least important items at the bottom.

9. *No Adjectives.* News releases do not contain flamboyant exaggerations of how great your business happens to be. Think of them as fact sheets. They only contain the facts. Seldom do you use adjectives. That is one of the reasons anyone can write one of these documents—just stick to the facts.

10. *The Five Ws.* Who, What, When, Where, and Why. Those are the facts in every release. Study the samples and you will see how the five Ws are used.

These are the structural rules. Once you have mastered them you are ready to write the release and find the correct news hook or angle.

What makes a news hook? Read the following news hook checklist carefully and see how some tie into your consulting practice.

News Hook Checklist or What Subjects Can Make a News Release?

1. *New Business or New Service.* You may have just opened offices or are offering a new service.

2. *Executive Appointments.* Someone has joined your firm or has been promoted.

3. *Community Involvement.* Your firm is sponsoring some local event or is involved with one.

4. *Awards.* Your firm has been awarded something from the community or your industry.

5. *Speeches.* You are giving a speech to a group. Make it newsworthy. For example, if a money manager gave a talk on investments, he or she could discuss a local economic forecast as part of the talk.

6. *Industry Surveys.* Every consultant, regardless of their specialty, is in some industry. There are more than 15,000 different industries in this country—meaning everything from autos and steel, to insurance, finance, personnel, engineering, and sales. You belong in one of those industries.

By surveying present and potential customers, suppliers, and others related to your industry, it is possible to come up with an industry survey, a forecast.

Let's take a hypothetical example—a personnel consultant. Personnel people are in the business of putting job seekers and jobs together. Suppose you are a personnel consultant who places engineers. It would be easy to survey one-half of your customer base (employers) and determine the average salary paid to engineers with experience, and the average wage increase these engineers will receive in the next year. You then structure a news release showing the salary range and the proposed increases. This is an industry survey.

If structured correctly, it may be published on the business or news pages of the local newspaper and your firm is given credit for conducting the survey. When engineers read it they immediately see a salary range. Suppose they are not making that much or suppose they are unhappy and want to change jobs. There is a good chance—in either case—they will come to your firm since it supplied the figures and knows where the job openings happen to be.

Many firms utilize this technique to attract customers. Study the local newspapers, watch for surveys, and you will see how they are handled.

7. *Topical Subjects.* There are usually two or three subjects that immediately interest the media. A few years ago, any release that related to energy, inflation, or consumerism tended to get printed.

Today the emphasis has changed. Consumerism is (and will continue to be) a hot topic for years to come, but other topics have replaced energy and inflation (of course, if inflation rears again, it will become topical).

Keep your eyes open for those topical subjects. There is a good chance your firm will tie into it. For example, terrorism was one of the hot topics in early and mid-1986. Think of all the firms that tie into that—consultants who coach CEOs and top executives on self-defense; companies that produce detection devices, and so on.

Let's look at one of those topics—consumerism—and see how companies throughout the U.S. utilize it to build business.

Consumerism Case Study

A classic case involves a magazine called *Entrepreneur. Entrepreneur* is a magazine that reports on the hot, new, small businesses. It is geared to the business opportunity seeker; the person who is thinking about going into business.

Some time ago, as a service to readers, *Entrepreneur* started to publish a monthly series of business opportunity frauds. That is, they wrote about the latest stings in the business opportunity field and told readers to beware. They ran one sting story a month.

Several years ago, the magazine decided to put 12–15 of these sting stories together in booklet form. The text, which ran 72 pages, was called, "Business Opportunity Frauds . . . and How to Avoid Them." They published the booklet and wrote a news release about its availability. The release—as every release—should be sent to *the media that best reaches your market.*

Entrepreneur's market was the business opportunity seeker. Most business seekers read the business page, thus one prime outlet for the release was the business pages of major newspapers throughout the country. The release contained the 5 Ws, and at the bottom a price: 50 cents per booklet, which would cover postage and handling.

Entrepreneur sent the release and waited. The company has a clipping service that has the capability of monitoring what happens. In the span of six weeks, it received more then $150,000 worth of free exposure.

Remember, however, free exposure has to result in sales. As a result of the media coverage, the magazine also received 55,000 orders for the booklet, worth $27,500. That, however, barely covers the cost. There is no profit in the figure. There is, however, something else—names—55,000 names of prime business opportunity seekers.

Although a small percentage of people will send for the booklet with no serious intent, more than 90 percent of those who mail in their money will be serious business opportunity seekers; potential customers for one of *Entrepreneur*'s $60 manuals, $25 tapes, and the like. With a mailing that cost less than $200, the company developed 55,000 prime prospects.

CONSULTANTS AND CONSUMERISM

Other companies do the same thing. Consultants can do the same as well. For example, let's say you are in insurance or real estate. Any insurance person could sit down and put a sheet of paper in a typewriter. On the sheet he or she would list 10 or 15 ways in which consumers (companies, industries, etc.) could save money when purchasing liability (or any other) insurance policy. The 15 ways would be in the form of a checklist. Then he or she could turn the paper over and on the flip side type a title: "How to avoid being ripped off by liability insurance." Take the paper to the local instant printer and have 100 copies run off.

What do you have? It is no longer a double-sided sheet of paper. Now it is a consumer-oriented pamphlet designed to educate and inform people how they can avoid being ripped off. It performs a service. Notice this is in contrast to the pamphlet that says, "buy your insurance from me."

The insurance person would then structure a new product news release similar to the one in this workbook, have it duplicated and sent to the media that will reach his or her market. Perhaps we are talking about print and radio; maybe the topic relates to a specific industry. Whatever it relates to, send the release.

At the bottom of the release, the cost of the pamphlet is listed. Perhaps it is free. People need only send in a stamped, self-addressed envelope or stop by your facility. Either way, you are going to develop a mailing list. Certainly people who have no interest in insurance will send for it (some people will send for anything as long as it is free), but more than 90 percent of inquiries will come from those who are thinking about insurance.

This type of release may be utilized by the media because of the service it performs. Your company gets the credit because the media has to say where and how the pamphlet can be obtained. This type of subject also makes an excellent seminar topic. The key—it is not self-serving. It is educational, informative, and it will help others.

That is the key to free publicity.

CHAPTER 6

EASY-TO-USE PROMOTIONAL TOOLS

Major companies generate millions of dollars worth of free and low-cost positive exposure for their products by effectively using the media. Consultants have the same opportunity.

In Chapter 5, news releases were discussed. They are one of the most potent and low-cost business building tools in the consulting field. In this chapter, there are samples of releases that can be used at any time as well as several other promotional techniques that can be utilized to increase sales.

One news release technique mentioned was the industry survey. The Big Mac release (Figure 6-1) is an example of a survey designed to get readers to buy a magazine. Consultants can build business in a similar manner. For example, a personnel consultant may generate business (seekers of employment) through a survey. Suppose the consultant has an inordinate amount of openings in a certain field. He or she could then write an industry-survey-type release in which salaries, and other benefits in the field were outlined. The release would then be sent to local business page editors.

When used, the media typically identifies the company that provided the survey results. A potential applicant reading the survey, and seeing the opportunities, might then be knocking on the door of the personnel consultant for one of those jobs.

Figure 6-2 is a new product news release. You can change the wording and put in your own new service, system, location, and so on.

Figure 6-3 is a summary of a speech. With timely speeches, you capsulize the contents and condense them into a one or two page release. The release is sent to the media the day of the speech. Ed Bobins, head of a large home warranty program, hoped to get realtors interested in his program—which he did.

The releases shown in Figures 6-4 and 6-5 are on seminars and would be sent to editors of the appropriate sections. If you are giving a seminar on taxes or the economy, it would be submitted to the business section; on relationships between men and women, or relationships on the job, it could go to the view, family, women's, or similar sections.

NEWS

ron tepper & associates
public relations
advertising
marketing

For Immediate Release

For Further Information
(213) 373-9335 Ron Tepper

BIG MAC KNOCKED
OFF BY CHICKEN

Los Angeles, Dec. 18--Move over McDonald's, the Kentucky Colonel
is Number One.

That's the conclusion of the Sixth Annual National Franchise
500 Survey, a year-long study conducted by Entrepreneur Magazine,
which ranks the top 500 franchises in the country.

The survey, which rates franchises according to numerous factors
including growth, number of units and years in business, placed
McDonald's #1 last year (1983), however, for 1984, the Big Mac
fell to fourth.

Following close behind the Colonel were Hardee's Family
Restaurants (2); Domino's Pizza (3), Wendy's (5), Burger King (6),
Midas Muffler (7), Taco Bell (8), Arby's (9) and Baskin-Robbins
ice cream (10).

This was the first year that only one non-food franchise (Midas)
was in the Top 10. The survey also ranked the "Ten Fastest
Growing" franchises (Carvel Ice Cream placed first). A list of
25, low-investment franchises, that is, franchises which

-More-

25550 hawthorne blvd. • suite 100 • torrance, california 90505 • (213) 373-9335

FIG. 6-1. Industry survey.

cost $10,000 or less to get into, are also included in the study.

The report, which is contained in the January issue of
Entrepreneur, was compiled with the aid of the International
Franchise Association and the Department of Commerce. The
Magazine's staff spent more than 4,000 hours researching and
compiling data.

Approximately 2,000 companies were contacted in order to
complete the study. Copies of the findings are available
from Entrepreneur Group, Inc., 2311 Pontius Avenue, Los Angeles,
CA. 90064. (213) 478-0437.

###

FIG. 6-1. (continued)

(This should be on paper that says "News Release.")

For Immediate Release   For Further Information
                             (213) 373-9338 Lysa Jenkins

"Critter Chaser" Adds
8, 16 Ounce Sizes

Torrance, Jan. 17--Dr. Dogkatz's Critter Chaser, an all-natural flea shampoo that is guaranteed to rid dogs and cats of fleas and flea eggs, has been packaged in 8 and 16 ounce sizes in addition to gallons for the flea season.

The product, which is being introduced by Growth Plus Laboratories (Torrance, CA), was developed after more than a year of research.

The product, which requires no gloves on the part of the user, is applied like an ordinary shampoo, however, it contains no insecticide and can be applied without the use of gloves.

Samples of the product can be obtained by calling Growth Plus Laboratories (213) 373-9338, or by writing to the company: 25550 Hawthorne Blvd., Suite 100, Torrance, CA 90505.

###

FIG. 6-2. New product/service release.

News...

For Immediate Release

For Further Information:
Ron Tepper, (213) 451-5743
(800) 421-7269

"WARRANTEES FOR LEGISLATION"
PREDICTS PENNSYLVANIA BUSINESSMAN

Alexandria, Virginia, August 31 -- In a speech before nearly three hundred Virginia realtors, Ed Bobins, president of Warranteed Homes of Pennsylvania, called for realtors to "take action and look into home warranty programs before the government and consumer protective legislation forces the industry to adopt a program."

Bobins, who heads one of Pennsylvania's largest warranty home programs, called upon the realtors in the audience "to look seriously at the warranty programs available and institute them as soon as possible. It doesn't matter whether it is our program or someone else's, the important thing is to adopt one."

Bobins cited the federal government's Housing and Urban Development Department's office of Interstate Land Sales as a government agency that "right now has the power to step in and oversee real estate home sales.

"Should the demand from consumers continue to rise for some sort of

-more-

DEVELEO

FIG. 6-3. Speech release. *(Figure continued on p. 178.)*

legislation that will guarantee them of a 'sound house' when they make a purchase, we could see the government step in.

"With the prices of houses soaring, consumers are becoming more concerned with the quality of the house they are buying."

Bobins cited figures from a two-year study which showed that 10% of all homes sales fell through in the Pennsylvania area while those homes that had warrantees showed only a 3% fall through.

"The key," Bobins said, "is not that homes that are warranteed are selling better but the thing you should pay attention to is that 'fall-through' rate. You might look upon it as a 'consumer dissatis-faction' rate and it shows that approximately 7% of those consumers were so dissatisfied with the condition of the homes they were buying that they cancelled out. That's an enormous amount of people---an amount that could lead to some sort of government action in the near future."

Home warranty firms provide insurance policies to buyers, sellers and realtors and guarantee that a home will be in proper condition when it is sold.

*   *   *

FIG. 6-3. *(continued)*

NOTE: This release should go
on your letterhead

For Immediate Release

For Further Information:
Ron Tepper, (213) 394-3787

FRANCHISE SEMINAR SET

Santa Monica, Dec. 20 -- "Pros and Cons of Franchising," an in-depth one hour and forty-five minute seminar covering the good and bad points of buying a franchise, will be one of the fifteen different seminars given at the Small Business Expo which opens Thursday (Dec. 28) at the Long Beach Convention Center and runs through Saturday (Dec. 30).

The Expo, which features seventy-five hours of "how to" seminars pertaining to small business and geared to the present--and potential --small business owner, will also have one hundred booths displaying the latest in franchises and distributorships.

The franchise seminar will be conducted by Jerry Fisher, former Small Business Administration Director and a veteran of more than twenty years in the franchise business. Fisher, who was responsible for the successful franchising of such companies as Sir Speedy, Copper Penny and Master Host Motels, will give the seminar on Saturday morning at the Center. Admission is $15 per seminar or $35 for all day which entitles consumers to attend as many as four seminars during the day.

* * *

FIG. 6-4. Seminar release.

For Immediate Release

For Further Information:
Ron Tepper (213) 394-3787

"HOW TO" SMALL BUSINESS
SEMINARS SET AUG. 5-7

Santa Monica, July 15 -- 50 hours of seminars covering all phases of
small business investment have been scheduled as part of the three-day
"Start Your Own Business Expo" at the Los Angeles Convention Center,
August 5-7.

The seminars, which will all take a "how to" approach, will cover
such diverse topics as "How To Finance Your Business," "How To
Market A New Product," and "How Women Can Start Their Own
Business." In all, nine seminars, each lasting two hours, will be
offered daily as part of the Expo.

The Federal Government's Small Business Administration; the Mayor's
(of Los Angeles) Small Business Assistance Office and the International
Entrepreneurs' Association are all co-sponsoring the seminars. In
Addition to the seminars, 101 different small business investment
opportunities will be displayed at the Center.

Information on the seminars and the Expo can be obtained through the
International Entrepreneurs' Association in Santa Monica.

FIG. 6-5. Seminar release.

Figure 6-6 is a typical personnel announcement release that could go to the local media as well as trade publications in your industry. When mailing to trade publications, address your envelope to the editor. If you are mailing a release locally and are unclear as to which section it should be sent to, address it to the city editor.

The next release (Figure 6-7) is a special report that was done. Consultants have access to similar news in their industries or they can develop similar releases.

The following releases (Figures 6-8, 6-9, and 6-10) consultants can use by simply filling in the blanks.

News releases are often accompanied by photographs. If you send a photo with the release, consult the following checklist first.

How To Get Photographs Printed

1. Study photos in newspapers to see the type of material that is used.

2. Notice the candid photo (nonposed) is used more often. Head shots or posed photos are used primarily for business stories.

3. Try to stage a photo that is candid. Consultants can get ideas for candid photos by examining their client's workplace. Perhaps there is a good photo idea in a group meeting, the operation of a new computer, engineers surrounding the construction of a building, or a personnel consultant talking to a prospect.

4. Hire a professional photographer to shoot the picture.

5. All shots, unless the publication utilizes something different (and you can tell by examining it), should be black and white.

6. All photos sent out should be glossy, 5×7 or 8×10.

7. All photos should have contrast. That is, the subjects in the front should not blend in with those in the background. If everything blends the publication will not be able to use it.

8. When mailing photos, place a piece of cardboard in the envelope to prevent bending.

News releases can lead to print, radio, and even television coverage. Probably one of the most effective news releases was written several years ago. It turned a $125 investment into a $750,000 business. It is covered in the following case study.

KETCH-ALL CASE STUDY

In the mid-1970s, Al Fluster was a retired engineer who had an idea for a new product. Al's only problem was that he did not have enough money to manufacture or market it. Al, however, strongly felt there was a market for his ketch-all, a 2½ inch plastic funnel. Al's ketch-all worked in the following manner. A near empty ketchup bottle was placed on one side of the table, the cap removed. A new ketchup bottle was opened and placed next to it. The ketch-all (funnel)

NOTE: This release should go
on your letterhead

For Immediate Release

For Further Information:
Name of Contact
(Area Code) Telephone Number

City, Date -- John Johnson has been elected (title of office) of the (name of company). The announcement was made by Jerry Jones (his title) of (name of company).

In his new position, Mr. Johnson will be responsible for (list the responsibilities). He will report directly to (name of person).

(This last paragraph should then have Mr. Johnson's background. Where he came from--his work background--and his previous responsibilities and credits that relate to his present one.)

FIG. 6-6. Personnel announcement release.

For Immediate Release

For Further Information:
(213) 394-3787
(800) 421-7260, Ron Tepper

Santa Monica, October 6 -- The Farm Home Administration, a little

known and seldom used agency that supplies start-up capital for small

business, is the subject of a special report in the October issue of

Entrepreneur, the small business research magazine published monthly

by the International Entrepreneurs Association.

The report outlines the operation procedures of the FmHA which has

1,100 offices nationwide and falls under the Department of Agriculture.

FmHA, however, does not limit its lending to either farms or homes.

The report also details advantages of an FmHA loan over SBA loans

and also reveals some of the types of small businesses (including

real estate loans) that FmHA supplies.

The report is available from IEA in Santa Monica.

*   *   *

FIG. 6-7. Special report release.

For Immediate Release   For Further Information:
                                         Name of Contact
                                         (Area Code) Telephone Number

City, Date -- The Johnson Construction Company will co-sponsor the

first annual (name of event) that will be held (date) at (where).   Proceeds

from the event will go towards (name of charity).

The object of the (event) will be to see which contestants can (whatever

the purpose) in the (time span).

Judges (or participants) in the event will be members of the Construction

Company (names of other companies involved or individuals).

                    *   *   *

This is a sample of "company involvement" type of release. It can be

used for both charitable and non-charitable events.

FIG. 6-8. Event sponsorship.

184

For Immediate Release

For Further Information:
Name of Contact
(Area Code) Telephone Number

City, Date -- "How To Insulate Your Home," a booklet outlining the dos and don'ts of home insulation, has been published by (name of company).

The booklet, which analyzes all types of possible insulation materials, tells consumers exactly how to evaluate each and select one for their home. It gives the pros and cons, describing the price and structural capabilities, of each system.

The booklet is available from (name of company), a fourteen-year-old home insulation company headquartered in (city). Copies of the report can be obtained free by writing to (name of company).

* * *

FIG. 6-9. Public service booklet.

For Immediate Release   For Further Information:
                                         Name of Contact
                                         (Area Code) Telephone Number

City, Date -- "The Dredge Socket," a new device that will enable electricians to (whatever it does) in half-the-time, has been developed by (name of company).

The device, which saves energy and costs less than other switches on the market, was developed (state length of time it took to develop) and is available from (name of company) directly.

The Dredge Socket lists for (suggested retail price) and in quantities sells to electricians for (price). Wholesale and distributor discount programs have been developed and details of the programs, including advertising allowance structures, are available from (name of company).

*   *   *

FIG. 6-10. New product/service release.

was placed inside the new bottle. The old bottle was then turned upside down and placed inside the ketch-all, which now was a connector between the old and new. The ketch-all balanced the bottles perfectly and the remaining ketchup from the old bottle drained slowly into the new one, thus saving food (for restaurants and housewives) and labor. No longer did a waitress have to shake the last drop out of the old bottle.

Al took several steps to promote his product. He wrote a new product news release and had a photograph taken of the product. Al did not just take a photo of the product, he showed it in action.

He had both the news release and photo duplicated professionally. His next problem was how to reach his market (restaurants and housewives). He picked up a copy of *Bacon's Publicity Checker* and looked under restaurants. In that category he found 26 publications that went to restaurants and restaurant companies. He picked the largest in the category, *Nation's Restaurant News,* called and asked, "Do you have a new products editor?" They said no, so Al asked for the name of the editor.

Al looked in *Bacon's* again under the general magazine category and found all the women's magazines that used new product news releases. Among them, for example, are *Better Homes & Gardens* and *Good Housekeeping.* He called both and asked for the name of the new product editor; each had one.

Al then sent his news release and photos (he put a piece of cardboard in each envelope to prevent the photos from bending) to the 26 publications in the restaurant field, and approximately 30 more in the women's field.

To the editors of *Nation's Restaurant News, Good Housekeeping,* and *Better Homes & Gardens,* he enclosed a note, "Dear _____ , Thought your readers might be interested in the enclosed. Sincerely, Al Fluster."

He gave each a week for delivery, called the three publications, and asked for the three editors by name. He introduced himself, asked if they had received the news release and photo of his ketch-all. All had, and he inquired if there were any questions he could answer. There were none, so he thanked them for their time and hung up.

What happened? A few weeks later, *Nation's Restaurant News* printed his news release and ran the photo. As with many publications that print new product releases, they also included the price and where it could be obtained. Within two days, Al received calls from three of the largest restaurant companies in the United States. One was International Foodservice, which owns restaurants throughout the country. They asked if he could customize—that is, put the International Foodservice logo on the ketch-all—and he said yes, of course.

He received enough orders from International Foodservice to put him in business. When *Better Homes & Gardens* and *Good Housekeeping* came out they also printed his release and photo. The result was thousands of additional orders from consumers.

Today, Al is one of the most successful manufacturers in the country. He makes a variety of products (plastic) for the restaurant industry. His entire business was launched through a news release; a news release that he wrote. His cost to get into business—$125. For $125 he opened his own business. That shows the potential of a news release if handled correctly.

Consultants have that same opportunity. As easily as the canned feature (the feature you write and place in a magazine or newspaper yourself) can reach a market for you, so can the news release.

Think about your consulting market. Where is it? What industries? What trade papers reach it? What type of releases do they use? Study them and use the releases in this workbook to expose and expand your business.

FEATURE STORIES

As you may have surmised, news releases, when printed, may run 6, 7, or 8 inches, sometimes longer. But the media may give you more exposure through a feature interview. For a feature, the publication assigns a reporter to come out and interview you, or a radio or television show invites you to be on the air.

Features have one thing in common with news releases. They both have angles or hooks. In other words, there has got to be something unique, something different about your consulting firm in order to get the media to come out and do a story on it.

In developing these features, it helps to study the pages of the local newspaper. Look and listen to the guests on talk shows. By reading and watching, ideas will come to mind. You will be able to develop similar topics. If you do, how do you get on the show or how do you get the reporter to come out and interview you?

The main selling tool is called a pitch letter. It is a letter that precedes almost every feature story you see in the newspaper or on TV or hear on the radio. The pitch letter enables the editor to evaluate the proposed angle for the feature. It details the angle. The editor never calls it a pitch letter. He or she may say, "Send me some information" or "Can you get me some additional facts?" But he or she will not refer to it as a pitch letter and neither should you when talking to editors. Pitch letters are as easy to write as news releases. They have a set formula. The following checklist details this formula.

Feature Story Four-Point Formula

1. Main angle or hook is in the first or second paragraph.
2. Supporting points are in the third or fourth paragraph
3. Background on you—your qualifications to speak on the subject—are in the next paragraph.
4. The closing paragraph should finish with, "I'll give you a call to see what you think" or a similar statement. In other words, you must follow-up with the media (make the call) to see if they will do the story.

Consultant Feature Story Case Study

Carlton Wagner is a color consultant who has a degree in design and psychology. Companies throughout the country hire him to advise what colors they should be using in offices (to increase productivity), hospitals (to put patients at ease), restaurants (to increase the appetite of consumers), and a variety of other locations. Wagner has, in fact, even done consulting for prisons, where he suggested colors that would have a relaxing effect on inmates.

Wagner, of course, would like to reach as many companies as possible. A short time ago, he determined he would try and to get a media interview to increase his business.

It should be remembered that when approaching the media you do not want to make your story self-serving. You want it to be of value to everyone listening, watching, or reading. The story has to be informative and educational—and in the process your business or practice will be plugged.

Wagner spent time thinking about what he could offer the media that they would buy. What could he tell the media that would interest them as well as their audience? Answer—what colors would be big next year and why. Or how color and the economy relate. And why colors differ from city to city, and why the favorite colors in this particular city (whichever one he happened to be in at the time), differed from others.

Wagner studied the media in his home city. He listened to the news/talk radio station and the guests that were being interviewed. He listened to the topics. Within a week, he had formulated a plan. He would call the local news/talk radio station and base a feature interview on how color and the local economy are related, what colors would be big in his city during the next year, and how they would relate to the economic health of the city.

He called the local station and talked to the producer of the show. The producer asked for more information, which he sent. He followed with a telephone call, and two weeks later he was a guest.

With the local newspaper, he developed a different angle. It revolved around the colors manufacturers would be selling to consumers the following year and why. For instance, he outlined the color of autos, clothing, refrigerators, and other appliances and explained why they were selected.

He called the newspaper and asked for the Living Section (some newspapers call this Family, View, or even Women's) editor. He outlined the idea, sent a letter, and a short time later he was interviewed by a reporter.

As a result of his radio interview, he was called by one of the leading manufacturers in the city. His newspaper interview attracted the attention of two hospital administrators and the corporate officers of a fast food chain of restaurants.

Figure 6-11 is a copy of the pitch letter that Wagner sent to the local newspaper. Consultants do not have to duplicate it exactly; however, notice the approach, where the ideas are placed, and the close. If you have a profile, as Wagner did, it can be sent along with the letter. If not, include your background in the letter.

Refer to the Feature Story Formula. This explains how to provide background information when you do not include a biography or profile.

When attempting to get the media to do a story of this type on your company, remember one important rule: Do not approach more than one newspaper, magazine, or radio station at the same time. In other words, avoid simultaneously approaching rivals. If one turns you down, it is acceptable to go to the other.

Determining whether or not a publication, TV, or radio show has a rival requires only common sense. For example, *Time* and *Newsweek* are rivals. They are both after the same audience.

(This should be on your letterhead)

Date

Name
Title (if any)
Company
Address
City, State, Zip

Dear

Many thanks for the time you took discussing a possible story with
psychologist/designer Carlton Wagner revolving around "color---how
people respond to it, how it shapes buying trends and the economy,
and what colors will have major impact in New Orleans in '87 and
'88."

Mr. Wagner will be in New Orleans next week (14th) for a meeting
of American Medical Interational (AMI). He'll be discussing
hospitals and the effect of color on patients and employees.

Mr. Wagner's thoughts and color background, however, go far beyond
the hues utlized in a hospital. For example, he has some extraordinary thoughts on color ranging from Nancy Reagan's use of
it, and the affect of the Libyan bombing on color choices, to the
impact of "Miami Vice" and its use of color to make it a top-rated
TV show.

He also has some fascinating opinions (which he backs with
empirical data) on the impact of color when it comes to the
relationships men and women have.

Mr. Wagner did his graduate work at the Carl Jung Institute,
taught psychology for more than a dozen years, and 15 years ago he
began studying color and its affects on men and women, and founded
his Wagner Institute of Color Research.

He has provided color consulting for a variety of companies and
organizations rangng from Sears and numerous fast food franchisors,
to hospitals, universities, and leading design firms and associations throughout the country. His knowledge of color's impact on
consumers is unmatched.

Last week, he participated in a week-long session in Seattle where
the leading designers in the country picked the "colors for 1988."

Although color has a psychological effect on the consumer, Mr.
Wagner's theories are based upon the fact there is a <u>glandular</u>

-More-

FIG. 6-11. Sample pitch letter to media.

response to colors--and men, women, manufacturers, etc. can increase their appeal by catering to that response.

For example, colors have been used to temper convicts and mental
patients; color has been used to sell fast foods; and color has
been used effectively by auto manufactures.

Color reflects the economic health of the country. For instance,
colors in 1982 and 1932 were similar...as was the economic climate. Different sections of the country vary in color preferences.

The color preferences of New Orleans differ greatly from Phoenix,
Los Angeles and New York--and there are reasons. Consequently,
the things people in New Orleans will buy are oftentimes different
from purchases made in other cities.

There are many other aspects to color that Mr. Wagner will be
covering that I think Living Section readers would find revealing
and thought provoking.

I've enclosed a bio for some additional background. I'll give
you a call to see what you think. In the meantime, many thanks
for your time and interest.

                                        Sincerely,

                                        (Your Name)

YN/si

encl.

FIG. 6-11. (continued)

Features are stories that can be reprinted and sent to potential clients. The following consultant idea checklist will give you some thoughts on utilizing the same approach.

Consultant's Idea Checklist

1. Certified Public Accountants can propose stories that revolve around new tax laws and how they will affect the local economy.

2. Money managers can propose stories revolving around the stock market, how high (or low) it will go, and what impact it will have locally.

3. Personnel consultants can propose stories about the jobs of the future, what subjects should be emphasized in school, and why.

4. Engineers could propose a range of stories dealing with buildings of the future, the relationship of the environment to building, and some of the new obstacles (and how to get around them) builders will be finding.

5. Engineers in other areas can talk about some of the new time and money saving equipment, procedures that are on the market, or that will soon be available.

6. Management consultants could talk about the new influences at the workplace—such as drugs, changing worker attitudes, and so on—and how they will affect companies as well as how companies should be addressing them.

7. Data processing or information consultants could talk about the innovations that are coming in computers and the impact on companies as well as workers.

Notice all these potential features are informative and educational for the reader. They all have local interest, and readers will benefit from them. That is the key to getting media exposure. Put something together that others will want to know about. Never call the media and say, "I am a new businessperson, would you like to do a story about me? I am in an interesting profession."

When you develop these stories there are many different media outlets. The checklist that follows supplies sources listing and explaining local and national media.

Media Sources

1. *Chamber of Commerce.* Most chambers maintain a list of local media and they supply businesspeople with that list.

2. *Bacon's Publicity Checker.* The two best directories that Bacon's publishes are *Bacon's Magazine Directory* and *Bacon's Newspaper Directory.*

    Together these two publications cover virtually every newspaper, magazine, and wire service in the country. The magazine directory also has valuable trade listings. For example, if you want to reach purchasing agents, the magazine directory has a complete list of all publications that go to them. It categorizes every profession and gives you the name, address, and telephone number of all the media in that category.

    The directories run about $100 each, however, major libraries have copies of *Bacon's* at the reference desk. *Bacon's* is located at 14 East Jackson Boulevard, Chicago, IL 60604. (312) 922-8419.

3. *Larimi Communications.* Larimi is a promotion firm but it publishes excellent resource materials including television, radio, and cable TV contact books. The TV book gives you a rundown on every television show in almost every city in the United States, large or small. It tells you what kind of guests the program wants, what kind of subjects they are interested in hearing about, who to contact, and how far in advance you should contact them. It does the same for radio and cable TV. Chances are the library does not carry them. Larimi books are a little more expensive than *Bacon's*. Larimi is located in New York City. Larimi Communications, Ltd., 246 W. 38th Street, New York, NY 10018. (212) 819-9310.

4. *Gebbie Press.* A reference book categorized similar to *Bacon's* newspaper and magazine directory, it also provides radio and TV listings. (*Bacon's* does have one thing that *Gebbie's* does not, a code which indicates what kind of news release various publications are willing to use.) It sells for around $100. Gebbie, Box 1000, New Paltz, NY 12561.

5. *Working Press of the Nation.* A five-volume work consisting of newspaper directory; internal publications directory; feature writer, photographer, and syndicate directory; magazine directory; and TV and radio directory.

   The books contain an enormous amount of information, however, it is best to look through them before you ever buy. They are expensive and present more information than the average consultant will ever use. The reference desk at most libraries carries the volumes. Look through them and copy the information you need.

For the successful consultant, business will ultimately come from referrals, and there is no better place to find referrals than in clubs and civic groups that have direct or indirect potential customers. For example, the engineering consultant may rely on developers for most of his or her business. By joining a local building trade association, an engineering consultant can meet potential clients. This would be direct contact.

Now, suppose the consultant joined a group that had bankers in it. Bankers usually finance buildings and bankers know developers. Hence, this would be an indirect way to reach potential customers, but it could also be extremely effective. Bankers could also be perfect contacts for consultants in management, personnel, and finance.

The same is true for every consulting field. Look at your potential customers. Which groups do they frequent? Is there a local trade organization? Can you join either one? When opening their doors, consultants may spend 25 percent or more of their time prospecting through one of these groups.

CHAPTER 7

LOW-COST EFFECTIVE ADVERTISING

"Who's Making a Bundle?"

How much does Joe's business make? Want to know the net profit, gross, or prospects for success of any business? Write . . . or call . . . .

That $44 ad and headline was the beginning of a 15 million dollar a year consulting business; a consulting business that reached $8 million within seven years, and $15 million two years later. The ad ran in the *Wall Street Journal* for three years and never slowed in its response.

It was the brainchild of Chase Revel, a management consultant who decided after 15 years in the field to start selling his advice through manuals, instead of making it on a one-on-one basis. The ad was utilized to create International Entrepreneur's Association and *Entrepreneur* magazine.

The headline of the ad illustrates a critical point in advertising—always try to answer the *customer's needs* instead of trying to *sell* him something. Customer needs can usually be divided into two categories, two categories (and needs) that have not changed since the beginning of time, two categories that will continue to be of prime importance to every potential consulting client regardless of their industry—ego and greed.

Acknowledging those needs will enable you to reach any audience. Study today's advertising on TV, on the radio, or in newspapers. The best ads, that is, those that pull the most response, address those needs. Often other needs are substituted for the words ego and greed. The following is a checklist of basic needs.

Basic Needs Checklist

To make money

To save time

To avoid effort

To be comfortable

To be healthy

To be popular

To be in style

To avoid criticism

To conserve possessions

To escape physical pain

To satisfy curiosity

To purchase wisely

To have beautiful possessions

To attract the opposite sex

To save money

To be an individual

To enjoy life

To be clean

To be appreciated

To protect family

To emulate others that are admired

To avoid trouble

To take advantage of opportunities

Equally as important in advertising as addressing needs, is specialization. Just as the specializing consultant has the best chance of succeeding in a particular field, the ad that has the best chance of succeeding (for a consultant) is targeted, not shotgunned. It is aimed at a specific audience.

Consultants do not market services to the masses. They are not retailers, manufacturers, or mass merchandisers who have millions of dollars to spend in order to bring someone—anyone—in off the street. Consultants have to aim—carefully. They have to select media that reaches a narrow market.

Before aiming, however, a consultant should know the market. In other words, Who are your potential clients and what are the most effective (and cheapest) ways of reaching them?

Often this takes market research. There is, however, nothing mystical about research. If, for example, an auto manufacturer wanted to know the dollar amount consumers would be willing to pay for a new model, all he or she would have to do is ask. The manufacturer can take a photo of the new model, show it to 500 previous buyers, and pose one question: How much would you be willing to pay?

Unsophisticated? Perhaps, but that is exactly how one of the largest manufacturers of luxury automobiles in this country put a price tag on a new model more than a decade ago. That model became one of the top sellers in the history of General Motors.

The same approach is used by other businesses. Look at the neighborhood cleaners. All a cleaner has to do is gather up his or her receipts for the past month (cleaners always give customers one copy and retain one when clothing is brought in to the store) and examine them.

Going through the receipts, the cleaners can determine which item (dress, pants suit, etc.) is being cleaned most frequently by customers. Suppose he or she discovers dresses are being cleaned more often than any other item. Logically, he or she could come to several other conclusions at the same time: The cleaner's customers are just a small segment of the entire market and if his or her customers are cleaning dresses more often than anything else there is a strong possibility that is what is happening in the remainder of the market. With that conclusion the cleaner knows what to advertise—a dress cleaning special—because he or she knows that getting dresses cleaned is one of the major needs in the marketplace.

That same approach applies to consulting. If you are already in business, all it takes is a perusal of your previous contracts to determine what kind or size company is most likely to hire you; what type of problems you normally deal with; what type of fees you are most likely to be paid; and what person within the company is most likely to retain your services. That information enables you to target your approach and ads; to focus on specific companies, industries, and people.

Let's assume, however, that you are just entering the field. Research can be valuable to the new consultant as well. For example, if you are thinking about marketing your consulting services to a specific industry, find out if the industry is growing and has a future.

This can be determined in a variety of ways. First, there are trade associations. Every industry has one. In most libraries you will find a book called, *The Encyclopedia of Associations*, which contains virtually every industry in the United States and the associations that represent them. By contacting these associations you can garner valuable information and insight into your field. You will also be able to detect trends and possible future needs.

There is also the market research department of the local newspaper. Most contain reams of information about specific industries in your area—growth patterns and potential. Newspapers have these departments to aid local businesses that may become advertisers. They usually have economic information about every industry in your area and it is available to you, the potential advertiser, at no cost.

The local chamber of commerce can supply data about industries and companies that are moving in and out. Personnel consultants can examine the Sunday classified ads to see which occupations are most in demand. Building, land, and government consultants can talk to people at city hall to determine developer activity.

Read national magazines and newspapers and look for items about new trends, businesses, and innovations. One of the best sources of material is the *Wall Street Journal*. On a daily basis, the *Journal* carries one of the best summaries of new developments of any publication in the country. The *Journal* also carries ads from agencies that put contracts out for bid.

A new computer system that allows companies to raise production may mean the demise of an old computer system (and perhaps even the company that produces it), but it is also an opportunity for someone (a data processing consultant) who knows the ins and outs of the new system.

CONSULTANT'S UNIQUE SELLING PROPOSITION

Once you determine the viability of your service and the industry you are going to target, there is one other critical thing to settle before you ever advertise—determine your USP (Unique Selling Proposition). The USP is an advertising term that goes back decades. It simply means you have to develop that one, single *unique* benefit you have that your competition lacks. Even if your competition has every USP you can think of, there is a good chance they are not using them when they market their services. The USP can be derived from pricing, service, or quality.

Why is your consulting service better than Joe X's? What one thing (USP) is there that you do (or can do) that no one else can?

What would you tell a potential client if they asked? Answer that question and you are on the way to formulating your USP.

Your USP, incidentally, will not only be used in an ad, but when making presentations. It is the selling point that sets you apart from the masses. You must develop a USP before any ad (or any presentation) can be effective. Look at the USP checklist and you will see that you recognize a number of them.

Unique Selling Proposition Checklist

Our 5 year 50,000 warranty

More dentists recommend our toothpaste than any other

Our automobile gets the best mileage

Our burgers are charbroiled, not fried

Five times the selection

On call 24 hours a day

Superior location

Convenience

Immediate delivery

Notice how each of these USPs sell a specific benefit. They offer something that the competition cannot match and it is something the buyer wants. Now examine the following USP checklist for consultants.

USP Ideas

Superior service

Unmatched quality and experience

Your money back if we do not solve your problem

We specialize in this (your) industry

Our program provides more benefits than others

Our prices are lower

Our technology is the latest

Of all these USPs, there is one that is weak insofar as consulting is concerned—pricing. Although pricing may be important in some fields (gasoline, milk, and other retail items), it will not have a significant impact in a consultant's business, unless he or she is priced far above or below anyone else in the field. The consultant who is priced too low will not remain in business long and the higher priced consultant will have difficulties as well.

Price usually only comes into the bidding when a client perceives both consultants to be exactly equal. Then price can be the deciding factor. That perception, however, does not happen often.

Whatever USP you decide on, be sure you can fulfill it. Once you can, then you are ready to advertise.

When advertising, there are 10 key elements in an ad—whether it is print, radio, or TV—that should be kept in mind.

Key Elements in the Consultant's Ad

1. Be honest
2. Avoid generalities
3. Be believable
4. Educate
5. Inform
6. Design the ad as if you are talking one-on-one
7. Do not hard sell
8. Stress the benefits you offer to customers
9. Push your USP
10. Answer the customer's needs

Can all those things be addressed in one ad? They can and must if your ad is to be effective. Consulting is a business unlike any other. You are not selling a 99 cent hamburger special, a $1.99 cleaning of a suit, or a box of detergent. You are selling a personal service, an intangible product—a product that usually requires investigation and thought before an investment is made by the client. Not every medium will enable you to sell your service, either.

Let's examine various forms of media, how they operate, and what kind of impact they can have on the consultant's clientele.

MEDIA CHECKLIST—SELECTING THE RIGHT ONE

The purpose of any ad campaign for a consultant is to generate *inquiries*. Do not expect an ad—by itself—to close a sale for you. The consulting business differs greatly from retail and many other businesses. The fee (or client investment) is usually high and the prospect usually will want to know more about you and your abilities than what an ad says.

Radio

Usually expensive. Radio sells through repetition. In other words, the more people hear it, the more prone they are to buy it. Some markets have 40–50 radio stations; others only a handful. Regardless of how many, note the characteristics of stations and who is listening to what.

1. *Rock Radio.*   Most rock radio is listened to by teens and young adults. There are, of course, a number of 30-, 40-, and even 50-year olds who listen to rock. They were brought up on it. For the most part, however, when a person reaches his or her mid-to-late 30s, they begin to switch and start listening to all-news or all-talk radio. If they are still rock radio listeners, they probably still have the same habit most rock radio fans have—they are dial punchers. That is, when the commercial comes on, they hit the dial and go on to the next rock station. Consequently, rock radio is not the media that a consultant would want in order to market services.

2. *All-News/All-Talk Radio.*   An excellent vehicle with which to reach potential customers. People who listen to all-news, and all-talk listen. They do not just have the radio on for background (as is the case with rock and most music stations). You will usually find an older group listening to these stations. They are the consultant's audience.

    It should be remembered, however, that radio sells via repetition. It would take an enormous number of spots (and expense) to reach and sell customers.

If you call the sales department of a radio station, they will try to sell you time across the board and throughout the week. In others words, they will sell you drive time, afternoon and evening time, weekend time, and so on. Use common sense. When would your potential customers (clients) be listening? Chances are they would be in their cars and would be tuned in only during morning and afternoon drive time—unless you are after salespeople who may be in their cars all day. Thus, if you buy radio, you only want drive time, regardless of the numbers the sales department will show you.

In the consulting business you do not just want numbers—you want qualified numbers. Thus the music station with high numbers in mid-afternoon may not be nearly as effective during drive time as the news/talk station which could have lower numbers.

Remember, too, that consulting is not a hamburger business. You will not get prospects to buy your services on the strength of a 60-second commercial. What you may be able to do, however, is open the door, pique their curiosity, get them to inquire, and ask for more information. This is where your USP comes in—if it is unusual and your spot addresses the items on the Key Elements in the Consultant's Ad checklist, you may be able to garner inquiries and open the door for a follow-up sale. Do not expect radio to close sales for you.

Television

In some time periods TV is expensive, however, in others it can be cheaper than radio. For example, prime time (7 to 10 P.M.) is a premium period and out of the reach of most consultants. You are also paying for a mass audience and the masses are not the consultant's potential clients.

You may be able to purchase time in a specialized TV program in an off-prime time period that will reach your audience. There may be a financial or "Meet the Press" type program that airs in a relatively inexpensive time period.

Once again, TV usually sells with repetition. A clever, well-worded spot, targeted directly at your audience could be effective. If structured correctly, it could generate inquiries but do not expect it to close sales.

Cable Television

This deserves special mention. Cable can be an excellent ad vehicle, although the numbers supplied by the stations are questionable. There are, however, two advantages to cable, especially if you pick the right programs and time periods. First, cable is still inexpensive, and second, you can put together your own program and have it aired. Numerous consultants throughout the country are doing this now. They buy a half-hour of time, put together their own program, and sell their services during the program. With a half-hour you can sell your services. The lengthy broadcast has one other advantage—it does not appear to be a paid advertisement. When you buy a half-hour, it looks (if it is put together professionally) as if it is part of the station's programming.

Usually, when a consultant purchases time in this manner, there is an 800 number that potential customers can use in order to respond.

In some cases—depending on the market—a consultant can go to the cable station and sell the sales manager on a Per Inquiry (PI) deal. (For a further discussion of PI, read the section on per inquiry advertising and its usage in this chapter.)

The station will air your program at no charge. You will, however, pay for each inquiry that comes in and the numbers are tracked by the station since the response comes directly to them.

You may have heard about Per Order (PO) time. This works the same as PI, except you pay a percentage for each order that is generated. Per Order would not benefit a consultant's practice, unless you were selling books and tapes. This type of arrangement has been successful for a variety of products and in recent years consultants began structuring the same type of deal.

The PI does require funds. For instance, the station will be willing to film the commercial for you but they will want to be paid for the production. If you are putting together your own 30 minute show, this can be expensive and you may pay to have an outside studio do the filming. If you do intend to experiment in this area, try to keep your filming confined to a studio. Once you go outside, the expenses can become enormous.

Per inquiries are not confined to cable. Depending on the market, you may find some commercial channels that are willing to listen to the same offer. Per inquiry arrangements put money in the station's pocket.

Print

Obviously, this is one of the least expensive methods for reaching customers. Targeting is the key. When considering print, think about the industry you are trying to reach. Think about the companies. Do they read certain trade journals? If so, your ads may be better placed in a trade and/or business journal.

Ask yourself questions before you place an ad. Let's say you are after firms in the aerospace field. Who within the aerospace companies will buy your services? Is it the president? Training director? Purchasing director? The training director may be reading a publication that has nothing to do with aerospace, but focuses instead on training. The purchasing director may read purchasing journals. The company president may be reading the business page of the local newspaper. Or perhaps there is an industry trade paper that is known and respected and all three read it. Once again, do not expect print to close the sale. Look for it to generate inquiries.

In contrast to radio and television, if your print ad is going to work, it will do so the first time out. Print does not take repetition. Do not let a salesperson at the magazine, newspaper, and the like convince you that people have to get used to seeing your ad before they buy your services. If the ad is intriguing, the needs are met, and the curiosity piqued, they will inquire the first time out. If they do not, reexamine the ad.

Yellow Pages

There are so many editions it is hard to keep track. You will do best if you go for the biggest—the metropolitan. Stay away from the small, neighborhood *Yellow Pages*. They are not cost-effective for consulting.

For which products and services are *Yellow Pages* effective? Think of when you use it. When you have a plumbing or electrical problem, or when you are searching for someone to repair or service something that does not cause problems on a regular basis. In other words, the *infrequent* used service is the one that benefits from the *Yellow Pages*. Consulting falls into this category and a *Yellow Page* ad may generate an occasional inquiry.

Regardless of which medium is selected, all advertising should be monitored to determine the response. When a prospect calls, always make it a point to ask, "How did you happen to hear about us?"

All businesspeople should make it a practice to monitor ads. If you find you get no response from a print ad, drop it. If you get good response from the *Yellow Pages*, you should not only keep it but consider expanding it. Determining where your business is coming from and how they heard about you is critical to success.

There are certain ways to structure print ads that will make them more effective and less costly, as explained in the following checklist.

Effective Print Ad Structure Checklist

1. *Borders.* Use something like a border that you see on coupons. This thick broken border stops the eye and that is one of the keys to structuring a successful ad.

2. *Vertical Ads.* If you are placing small space ads, you will usually get better placement with a vertical ad instead of a square ad. Instead of buying a 2 column by 2 inch ad, buy a 1 column by 4 inch ad. The amount of space and cost is the same. Why vertical? Study your local newspaper

and the magazines you receive. You will notice that square or horizontal ads (i.e., 2 column × 2 inches) can fit anywhere on the page. They are just the right configuration. Vertical ads are not. They are difficult to place; often they float to the top of the page, and you get better position.

3. *Headline.* Make it simple, intriguing, and keep it short. Headlines are the key. Seventy percent of an ad's appeal is in the head. You should spend more time on this than anything else. Sometimes, with a one or two word change in the head, you can increase your response dramatically.

4. *Content.* Keep the ad guidelines in mind. Be honest and avoid generalities. Address the prospect's needs.

5. *Ask for It.* Be sure to close by asking the prospect to respond. Give him or her a telephone number, address, and so forth.

6. *Avoid P.O. Boxes.* Many consultants operate out of their home. They may rent a P.O. Box for business purposes. P.O. Boxes cut down response. They say to the prospect, this person is not substantial enough to have his or her own office. If you need a box, check out some of the Private P.O. boxes available. They allow you to use a street address and your box becomes a suite. You can rent Private P.O. boxes with prestigious addresses.

SAMPLE ADS

The following ads (Figures 7-1 through 7-6) all proved to be effective because they followed the ad guidelines outlined previously.

Notice how specific they are. Look at the headlines and see the USPs. Read the body copy and see how the USP flows into the copy.

Notice, too, how these ads tell a complete story. None of them say buy our brand or retain our services without giving the prospect a good reason to make the purchase.

These ads are also directed at specific audiences. There is no confusion; no misleading headlines. These are principles that consultants should keep in mind. Do not put a clever head on an ad simply because it is clever. Be specific and try to appeal to your potential audience.

Each of these ads was designed to generate immediate response. In each there is a telephone number that is prominently listed. The companies that created these ads will be able to judge the effectiveness with little problem. If the telephone rings, the ads are good; if not, something is missing.

In each of these cases, the telephone rang.

PER INQUIRY AND PER ORDER ADS

For those contemplating per inquiry advertising, several things should be kept in mind. Per inquiry is not just a matter of going to the local TV station and convincing them to run a commercial on your practice. Before seeking any PI arrangement, the consultant should determine which media *reaches* his or her market. It is senseless to sell a local TV station on a 15 or 30 minute show

3 Critical Qualities You Should Demand From Your Lawyer.

1. *He should listen to you*—to find out exactly what you need. When you first meet it's a good sign if *you* do most of the talking: your case may be won or lost on just one small detail.

2. *Fast Working*—you pay a lawyer by the hour. Make sure your lawyer goes straight to the point without dilly-dallying. His time is. *your* money.

3. *Easy to get a hold of*—he's got to be available when you need him. It could be 8:00 p.m.—it could be on a weekend. Don't settle for a 9-5 man.

"When you need a lawyer, you need someone who can stand up and fight for you.

My approach isn't timid. I'm a hardhitting lawyer and I've been handling all manner of legal problems for local clients for 10 years."

"I've built my whole practice on these 3 points. Give me a call. My number is 889-0523. We'll work out a plan to solve your legal problems . . . then put it into action."

—Marvin Friedland

Melvin L. Friedland

Attorney-at-Law

357 West Second Street, Suite 12
San Bernardino

889-0523

FIG. 7-1. Sample ads.

which they will air in mid-day, opposite network soap opera programs. A consultant's clientele is usually not watching at that time.

That is why it is important to analyze your market first. What media do they watch? What publications (both trade and consumer) do they read? What radio stations do they listen to? As a rule, the bigger the media, the less likely they are to consent to a PI offering. Networks and network affiliates are not likely candidates, nor are major metropolitan newspapers or national magazines.

Cable stations may be ideal—and demographic studies show that many reach the consultant's market (businesspeople). Local newspapers that are owned and run by an individual offer good PI potential. They are more likely to listen to your proposition and they can track the leads without rearranging an entire accounting department. Some stations will ask for an exclusive when it comes to PI. That is, they do not want you running the spot on any competitor station in the same market.

For consultants, the two best types of PI arrangements would be with a trade magazine (that reaches your potential market), a local magazine that is business oriented, and a cable or local independent station that will accept a half-hour program. Realistically, in order for a consultant to generate inquiries,

FIG. 7-2. Sample ads.

he or she is going to need time (more than a 60 second commercial) or space in print.

If you can convince the station and/or magazine/newspaper to give you those things, then PI may be an ideal vehicle for your practice.

The PI checklist which follows is designed to aid the consultant in putting together a commercial or spot that he or she intends to air on television without cost. Per inquiry has been utilized extensively on cable and commercial television. It also can be used on radio, and in many cases, print.

Per Inquiry Checklist for Consultants

1. Determine which station (stations) in your market may appeal to or reach your potential audience
2. Look at time periods that are most desirable
3. Call sales manager (or station manager) and ask if they have any PI time available
4. If PI time is possible, make an appointment to see manager

Carpet Cleaning 24 Hours a Day 365 Days a Year

When water damage occurs, even a few hours can make the difference in saving expensive carpeting and furniture.

As a special service to our customers, **Westside Carpet Care** is instantly available in emergencies . . . 24 hours, year round.

The minute we receive your call, we're on our way to help.

Non-Emergencies too

Our steam and shampoo treatment will leave your carpeting and upholstery sparkling. That's because we take the time and have the knowledge to do the job right.

Our powerful, professional equipment will remove the stubborn dirt that do-it-yourself rental equipment leaves behind.

Free Estimates

Call us today. We'll be happy to give you a free estimate for a sofa, a room or an entire house.

Westside Carpet Care 558-4977

3376 Motor Avenue, Los Angeles

FIG. 7-3. Sample ads.

5. Prior to seeing manager, prepare a presentation of what type of approach you will utilize, who your audience will be, why this station is perfect, and how the station will benefit from your deal (remember, the station does not care about you, but about making profits)

6. See manager

7. Negotiate terms

8. Get go-ahead for commercial

9. Get signed contract with terms and so on

10. Price studio time and so forth at station

11. Price studio time at independent studio or station

12. Script commercial

    a.   Examine for USP

    b.   Examine for beginning, middle, and end

    c.   Make sure it requires action from the prospect

13. Check studio announcer availabilities

14. Check other announcers available

15. Check pricing of each

16. Hire announcer

17. Arrange for filming

18. Arrange for editing

19. Obtain original of commercial

20. Supply station with copy

21. Utilize commercial on other stations (if there is not a nonrestrict clause in your agreement)

LOW-COST ADVERTISING ASSISTANCE

Where can you get someone to help you with a print, radio, or even a PI ad?

Obviously, if you deal with an ad agency the problem is solved. However, most consultants do not have a budget which enables them to hire an agency. Usually, you will be dealing with the media directly.

FIG. 7-4. Sample ads.

FIG. 7-5. Sample ads.

All media have an ad or sales department. It is up to these people to lend assistance to advertisers whenever possible. They will even provide, at no cost, layouts of ads and ideas. They will also help you write the ad. Do not, however, rely on these people to do everything. Their job is selling and getting the ad dollars in the door. Although they have creative ability, you will find it may be limited. Some may not even understand (or agree with) your thoughts on a USP or the content of the commercial.

Consequently, do not hesitate in looking for other help. Try the graduate business department of the local university or the local Small Business Administration (SBA), which has an abundance of literature providing hints and copy approaches for putting ads together. These brochures and handouts are some of the best resources you will find. Your best bet may be to find a *small*, local publicity or ad agency that will work on a one-shot basis and do the writing and supervising of the commercial for a fee.

If you are contemplating PI commercials, you will need professional help if you do not have writing skills. That help is available through the station you will be utilizing or other cable outlets that have spare time and would be willing to aid in the production of a commercial for a lower or reduced fee.

Do not try and get network affiliates (i.e., those stations that program ABC, NBC, and CBS series) to help with the filming. You will find they do not have time and they are expensive.

Drunk Driving Injury

Why Nagelberg & Weissberg should be your attorneys.

Drunk Driving, Shoplifting, Drugs or other criminal charges?

Or have you been hurt in an auto accident or by a defective product or, by someone else's negligence?

We handle cases like these and many others every day. Chances are we can help you too.

No 'up front' fee . . . on any injury case. You pay us only after we've collected a settlement for you. No settlement - no charge.

Not only that we'll advance all filing fees, process serving charges, court reporter fees and jury deposits.

First visit free

We're located on the 11th floor of the Avco Center in Westwood, at the corner of Wilshire & Glendon, no charge for your initial consultation.

Call us for an appointment today. **475-7049**

Larry Nagelberg

Bill Weissberg

Nagelberg & Weissberg

10850 Wilshire Blvd., Suite 1101   Los Angeles,   (213) 475-7049

FIG. 7-6. Sample ads.

If you do not have a writing background, spend time at the library and research some of the advertising literature that is available.

Interestingly, some of the best books on writing ad copy have been out for years. Look for *Ogilvie on Advertising*, by David Ogilvie and *Scientific Advertising*, by Claude Hopkins. These texts were published long ago, however, the principles that must be used in order to sell services have not changed. You will find them clearly outlined in these and similar books. Hopkins, who virtually wrote the rules for advertising, makes some interesting comments throughout *Scientific Advertising* that consultants can benefit from.

When you plan and prepare an advertisement (always) keep before you a typical buyer. Don't think of people in the masses, think of individuals. With your ad only try talking to one.

Remember that the people you address are selfish, as we all are. They care nothing about your interest or your profit. They seek service for themselves. Ignoring this fact is a common mistake and a costly one in advertising.

Headlines in an ad are like headlines in a newspaper. Nobody reads a whole newspaper. We pick out what we wish to read by headlines, and we do not want those headlines misleading.

We have learned that cheapness is not a strong appeal. Americans are extravagant.

Being specific in your claims is important. A person who makes a specific claim is either telling the truth or a lie . . . and potential customers recognize this fact.

When writing your ads consider only new customers. Do not consider the person who has already bought from you. Explain everything for that new prospect.

Always know your competition. What have they in price or quality or claims to weigh against your appeal?

A person who desires to make an impression must stand out from the masses and in a pleasing way.

To attack a rival is never good advertising.

Letter writing has much to do with advertising. Letters to inquirers, follow-up letters. Ads and letters will have the same differences insofar as response is concerned.

A letter going to an inquirer is like a salesman making a call on an interested prospect.

CHAPTER 8

STRUCTURING/USING DIRECT MAIL

His name is Jay Abraham and he has become one of the best known direct mail marketing consultants in the country. He took a company that was grossing $50 million a year, and in just a few years, built the firm into a $500 million a year company.

Jay specializes in selling precious metals such as gold, silver, and collectibles. When consumers in the United States were paying 21 percent for an auto loan, inflation was only a few points behind, and consumers were panicking, Jay's clients were doing well. In fact, every precious metals company was doing well. Suddenly, however, inflation abated, unemployment began to drop, interest rates came down, gasoline became affordable, the dollar increased in value—and you could not give away gold, silver, and collectibles to investors.

Jay, however, did not panic. There is a truism in sales: If you have a good product, a product that has benefits to those who purchase it, you can sell it with the correct approach.

While others in the precious metals field took their money and ran, Jay studied the market. He realized several things. Gold, silver, and collectibles were still good investments. They belonged in a balanced portfolio. What investors had to realize was that they would not show the quick return or rapid rise that they had during the previous three to four years.

What did Jay do? He utilized direct mail as an educational and informational tool. He did not make rash promises or shout (through the written word) at his company's potential customers.

He acknowledged, for instance, that gold had plummeted. At the same time, he would include copies of reports from economists, analysts, and the like who maintained that although gold was on a downswing, it could be a good investment in the long run.

He sent reports from respected investment analysts who maintained that gold, silver, and collectibles should be regarded as part of an overall investment plan.

He even included reports that did not mention gold but talked about other aspects of the economy. In many of these letters he made offers and proposed guarantees. He spent months educating and informing buyers.

Only when he was convinced that his potential customers had all the information they needed, did he make an offer, and it was always followed by a guarantee.

People will not buy unless they first believe they know a great deal about what they are buying. Nor will they buy if they detect you are trying to hide things about your products or services.

Jay wrote and rewrote direct mail pieces. He developed USPs that made sense in a noninflationary environment. Jay's letter often ranged five, six, or seven pages in length explaining the economy and its impact on gold and silver. He included 50 page reports from outside sources, paid for them, and gave them away to prospects.

There is a fallacy among many advertising people that says potential customers will not read, so make everything short, from headlines to body copy. People will read if the mailing piece has beneficial information, answers their needs, and has a USP.

MARGINAL NET WORTH OF YOUR CUSTOMERS

In sending lengthy reports and letters to his market, Jay often spent more than he made from the prospect. Why was he investing in prospects who did not show a return? Because of a concept that is crucial in the direct mail field—the marginal net worth of a customer. It is of importance to every consultant.

Marginal net worth simply asks the question, "If you have a customer, how much is he likely to spend with you while he is a customer?"

For example, an insurance agent may spend $300 in advertising, direct mail, and time generating a buyer who will purchase a homeowner's or similar policy. Let's say he or she makes $300 from the policy. Why pursue the customer if only to break even? Because of the customer's potential future purchases. For instance, the insurance person may know the average customer will make four additional policy purchases after his or her initial plunge. Each of those four may be worth $100, $300, or even more. In that case it pays for the insurance person to break even on the first sale. He or she knows that the customer, if taken care of, will buy four more policies, worth anywhere from $400 to $1200 in profit.

Consultants have the same opportunity. A client could end up giving them four or five different projects, not just one. That is one of the reasons why it pays to supply prospects with information.

Some day those prospects may become clients and they may make multiple purchases. Jay Abraham operates under that theory. He is willing to break even, even lose money in some cases, if he can nurture a prospect into a client. He knows that once he has gained the prospect's confidence, that prospect's first purchase may be a loss, but he or she will remain a customer for two or three years and spend thousands of dollars in the process—and Abraham's company will profit.

Consultants should keep this principle in mind. A consulting client may be around for numerous additional purchases if he or she is treated correctly and the consultant does the job that is expected.

The following case study is an example of the impact of a customer's marginal net worth.

Icy Hot Case Study

Icy Hot was a product designed for those with arthritis or symptoms of the ailment. It alleviated the aches and pains, and the company had done well with it.

The owners of the firm decided they could do much better. They brought in a young, aggressive direct mail specialist to work on the product.

The specialist developed numerous mailing pieces, however, he believed that the most promising marketing media for the product was television. The owners had never tried TV and relied almost entirely on sales from the retail store level. The consultant convinced them to let him try and negotiate a PO arrangement with a local TV station.

Before going to a station, the consultant examined past sales records. He found that once a buyer purchased the ointment, they became regular customers, and in 90 percent of the cases, buyers would make at least six more purchases of the product. Icy Hot was not expensive and a percentage of its small suggested list price was not particularly appealing to the local TV station. The consultant, however, made them an offer they could not refuse. In exchange for the commercial time, he gave them all the proceeds from the sale. All he retained was the name and address of the buyer.

The station jumped at the proposition. Realizing it could make significant profit from the spot (and not have to split it), the station aired the commercial endlessly. They generated thousands of Icy Hot customers—and the consultant got the names and addresses in return.

Those names built Icy Hot into a $13 million a year company within 18 months. It was a lesson in the value of marginal net worth of a customer, and is an example of what a customer's buying power can mean to a company once he or she becomes a satisfied customer.

The young consultant who convinced Icy Hot to go with the program was Jay Abraham. One of Abraham's most effective direct mail pieces follows (Figure 8-1).

It runs 12 pages but contains important basic elements that every consultant should keep in mind. It sells, resells, and repeats. In direct mail you tell the prospect once, and you tell him or her again in a different manner.

Notice the headline. The fact that you can hire a marketing genius for $9.52 a week is intriguing. Notice, too, it is not the marketing genius who says he is a genius—it is a client, the best reference you can have. (In this case, the client was Howard Ruff who signs his name on page one of the piece.)

There is a tremendous amount of copy for anyone to read, so the authors have made the task easier by underlining passages, putting bulleted items (bold-faced dots) beside certain points, breaking the piece into small paragraphs, using numbers alongside certain key items, and putting subheads (bold-faced headlines in the middle of pages 2, 8, 9, 10, and 11).

"I PAID THIS MARKETING GENIUS $600,000 LAST YEAR, BECAUSE HE MADE ME $2,000,000.

Now You Can Hire Him For $9.52 A Week"

Howard Ruff

Dear Friend:

Yes, that is <u>absolutely true</u>! I paid Jay Abraham $600,000 because he was worth every penny of it. <u>He made me much more than that</u>. The money I used to pay him came from the profits he produced for me with no cost to me.

AND YES, IT'S ALSO TRUE THAT <u>YOU CAN HIRE HIM FOR $9.52 A WEEK</u>.

This offer is <u>not for everyone</u>. In fact, it will probably be a waste of ten minutes for you to read the rest of this letter unless you meet one of the following criteria:

• <u>You are a small businessperson</u>—in any business—not getting as much business as you would like.

• You have a <u>terrific idea</u> you think is saleable, and you'd like to sell the idea to your boss and share in the profits, but you don't know how to market it or make the deal. Or your idea has been turned down by your company, and you want to know how to market it to someone else.

• You have come up with <u>an invention, an idea, or a concept</u> and want to start a business of your own, <u>but you don't know how to get the capital</u> to start up without giving away most of your company, and you are afraid to quit your job until you can find out if your idea is any good.

• You have <u>a product or service you are trying to sell,</u> or would like to sell.

• You're <u>frustrated with advertising agencies</u> to whom you give a fortune and get little or no business in return.

• You are retired or semi-retired and you want to profit from your past business experience.

• You have a <u>"dead" customer list</u> or lots of prospects you're not converting.

• You are a <u>manager</u> working for a corporation, responsible for spending some of the marketing or advertising budget and generating sales—and you're not doing as well as you'd like—or your boss would like.

• You own a reasonably successful business, but <u>you have stagnated</u>. Competitors are catching up with you and it's getting harder and harder to make a buck.

• You have just seen a 20-year veteran at your company fired and you are beginning to wonder about your own future.

• <u>You could make a lot more money</u> if you had a marketing genius working for you.

If any of the above statements are true, you simply must read this <u>no-risk offer</u> to at least find out whether Jay Abraham can help you.

FIG. 8-1. An effective direct mail piece—sample.

Before going further, let me introduce myself.

My name is Howard Ruff. You may have heard of me.

I am the publisher, editor, and principal author of the largest-circulation financial newsletter in the world—THE HOWARD RUFF FINANCIAL SUCCESS REPORT. I also wrote the biggest-selling financial book in the history of publishing.

This is the first time (and probably the last time) I've ever written a letter like this over my own signature to sell another publication. Here's why.

I'm a pretty darn good marketer. My own newsletter's circulation growth didn't come by accident. When you invent a better mousetrap, the world does NOT beat a path to your door unless you develop effective ways of telling them about the virtues of your mousetrap, and inducing them to try it. Even though I think I write a terrific financial newsletter, the key to its commercial success was and is marketing.

But as good as I think I am at marketing, Jay Abraham is better. He is the finest marketing mind on this planet. He generates marketing ideas as compulsively as my Labrador, Sassie, fetches tennis balls. Now he will be writing a monthly publication to share and teach in minute detail the principles which he has used to help dozens, if not hundreds, of businessmen make fortunes, while making a fortune for himself out of his share of the profits he produced for them.

Jay is so good that his current income doesn't come from hourly billings, fees, or commissions from the placement of ads. He only asks his clients to share with him the additional profits that he generates for them, often with no cost at all to the client.

When Jay first described this publication to me, and told me he was going to spill his guts about everything he knew about marketing, my heart started pounding, as I knew that I would become a hero to everyone who I could induce to subscribe. Not only am I writing this letter, but I'm going to help him produce and edit his publication.

From Skeptic To Believer

It took me three years after I first met Jay to recognize his genius. Frankly, at first, he turned me off. The reasons, in retrospect, are hilarious.

First, because I consider myself such a good marketer, my ego sometimes prevents me from recognizing that virtue in others, but the problems weren't just on my end.

When I first went to Jay's home in Palos Verdes, California on a cliff overlooking the Pacific, I found him hanging upside-down like a bat from some contraption that was supposed to improve his health.

He sleeps like a bat too, going to bed at 4:00 a.m. and sleeping until noon, probably because his brain is still compulsively racing when you and I are pooping out.

Not only that, he's a fitness freak who works out two hours a day—but at the same time seems to subsist on gallons of Diet Coke.

If you think that's strange, listen to this. Four years ago, he refused to come see me because he was afraid to fly. I had to go to him. But last March when I was having breakfast at a hotel in Hong Kong, I looked up and there he was. He had suddenly decided to no longer be afraid to fly, and promptly took a vacation trip to Singapore, Bangkok and Hong Kong.

He's obsessed with cars and buys and sells Porsches, Rolls Royces and Mercedes like you or I might change socks.

Worst of all, each time I saw him he spent the first hour telling me how wonderful he was.

Page 2

FIG. 8-1. (**continued**) (*Figure continued on p. 216.*)

You can understand why it took me a while to wade through all this to recognize his extraordinary gifts, but his work for others was so wildly profitable, I decided to get to know him. I finally was forced to surrender to the fact that Jay Abraham is an honest, loveable, eccentric, <u>unorthodox genius</u>, the likes of whom I will probably never meet again. Once I accepted that, he made me millions. In fact, this eccentric man not only worked for me <u>strictly on a contingency basis,</u> taking his compensation out of the increased profits he produced, he even put up his<u> own money</u> on most of the deals we did together.

He's done precisely the same thing with literally dozens of other companies.

Jay has been caught in a conflict between two seemingly immovable facts.

(1) <u>He loves to teach everybody,</u> regardless of whether they are in a big business or small business; but,

(2) <u>He can't work individually with smaller clients</u> because it takes him just as much time to work on a deal that will make him $10,000 as one that will make him half a million.

Now Jay has become convinced that it would be worth his while to sit down <u>once each month</u> to write an in-depth, comprehensive, step-by-step explanation of <u>one major marketing principle</u> that he has used to make himself and others millions of dollars—a principle that can be used by <u>all</u> businesses, small, medium or large. Now he can make more money with less work <u>and</u> help more people.

<u>As a newsletter editor and publisher</u> who has had to discipline himself for a decade (I haven't missed a weekly deadline in those ten years), I know how to pull out of Jay Abraham those ideas that will make big bucks for anyone, <u>things you will never get from anyone else, anywhere else.</u> We will do this for you, once a month for a year.

We struggled with <u>what to call this publication.</u> It isn't a magazine because there is no advertising, and it isn't a typical newsletter because there isn't any news. Finally we just decided to call it YOUR MARKETING GENIUS AT WORK, because that's precisely what it is.

My job is to ensure that Jay's lessons come to you on time, in the most compact, compelling, lucid, practical and useful way possible, <u>in clear and simple prose.</u>

Let me share with you a few of the actual ideas Jay Abraham teaches. As terrific and useful as they will seem to you, they just scratch the surface. Consider these ideas free samples. You will learn:

(1) The principle of the <u>Unique Selling Proposition</u>, or USP.

Every business has or can create <u>that single compelling idea</u> that differentiates it from its competitors. The very statement of that idea makes people want to do business with you.

The Unique Selling Proposition crisply describes or illustrates those benefits to the customer <u>that ring an automatic bell in his mind.</u> The customer doesn't really care about you. While all of your competitors are bragging about themselves, you are concentrating on the unique benefits that will make the customer's life richer, easier, less expensive, and more rewarding.

This single principle will give you an <u>unbelievable advantage</u> over all your competitors.

You will change all your advertising, marketing, and sales force efforts (if you have any) to convey how you are dedicated to serving the customers' needs, saving <u>them</u> time and money, making <u>them</u> more effective, and improving their circumstances. The Unique Selling Proposition makes that clear and simple.

<u>Sometimes it's an old idea</u> looked at from a new perspective. <u>Sometimes it's a new idea,</u> which lets you pull away from the pack.

Page 3

FIG. 8-1. (*continued*)

Would you like an example? All right. Let's take me. Before me, nearly all financial newsletters catered to rich clients. My Unique Selling Proposition is that I am "The Financial Advisor To America's Neglected And Abused Middle Class." That Unique Selling Proposition was my niche which let me pull away from the pack by attracting hundreds of thousands of people who never before thought a financial newsletter was for them.

Need another one? Avis' USP is that they had to try harder, because they were #2. It gave them a far bigger share of the market and made them a household word.

Jay will teach you how to find or create your own Unique Selling Proposition, to look at your business in totally different ways, and more than that, to help your prospective customers single you out in the most positive way possible.

(2) Jay will show you how to squeeze several times more immediate return out of an advertising budget. In fact, Jay will do things for you that no ad agency ever could or would do.

For example, ad agencies are compensated by commissions on the advertising they place. They are never compensated on a percentage of the results they achieve. Perhaps you can guess why.

No ad agency would cut its own throat by helping you cut the advertising budget to get the same result. Jay does that all the time. And remember, he has been so effective, in all his deals he prefers to be compensated on the basis of results, not on advertising commissions. With his techniques, the money usually comes in even before the ad bills come due.

Jay believes only in "direct-response" advertising, never "institutional advertising."

What's the difference? Institutional advertising simply puts your name in front of the public. It rarely presents a proposition or asks the customer for a specific action or response. Maybe it wins prizes for artistry, but it puts no money in your pocket within a predictable time frame, in predictable amounts, so you can quickly evaluate the ad, letter, commercial, or sales pitch, improve it, and roll it out to make more money.

Direct-response advertising, however, must generate immediate sales—bringing customers in the door, and leads or checks in the mail—NOW! In fact, the results must be complete in 60 days or less, usually in 7 to 10 days. It must be efficient, not waste one inch of space, tell the full story, elaborate on the Unique Selling Proposition, tell customers why they must respond now, and be profitable from the word "go."

These powerhouse principles of direct-response advertising are understood and practiced by only one business in 1,000.

(3) Jay will teach you how to ethically make money from customers who are no longer doing business with you.

For example, you can sell, rent or joint-venture your old inactive customer or prospect names to other companies selling related or even possibly competitive products or services, for as much as $10-$25 each, often more. It costs a lot of money to secure a customer or prospect. You can get it back, and then some.

Or you can have your salesmen sell other companies' products or services to your customers for a big share of the profits.

You can even make a bundle from every one you DON'T sell. Perhaps your product is too expensive, or too cheap, or too sophisticated, or too basic. You make a deal with a competitor whose product more completely fills the customers' needs. Once you have given up on a prospect, you notify your competition. He sells them and splits with you. Jay has taught many companies how to profit from their competitors.

He'll teach you the concept of "the moving parade"—the fact that customers' desires and circumstances constantly change. Here's an example Jay loves to recount.

Page 4

FIG. 8-1. (**continued**) (Figure continued on p. 218.)

"I bought a small house some years ago and used an interior designer to help me decorate. I could only afford to do a modest job on half the house, spending about $20,000. The designer knew the house needed a lot more work; I had just run out of money. The designer never called again.

"Had she called me six months later when I saved $10,000 more, and shown sincere interest in what I was doing, she would have gotten the living room remodeling job I gave to someone else. Had she called me again a year later, she would have gotten the recarpet job and wall and window covering business I gave to someone else. Had she called me with a piece of furniture she thought I would like, she would have sold me the $5,000 sofa I bought from someone else. And had she called me 18 months ago as I was about to move into a new 4,000 sq. ft. home, she would have gotten the $150,000 I spent decorating."

The point is that people's circumstances keep changing. By merely showing regular interest, you increase your chances of prospering.

(4) He will teach you how to profitably make deals for your product or service to be used as an immensely attractive premium to be given away by other businesses, generating money from other people's customer lists and ad budgets. You will learn how to persuade the other businessman to put up the money and do the work.

Jay once "bulk" bought 20,000 six-month, $95 memberships from a health club, for 75¢ apiece—that's right, 75¢. He then went to a clothing store and persuaded them to give any customer buying $200 worth of clothes a free membership to the health club, which he sold to them for 75¢.

The health club got an immediate check for $15,000, plus they had 20,000 prospects willing to try their facilities for six months. The club didn't have to spend a dime in advertising and promotion.

At the end of the six months, the health club closed at least 5% of the 20,000 as fully paid renewal members at $95, generating $95,000 in renewal membership income (almost all of which was pure profit), and $15,000 in immediate front-end cash.

The retailer client gave his clothing customers a real $95 gift that only cost him 75¢!

Needless to say, Jay had deals both with the clothing store and the health club that made him a lot of money.

Here's another example of the same principle.

A florist told Jay that roses, which normally sold for $48 a dozen retail, and cost him $15 a dozen wholesale during the winter, were in oversupply in the summer and that he could buy them for 35¢ a rose—about $4 a dozen.

Jay made a deal with a formal clothing rental chain. Whenever anyone rented a tux or gown, they got a dozen roses free. It cost the rental chain $5 a dozen (Jay's client made $1 a dozen on the bulk sale) to secure hundreds of extra sales their competitors would otherwise have gotten—plus the client ended up selling hundreds of dozens of roses and the rental firm gave a $10 discount coupon for the flower store.

(5) Jay will teach you how to apply his principle of " Concentric Circles."

For example, Jay persuaded coin company client to offer customers a $23 starter coin set at cost. Through advertising and direct mail, 30,000 people sent in for it. The client then went back to those 30,000 people and got 3,000 to buy at least $1,000 worth of coins (that's $3,000,000 in sales).

Within six months, he went back to those 3,000 people and sold 1,000 of them $3,000 to $5,000 worth of coins (that's at least $3,000,000 more). Then he went to those customers and sold 150-250 of them an average of $10,000 more (that's another $1,000,000-plus).

Page 5

FIG. 8-1. (*continued*)

The original 30,000 people who spent $23 on which the coin dealer made nothing, eventually bought more than $7 million worth of coins in concentric circles, all profit for the dealer.

That idea has been worth $50,000 a month in commissions and fees for Jay, paid happily by a grateful client.

Jay believes that everyone should turn a one-shot sale into a perpetual sale.

If you sell swimming pools, why not add a yearly maintenance and cleaning contract?

If you sell dry cleaning, why not give good customers a monthly or yearly flat rate for all their business?

If you sell furniture, why not give away free a $95 quarterly decorating consultation in the home whenever someone buys something, giving you four more chances each year to sell them something else?

(6) Each monthly in-depth report from Jay will never be the typical, superficial concoction of abstract, so-called "marketing" concepts, but a complete detailed counseling, explaining every relevant aspect of a strategy which, when used properly, can project anyone far above his competition in a matter of months.

Let me give you another example. Jay will teach you how to educate your potential customers to appreciate the inherent value of your product or service by using "pre-emptive educational marketing"— explaining to your customers just how you make, produce, or render your product or service so it comes to life and has more credibility in the customer's mind. When you educate someone before asking them to buy, it gives an important dimension to your proposition.

Schlitz Beer in 1919 was the first beer company to explain how their beer was made. They told about the one Mother Yeast Cell which was a result of 1,525 different yeast experiments, the 4,000 ft. deep artesian well the pure water came from, the five plate-glass-surrounded rooms where the beer was condensed and repurified, the bottles that were sterilized five different times to insure purity, the 12 pounds of barley in every six pack of beer, the tasters who checked and rechecked each batch of beer seven different times before the bottles were cased and shipped out.

ALL BEER WAS MADE THAT WAY, but Schlitz was the first company to explain the beer-making process, and they pre-empted every other competitor.

Once we explain how such a basic concept works, we'll carefully explain how to use this technique successfully in ads and sales calls, in letters and on the phone.

Next we'll furnish copy and text you can use, filling in the blanks with your own applications.

Then we'll illustrate a hypothetical application of this technique for a retail, wholesale, or field sales promotion, a direct-mail solicitation, a newspaper ad, an intangible, or a service organization.

Then we'll list the bibliography worth reading on the subject and cite specific situations where companies leaped ahead of their competitors using the technique.

(7) Jay will show you a wealth of overlooked and hidden profit and cash flow opportunities in your business that you have never thought of. He'll also show you how to find other opportunities that he didn't think of, and precisely how to exploit them for all they're worth. He will profitably emancipate, liberate, deploy and redeploy your overlooked assets. It's a whole new way of thinking that you can apply to any product or service.

For example, most businessmen, once they have sold their basic product, make no effort to sell the customer anything else. This "back-end" marketing is usually more profitable than the sale of the initial product because you don't have to pay to find a prospect.

For example, most successful people in the direct-mail business have found a myriad

Page 6

FIG. 8-1. (*continued*) (*Figure continued on p. 220.*)

of opportunities to make money from their prospect list, such as mailing-list rentals, or joint-ventures with other people whose customer profile is similar to their own.

(8) You will be taught how to set up non-competitive and synergistic joint ventures with other companies who want access to your customers, who will allow you access to theirs, giving you 100% control while you get a big chunk of all profits of the joint venture.

Let's say, for example, you have a tennis club with 10,000 tennis enthusiasts on your roster. If you make a deal with a tennis court builder to let him solicit your membership, he would probably pay you $5,000 on every court he sold. You'd have to keep a membership for 15 or 20 years to make that much.

If you were a book publisher and you published a book on stress, and a group of psychologists wanted to put on a seminar on stress, your customers would be perfect prospects. Jay arranged a similar deal for a publisher who made $75,000 for making his list available and endorsing the seminar.

You know those bank charge card bills that always include the "statement stuffers?" Why do you think they keep doing it? Because they are profitable and the bank has their statement costs paid for by the people who supply the stuffers. That could be you, either supplying stuffers for others or selling stuffer space.

(9) After you have applied these blindingly simple but unorthodox principles to your own business, Jay will then show you how to license or sell the equivalent of a franchise on these techniques—your intellectual property—to either similar or totally dissimilar firms which would benefit from adapting them to their businesses. He will show you how to get them to pay through the nose on contingency. There are endless possibilities.

Let's say, for example, that you learned a valuable technique that was a vast improvement over any previous advertising.

You could license or teach this technique to other people in your kind of business in non-competitive geographic areas, and also to companies outside your field whose sales efforts could be expanded by your techniques.

If you create powerful newspaper ads or mailing pieces, you could sell or "lease" the ideas to others in or out of your field.

Some old ads or old sales techniques you no longer use might still be superior to the techniques currently used by your peers. You can license or sell those old ideas as well.

If you've mastered a way to resell customers, upgrade customers, reactivate prospects, or joint-venture your prospects, we'll show you how to license that technique as well.

Not one businessman in 10,000 ever sees the value of these lucrative, hidden or intangible assets and sales-enhancing techniques that other people would pay through the nose to get. Jay will teach you how to sell them for the maximum, and also how to acquire licenses for other people's techniques for the minimum amount possible, either for you to use or to license to others. Every successful ad promotion or sales pitch letter you ever did could turn into a $5,000 or $500,000-a-month profit center.

(10) Here's one Jay did for me. He can teach you how to increase the performance of every marketing dollar you are currently spending from 2 to 17 times. There are very few businesses that could not immediately increase their business several times over with their present marketing and advertising budgets.

The use of a better headline in advertising alone can quadruple the effectiveness of almost every ad letter or radio or TV commercial you ever use, regardless of whether you are a retailer or a wholesaler.

I did $84 million of business for my newsletter over more than seven years with a simple headline that said, "Can You Afford To Be Without This Man's Advice?" It out-pulled

Page 7

FIG. 8-1. (continued)

every other headline by several times using the very same body copy.

Advertising history is full of examples like "They Laughed When I Sat Down to Play the Piano." The same "headline" concept applies to sales pitches in the newspaper, the mail, the store, the field, or on the telephone.

We'll teach you how to identify and rank in order of effectiveness all the conceivable hot buttons you can incorporate in every marketing aspect of your business, and how and why one hot button evokes 2-10 times greater response than another one.

Your biggest competitive and financial advantage over your competitors lies in your ability to market and their inability to do so. Whatever business you're in, you're a marketing company whether you like it or not.

Success does not depend on how much money you can borrow from the bank. It's much more profitable to get that money out of every marketing dollar you spend. It is conceivable to get many times more response from the same marketing dollar. That's tremendous leverage!

You Can Do It!

Even though it took a marketing genius like Jay Abraham to dream up these principles, they can be taught to anyone of average intelligence, an open mind and an entrepreneurial spirit. Every month he will teach you clearly and lucidly so you can go out and do it—now.

Jay's strategies are for any and every type of businessman or woman, not just those who are running ads or sending out mailing pieces. If you have salespeople—either inside or outside—or customers or prospects you can identify by name, or new prospects that come into your business or that you visit, Jay's advice can transform your business. The type of business simply does not matter, even if you're just starting up.

For example, Jay taught a car wash owner who had devised a new way to increase the number of customers adding hot wax to their car wash how to sell that intangible technique to 500 other car washes for a fee and percentage of the increased hot wax business it produced.

He taught a dry cleaner how to get three times as many people to bring their leather coats in for cleaning, which is very lucrative, and then how to license the technique to another 1,000 dry cleaners for a percentage of the increased business it produced.

The principles Jay teaches are practical and real; and you can do them. He lays them out so clearly they can be embraced even by someone who was previously a nonconceptual thinker. He will pull out the latent entrepreneurial instincts you all have lurking in the backs of your heads.

(11) He will teach you how to sell some of these ideas to your employer and make a deal with him, becoming an independent contractor and sharing a percentage of the profits. You can be a corporate hero. You can have the best of all possible worlds—you retain the security of employment, along with the unlimited opportunity of the entrepreneur.

(12) Now we come to one of the most powerful benefits Jay can give you.

He teaches aspiring entrepreneurs how to put themselves into business with next to no capital. He had $10,000 when he started, but I believe he could have done it with nothing at all.

Literally thousands of my subscribers have asked me how they can raise capital to start a new business. I tell them how I did it. I marketed on a shoestring and produced immediate cash from direct-response advertising. If you raise capital the traditional way from professional venture capitalists, you usually give up control, and they're usually impatient to cash in, so you don't know who your future partners will be down the road when they

Page 8

FIG. 8-1. (*continued*) (*Figure continued on p. 222.*)

sell out.

Jay will show you several other ways to use your business idea and other people's capital to raise the money to fund your business without giving away your own future. If you have a viable idea, Jay will teach you how to find the Unique Selling Proposition and structure a deal so other people will be anxious to put up money while allowing you to retain total control. I*'s at least as good as nothing down real estate.

Hidden Motives?

Why are Jay and I doing this? Normally we wouldn't want the aggravation of another regular deadline for a publication.

First here are Jay's reasons.

(1) He is a compulsive teacher. If he can help 5,000 people be successful, they'll love him, and I think that's important to Jay. I guess he needs his ego stroked, just like a lot of us.

(2) He can benefit from potential relationships with thousands of businessmen. Out of those relationships may come a few clients with whom he will want to joint venture personally, deals that could make him millions of dollars. Frankly, it's a terrific way of developing clients.

(3) Newsletter publishing can be profitable, and, of course, this one will make money for Jay. He hopes to make more money for less work.

(4) Jay needed something in his life to force him to sit down and articulate and summarize all of the principles he's developed over the years. He didn't want to write a book (I don't blame him; writing a book is one of the greatest ordeals known to man. I know, I've written five.), but on a month-to-month basis, Jay can handle it.

Now, why am I doing this?

(1) Knowing how much Jay can help you, this is one of the most fantastic financial publishing opportunities of all time. As a financial publisher, I want to be part of it.

(2) Our close association will produce marketing ideas for me that will make me millions of dollars.

I don't really need Jay Abraham. I was doing fine before I met him. But when a man makes you $2 million with no risk of your own, who can resist the opportunity to stay close to him?

(3) Jay is an honorable man. Whenever we've made a deal, if it turned out that it was unfavorably balanced in his favor, he has voluntarily come to me and said, "Howard, let's redo this." He has always knocked himself out to make sure that the deals put me in his debt rather than the other way around. I like his style.

You may have trouble believing this, but I wrote this for Jay before I worked out a deal with him. I trust him. He's helping me on some projects, and I'm helping him with this one.

How Much?

Now, the price for all this:

It's $575 for one year (or $495 depending how you pay for it), which is either a lot of money or a pittance, depending on what you compare it with.

If this were just a newsletter, it would be one of the more expensive ones. But if you hired Jay, you would pay him $2,000 an hour, and that's a real-world figure. That's exact-

Page 9

FIG. 8-1. (continued)

ly what clients have paid him when they have chosen his hourly rate.

For the dollar equivalent of less than 15 minutes of Jay's time, you can have access to all the concepts he has honed to a fine edge over 20 years of trial and error. He wasn't born with this knowledge. He has worked with more than 165 companies and industries as he has earned his education. He's made every marketing mistake possible. You will be paying pennies to avoid the costly mistakes he has paid a fortune to uncover through personal experience, mistakes nearly every business in America still makes every day.

No-Risk Guarantee

Besides, if after the first two reports from Jay you don't feel it's worth it, YOU CAN GET ALL YOUR MONEY BACK WITHOUT EVEN HAVING TO GIVE A REASON. You'll still be hundreds of dollars ahead, because you can keep all of the incredibly valuable premiums I'll describe in a moment.

What do you actually get?

Every month, you will receive 16-24 closely spaced pages exploring all of the techniques, implications, and applications of one major marketing concept that will work for almost any business and will produce immediate profits.

These are not random, ivory-tower ideas, but organized, proven, unorthodox, scrupulously ethical strategies which have made millions of dollars in the past and will continue to work in the future.

We will accept your subscription only for one year, as I have not yet persuaded Jay to write more than 12 reports. Whether or not you will be able to renew your subscription is undecided as of now.

All I can guarantee you now is 12 issues, beginning in January, 1986.

Also, we plan to accept no more than 10,000 subscribers, because any technique can become ineffective if everyone is using it. 10,000 people in hundreds of different kinds of businesses scattered over hundreds of communities will not saturate the marketplace. You will be one of an elite corps of successful marketers.

As this opportunity is being offered to several million people whose names are on rented mailing lists, we're sure it will be over-subscribed. If you are too late, your check will be returned and your name will be added to a waiting list. If someone doesn't have the vision to utilize the lessons and cancels out, creating an opening, we'll send you a subscription, all the back issues, all the bonuses, and a bill.

An Offer You Can't Refuse

The cost is either $575 or $495, depending how you pay for it.

Option #1 - You can send us $275 now, plus two monthly payments of $150 each (we'll bill you) for a total of $575. With this option, is a basic course to help you get started while you are waiting for the first report (which will be mailed in January), you will receive these valuable premiums, absolutely free:

(1) A special report on THE TEN BIGGEST MARKETING MISTAKES EVERYBODY IS MAKING AND HOW TO AVOID THEM. This report is sold for $75. It costs you nothing.

(2) A three-month subscription to my newsletter, THE FINANCIAL SUCCESS REPORT, America's biggest circulation financial newsletter aimed at America's middle class, with the highest renewal rate in the newsletter industry. That means not only will you get a letter from Jay once a month, you'll get one from me every week, including unlimited free con-

Page 10

FIG. 8-1. (*continued*) (*Figure continued on p. 224.*)

sultations on our toll-free Hot Line on almost any financial matter you can dream of. If you are already a FSR subscriber, we'll either extend your subscription or send your premium three-month subscription to a friend of your choice (in your name). Market value, $35. You get it free.

(3) A special report entitled "The Art Of Redeploying Your Company's Assets"—including "How to Resell, License, Cross-Sell, Up-Sell, Reactivate or Joint Venture Your Assets." 100 powerful pages of confidential information. Its market value is $250. You get it free.

Option #2 - Our Best Deal: Send us only $495 now, we will add two more valuable premiums which will enhance your marketing.

(1) A complete transcript of an all-day marketing seminar conducted by Jay, which only ten people were allowed to attend. They each paid $2,500. The marketing ideas and concepts came fast and furious. This transcript is worth at least $500. Remember, the people who attended the seminar paid $2,500 for it. You get it free.

(2) A transcript of a private interview Jay gave to a research organization which paid $6,000 for it. It's easily worth at least $500. It introduces several of his basic concepts. It's an essential primer to help you get the most out of your subscription.

Even if you cancel your subscription and get a full refund, you will come out at least $1,360 ahead, since these premiums are all yours to keep for your trouble. You can't lose. You can only win.

If you're ordering for a business, we'll even bill you. Just check the "bill me" box on the order coupon. You'll still get all 5 premiums at our discounted price of $495. You can order by mail, using check or credit card. Or, for faster service, call 800-654-4455 (USA) or 800-654-4456 (CA) between 5:00 a.m. and 10:00 p.m., Pacific Time, Monday through Thursday and 5:00 a.m. to 5:00 p.m. Friday, Pacific Time. Just give our subscription desk your credit card number or ask us to bill your company.

We know we are asking you to pay a lot compared to other newsletter offers. It stands to reason that the guarantees should be stronger and the compensations greater if you don't believe our promises have been fulfilled. I can't overemphasize the value of the free premiums you will receive. If you bought all 5 premiums, you'd pay more than $1,000. And the wonderful ideas they contain can make you many thousands of dollars, and you can't get them anywhere else. There is no Stanford Research Institute for marketing, and if there were, they would charge you many thousands of dollars for such reports, and only big companies could afford them.

Also, Jay wants you to think well of him, even if you ask for your money back. Remember the "moving parade" we mentioned earlier? You may keep this offer in the back of your mind and want to do a profitable joint venture in the future, so Jay wants your good will.

Our Guarantee

Let me reiterate: Jay and I both promise you that if after receiving two issues you find this publication is not for you, for any reason whatsoever, we will send back all of your money immediately upon request, and you may keep all of the premiums, special reports, and issues you have received to date.

If you wish to discontinue your subscription after the third issue, then we will send you a pro rata refund, and you can keep the premiums!

This letter was not written by an ad agency or some hired-gun copywriter. I wrote it myself because I am so excited about this publication that I can hardly stand still. I

Page 11

FIG. 8-1. (continued)

believe in it, and I'll personally stand behind it. I also intend to personally edit each issue.

I have a financial self-interest in this publication, and because my name and reputation are on the line, I of course guarantee it is everything we claim and more.

Sincerely,

Howard

Howard J. Ruff

P.S. Six months from now, this will very probably be the most talked about business publication ever produced. Every businessman or woman or aspiring entrepreneur who is the proud owner of one of the 10,000 available subscriptions, will have an almost unfair advantage over his or her competitors.

P.P.S. Don't forget, this subscription fee may be tax deductible under IRS Code Section 162 or 212.

YOUR MARKETING GENIUS AT WORK

Target, Inc • P.O. Box 25 • 6612 Owens Drive • Pleasanton, CA 94566-0625

For Rush Service call toll free 800-654-4455 (USA) or 800-654-4456 (CA)

✔ **YES,** I want Jay Abraham's Marketing Genius to go to work for me!

☐ **Option 1** Send $275 now and we will bill you in two monthly installments of $150 each for a total of $575.

You will receive twelve tightly written marketing reports from Jay Abraham plus the following bonus gifts: **The Ten Biggest Marketing Mistakes Everybody is Making, and How to Avoid Them** (a $75 value) USA65; A three month subscription to **Howard Ruff's Financial Success Report** (a $35 value) USA61; **The Art of Reploying Your Company's Assests** (worth $250) USA63.

No-Risk Guarantee
I understand that I may cancel my subscription after the first two issues for any reason, keep all the free premiums and receive a complete refund. If I decide to cancel my subscription after the first three issues, I may still keep all the premiums and receive a prorata refund. I'm taking absolutely no risk.

Tax Deduction
The fee for this publication may be tax deductible if it is used in your business or trade, so your real cost may be only a fraction of the listed price! Check with your accountant.

Mail Coupon to:
Target Publishers, P.O. Box 25, Pleasanton, CA 94566 or call 800-654-4455 (USA) or 800-654-4456 (CA)

☐ **Option 2** Send $495 now and you will receive everything in Option 1 plus a transcript of a fast and furious **Marketing Seminar** (worth $500) USA62 and an insightful **Interview Jay Abraham Gave to a Leading Research Organization** (worth $500) USA64. You will receive a total of $1360 in marketing gifts with Option 2.

Send Reports To:

Name_____

Address_____

City_____State_____Zip_____

☐ **Bill My Company for $495.** We will receive all of the premiums.

Name_____

Name of Company _____

Address_____

City_____State_____Zip_____

☐ I have enclosed a check or money order for _____
Make checks payable to Target, Inc.

Foreign Subscriptions : $545 (we cannot bill foreign subscriptions)

Charge my: ☐ VISA ☐ MasterCard ☐ AmEx ☐ Diners

Card Number _____ Exp. Date _____

Signature _____

S/C 12626

FIG. 8-1. (continued)

These subheads do more than break up the page. They reiterate selling points. On pages 8 and 9, notice the use of no risk and guarantee, and how they are emphasized. Everyone would like to learn something, make more money, especially if it is no risk, and fully guaranteed.

The mailing piece also addresses one of the reader's main concerns: if this marketing genius is so great, why is he willing to sell his information at such a low cost? Knowing that readers will raise this question, the authors address it under "Hidden Motives" on page 9.

Honesty is needed—and it works—in advertising.

Notice the USP of the mailing piece. It is in the headline. This mailing piece attracted nearly 3000 subscribers who each paid nearly $600 a year for the newsletter.

When constructing a direct mail piece, the following checklist will be of help.

Direct Mail Checklist

Have a good strong opening line to grab the reader's attention

Have a USP within your headline or within the piece

Tell them a basic story or pitch with beginning, middle, and end

Do not hard sell or try and twist arms

Make them a proposition or an exact offer

Supply them (or offer to) with information they need

Be sure to explain (and re-explain) the value of the information/offer

Give them a guarantee to allay their fears

Conclude with a call to action (they ask for additional information or you follow with a telephone call)

At times, direct mail has been dubbed junk mail and for good reason. It is often sent to occupant, owner, the president, or purchasing director without any thought. In consulting, however, direct mail can be one of the most potent marketing tools utilized.

Do not think of direct mail as a package of discount coupons from neighborhood retailers, nor as the letter you receive from the local realtor looking for another listing.

Direct mail is actually the consultant's most efficient and cost-effective method of marketing. For a fraction of the cost you would pay for a radio, TV, or print ad in a major metropolitan newspaper, you can rent a mailing list and reach your customers.

The advantage of renting lists is that you can rent names for specific industries and target prospects. For example, if you were trying to reach purchasing agents in the aerospace industry, you might take an ad in an aerospace magazine or a purchasing publication. With direct mail, however, you could rent a list of purchasing agents who deal exclusively in the aerospace field. Thus you get to your market immediately. There is no wasted circulation.

There are several ways to obtain lists. Every industry has an association (i.e., personnel directors have an association, attorneys, doctors, and accountants as well). You can contact the association and ask if they will rent their list.

You may be able to obtain a list with telephone numbers. You can usually obtain a list divided into a specific geographic area.

Contact trade magazines that reach your market. Often they rent subscriber lists.

List rental services can be found in the *Yellow Pages*. Be sure you specify exactly what you are looking for when you talk to them. List rentals will cost from $30 to $100 per thousand names. This is an inexpensive cost for a list of prospects.

Once you obtain the list, you must write the direct mail piece. For the consultant, effective direct mail should be personalized. It should be written as if you are addressing one person, not a mass of potential clients. Think of it as a one-on-one conversation.

Effective direct mail is similar to an in-person sales call. If you had 2 minutes in front of a prospective client, what would you tell him or her; what is there about your practice that would intrigue him or her; what is the USP? The same things that would go into that 2-minute presentation belong in a direct mail piece. Once the piece is structured, it can be used in several ways.

Consultants can stimulate inquiries by offering the prospect material or information of value that he or she may want.

Abraham supplied potential investors with 50-page reports on the economic climate and its outlook. These reports informed and educated the buyer. All the person had to do was call or return the postage-paid card that was enclosed—no strings attached.

The report did not blatantly try to sell Abraham or his investments in any way. It was an educational/informational tool—the most potent weapon in sales. It is a subtle sales technique.

A management consultant specializing in productivity could isolate prospects and offer them a report—at no charge—which might outline some of the latest innovations in productivity.

A personnel consultant could offer a report on the status of benefits, what kind, and whether they would be increasing, leveling out, or dropping in the future.

A money manager could offer prospects a report by a group of respected economists discussing the outlook for investment.

An engineer specializing in certain types of equipment (or an industry), could offer a report on the latest innovations in equipment, production, and so forth.

These are things that prospects can use—and they appreciate the consultant for supplying it. They are sales weapons; they educate the prospect, and when prospects are educated they are ready to buy.

Certain types of direct mail take follow-up. For example, you may send something to a prospect with an offer (i.e., free consultation, evaluation, or analysis) in which they reply with a card, or you must stimulate the reply with a telephone call. Cold calls are not recommended, but once someone has responded to one of your offers the call is no longer cold. The response, or request for information, is a sales step that opens the door.

Do not leave it up to the prospect to call. They may never pick up the telephone. Certainly, companies that are selling $9.95 books, knives, tapes, and the like leave the response to the recipient. However, the consultant sells an expensive, intangible product. It will take follow-up. The order will not come in via a postage-paid card.

Remember that direct mail is a sales tool—even after the sale has been made. It should be used for more than soliciting. It is a communication tool as well. For example, when you begin working with a client, keep him or her informed as to what is going on regarding the project. Although you may see the client or talk to him or her once or twice a week, a written summary is advisable. It is something tangible. It provides a link between you and the client.

In some fields, the consultant may be hired (i.e., data processing or engineering) and may not see the person who has hired him or her until the job is done. Written communication is critical in this area.

POSTPURCHASE SELLING

Banks, savings and loans, insurance companies, automotive dealers, and many consultants spend thousands of dollars to get the buyer in the door and then communication and personalization suddenly end.

You occasionally hear from the bank via a mass-produced stuffer that comes in your statement. There is a piece that arrives once in a while from the auto dealer to tell you your service is due or there is a recall.

For the most part, businesses forget about customers once they have made a purchase and the job is done or they have left the store. Yet, previous or existing customers can help a business increase its sales by up to 50 percent.

How? Through referrals and additional purchases. If you did consulting for a developer six months ago, there is a good chance he or she may need you again. But have you kept in touch? Have you kept a correspondence and relationship going?

If you approached a potential client last year and did not get the business, perhaps it is time to approach him or her again. Maybe the situation has changed. But have you kept in touch, communicated on a regular basis?

Successful consultants always keep communication channels open. When the job is done, put the customer in a tickler file. Make sure you write him or her every two to three months. Try to design your letters as informational and educational pieces. Tell the previous (or potential) client about some new development, process, event, and so on in his or her field.

The following list suggests some possible items that consultants can send to potential or present clients on a regular basis.

Direct Mail Ideas for Consultants

1. Congratulatory notes on promotions, earnings, speaking engagements, or whenever you see a client's name in a newspaper or magazine.

2. Copies of stories and/or surveys that you see in a trade magazine (or newspaper) that may be of interest to clients.

3. Thank you notes for something the client has sent to you or some service the client has rendered on your behalf.

4. Tax and/or legislative stories that you may have seen in a trade paper that may affect the client's business.

5. Special reports you may have access to that relate to the client's business, industry, or your profession.

6. A thank you note to show you appreciate his or her business and regard his or her company as something special. This helps to reinforce the client's belief that he or she made the right choice.

7. Updates on your progress with the account and/or project. Be sure to carbon copy (cc:) the proper parties.

8. Anything else you feel may be of value or interest to the client.

9. Send to past clients as well as present and potential ones. Your greatest source of new business will come from your clients.

Whatever you send the client, it should be of interest. If it is not a congratulatory or thank you note, it should be educational and informative.

By keeping these lines of communication open you will not only be on the client's mind when it comes time for him or her to hire again, but also when he or she is talking to others within the industry who may need help as well.

CHAPTER 9

NEWSLETTERS AS BUSINESS BUILDERS

Once you get your business rolling, a newsletter can be an excellent selling tool. Used effectively, it can develop a better image for your firm, attract prospects, and lead to more dollars in your pocket.

What makes a newsletter effective?

Good newsletters have common ingredients. They are targeted at specific industries and/or professions—in other words, your potential and present clients. They are not generic products that have your name and picture imprinted at the last minute. They look distinctive and have a message loaded with benefits for the reader. They are educational and informative, and contain information that the recipient (client) is so interested in seeing that he or she keeps it for weeks..

For example, suppose you are a personnel consultant specializing in some type of placement. Your audience is personnel or human resource directors. Those are the people who are in the market to retain your services.

What kind of newsletter would appeal to these people? It would have ingredients such as:

Newsletter Checklist—What Belongs in One

1. *News* relating to the latest innovations and so forth in the personnel field. It could have a roundup on pending new laws, changes in labor relations, and the like.

2. *A column* and/or interview with (perhaps) a panel of personnel experts covering a specific current problem (and solutions) in the field. For example, the Q&A session could revolve around worker absenteeism, drug abuse at the workplace, or handling problem employees. If you are in this field, you can probably name at least a dozen other issues that personnel and human resource directors would find fascinating.

3. *Success stories* about successful placements. The stories would show how each has contributed to the company in which they were placed. It could

contain quotes from the employee's supervisors and quotes from the personnel people that the consultant was working with at the time of the placement. It might have hints or ideas that other personnel directors could adopt. It might also have thoughts on why the employee decided to go to work for the company; what employment elements meant the most to him or her.

This approach works in other fields. For example, a data processing consultant could run a success story centered around a redesigned system, why it was redesigned, and how it improved productivity when it was completed. The story could contain hints on spotting trouble areas within computer systems.

The data processing consultant could have two audiences: top management outside the data processing department and managers within the department.

4. *Profile* of a personnel director. In each issue you could profile (run a short bio on) a selected personnel director. Select someone who is well-known, has accomplished some special goals, or solved an unusual personnel problem for his or her company. This gives recognition to the personnel director—and if there is one thing everyone has in common it is the need for recognition.

5. A *column from the consultant* covering an area that would interest personnel directors could be another feature. For instance, in one issue you could discuss the changing motivation of workers, and in another, whether money is the bottom line for taking a job. These are issues personnel people wrestle with daily and any insight would be appreciated.

6. *Wild photos* that do not have a story with them. Underneath each would be a caption, a two or three line explanation of what the photo is all about. These photos can be slipped in whenever there is extra space. They should all relate to the subject in the newsletter. For example, you might have a photographer take a picture of the personnel department's new offices; the engineering consultant could have a shot of a new safety device; and a money manager could have a photo of the interior of the stock exchange.

7. *Shorts* to fill an inch or two of space here and there. Not all newsletter columns will fit to the inch. Plan short fillers all pertaining to the theme of the newsletter. These shorts can be run anytime.

The personnel newsletter could have a short about a newly developed placement test for human resource departments. The item would only run a paragraph or two. It would briefly tell what the test was, who developed it, and where more information could be obtained. Typeset, it would be no longer than an inch or two.

The messages in a newsletter are multiple. They address the needs of the reader, show him or her how to solve problems, and educate and inform.

Nowhere does the newsletter contain a message from you that says, "Hire me as a consultant." Rather it says, "I am a well-informed consultant who wants to share information with you. If you like what you read, perhaps you may want to utilize my services for something other than gathering newsletter information."

In other words, newsletters are a soft sell. They show your knowledge, but they do not twist the prospect's arm.

NEWSLETTER PROCEDURE/TIMETABLE

The newsletter has both objective and subjective editorial ingredients. Objective elements would be the news stories, developments, profiles of people, success stories, and Q&A columns. Subjective material would come from the consultant through a column. Subjective material would be your opinions, supported by empirical evidence, of things such as the changing attitudes of workers, drugs and the worker, how to handle excessive absenteeism, and so forth.

Ideally, a newsletter should be published quarterly. More frequently and people take it for granted. There is also the question of the value of the material. Quality, informative material is not found in a few days. At times it may take you a week or two to follow-up on an important trend or development. Newsletters are not cheap. A quarterly would be costly enough for most consultants.

Newsletters are like ads. They should have catchy headlines that spark the reader's curiosity. You do not want to go to the expense of producing one and having it tossed aside because the heads say nothing to intrigue the reader. The average executive—the usual customer for the consultant—is deluged by mail. Most of it goes directly in the round file because it does not catch the eye of the reader. A good, intriguing (but not misleading) head can help improve your readership.

Be specific in your heads. If you are a management consultant running a story on new productivity techniques, come up with a head that is worded like, "Six new ways to improve production." Six is more specific, and certainly more intriguing to the reader than, "Ways to improve productivity." Consult Chapters 7 and 8 in this workbook for hints on effective heads.

Make the newsletter easy to read—pay attention to the layout. For example, a newsletter configuration may be 8½ inches by 17 inches, folded. This gives you four, 8½ inch × 11 inch pages. It is easy for the reader to handle. Run two or three columns on each page, no more. If you try to put four columns on an 8½ inch × 11 inch format, the type will be too small.

Put your newsletter on glossy stock. The cost differential is minimal and glossy stock reproduces photographs better. It also has a richer, classier appearance, and enhances the image of your firm.

A two-color newsletter (there is a slight additional charge of perhaps $50 for the second color) is effective. You might also look at using screens (see Chapter 3 on brochures for an explanation of screening).

Photography is a necessity. The most desirable pictures are candids, that is, photos which appear unposed. This type of photo is interesting in itself and attracts the reader's eye. (Note some of the examples of candid shots in this chapter and how they can be used in a newsletter.)

There should also be a photo of you. This would go on page one or wherever your column will appear. Page one is best, since it will have the highest visibility. You would use a head shot, which pictures a person from the chest up. Usually they are looking straight at the camera. This particular photo is used in personnel announcements that are often seen on financial pages.

For success stories, go for the candids. Have a photographer take some pictures at the location where the worker is employed. If you have a group of panelists discussing an issue, you might have each of them give you a head shot and disperse them throughout the story.

Photographer's fees will vary; however, you will be shooting all black-and-white for the newsletter. (Although color adds a nice touch it is expensive—for separations and printing—and is not necessary.) Some photographers will quote you a fee by the day or hour. It is important to get all shots lined up before doing the photography. If you do, you can usually get the shots in one day or less and keep your costs down. Some shots can be used in future issues.

Ask the printer about a Z fold. In this configuration, the newsletter is folded twice. The name of the newsletter and your photo show on the front side; on the back is the recipient's address, and the return address.

Designers are not needed. Talk to printers and find out which ones have put together newsletters. Ask for samples. Most printers have little trouble laying out and pasting down the type and handling the photos when they come into the shop. If in doubt, copy one of the formats in this workbook, and ask the printer to use it.

Typestyles

Make sure you pick a readable style. Helvetica is ideal. It is easy to read. If the printer does not have this style, he or she will have something similar. If you are in doubt, look at the daily newspaper and pick a typestyle similar to what you see.

Headlines

On page one, make them bold so they stand out. This gives the newsletter the appearance that something important is contained in it. Inside, vary head sizes and styles. Look at the sample in this chapter for ideas. Read through the Sunday paper for more ideas. Borrow a few ideas from the professionals—the newspaper editors.

Be aware of printing deadlines and timetables. It will take a printer anywhere from 5 to 10 working days to print and fold your newsletter once the type has been pasted down and the photos delivered. With a Z fold, the printer may have to send the newsletter to a bindery, which will take another production day.

If you mail your newsletter bulk rate, it can take up to seven days to be delivered locally. There are also sorting requirements and fees for a bulk rate number. Obtain the bulk rate number so the printer has it for the newsletter before going to press.

There are freelance writers who will write and supervise the newsletter for you. They must, however, understand the newsletter, the market, and the editorial approach. The consultant, of course, has the ultimate voice—it is a newsletter going to your prospects.

A consultant may also find a wealth of additional material in magazines and/or other publications that go to his or her market. If you find an interesting article, request permission to reprint it (from the magazine). In most instances, there is no charge as long as credit is given to the publication that initially ran the story. Publications within the trade are an excellent source of material for the newsletter.

Freelance writers can be found at newspapers, college journalism departments, and advertising or public relations agencies. Make sure they have a news background. Consult Chapter 7 on advertising and free promotion for ideas on where to get freelance writing help.

Before launching a newsletter, go through the following procedure, which will also give you an idea of the time involved in producing one.

Newsletter Procedure/Timetable

Task	Days Needed
1. Determine audience for newsletter	(1)
2. Hire writer/supervisor if needed	(2)
3. Develop theme	
4. Develop format with aid of printer	
5. Begin interviews/writing	(10)
a. Develop lead story	
b. Develop consultants column with subject	
c. Develop success stories with people/companies	
d. Develop other features within newsletter	
e. Develop shorts as filler material	
f. Obtain bulk rate permit	
6. Lay out of newsletter by printer	(1)
7. Copy set and proofread	(3)
8. Double check spelling of names	
9. Finalize photo ideas	
a. Hire photographer	
b. Arrange photos	(2)
c. Get candid shot of anyone in editorial	
d. Get head shot of consultant	
e. Get head shots of panelists and others	
f. Get other posed shots	
g. Have success story shots taken	
h. Receive contact sheet from photographer	(5)
10. Select photos	
11. Deliver photos to printer	
12. Purchase mailing list if needed	
13. Decide on printing quantities	
14. Paste down corrected copy with photos	(2)
15. Approve blueline/brownline	(1)
16. Newsletter printed/folded	(10)

17. Deliver newsletter to consultant
18. Affix labels for mailing
19. Mail newsletter at post office
20. Newsletter delivered to prospects   (7)

Notice there are approximately 44 working days to complete a newsletter. This allows everyone enough time to do their job and gives you an idea of why it is impractical to do a newsletter more than once a quarter—unless your business is producing newsletters.

If you are looking for a December newsletter, planning should start in late September or early October. Naturally, once the first issue is out, the following issues will not require the same amount of time.

Some consultants avoid the deadline rush by purchasing mass-produced newsletters from marketing firms. These newsletters have one advantage— someone else is doing all the work, but they have disadvantages. They are not focused (or targeted) at your market. Newsletters are communication tools. They should be designed so the consultant gets feedback from the prospect or client. If you customize your own newsletter, you can put offers in that will provide insight to readers. For example, if you are an engineering consultant marketing to developers, you might offer readers a copy of an upcoming report on the environment or a summary on new building codes in your area. The newsletter recipient can obtain a copy by calling or writing your office. This enables you to test the readership and monitor what is happening with your newsletter. Are people reading it? This is one way to find out.

On the following pages, you will find newsletters with varying formats; comments precede each.

SAMPLE NEWSLETTERS/CRITIQUE/ANALYSIS

Inside Park Del Amo is a newsletter that was designed for the buyers of a townhouse development. The builder (Watt Industries), sold the townhouses (i.e., they obtained deposits) before they were ever built. Between the time of the selling and the actual close of escrow, nearly 7 months elapsed. The builder saw the necessity to communicate regularly with buyers and prospective buyers. (There were 2000 others on a waiting list. They would be prospects for future developments. They were placed on the newsletter mailing list as well)

The builder selected a monthly newsletter because there was enough material to fill the publication; he could show buyers (visually) what was happening with the development; and it was important that he continue to sell them on the benefits of the community.

Postpurchase selling, as it is called, is important. If you sign a letter of agreement with a client, one of the first things that occurs in his or her mind is doubt. Should he or she have committed to the expenditure? Was it too much? Can you do the job? What if something happens? Should they have waited? The same is true in building. Should we have spent the money on the house? Is it worth it? Can we afford it?

These are natural feelings. People buy for emotional reasons and later seek to support those feelings with logic. With postpurchase reassurance you give them reasons.

In the case of Park Del Amo, the builder is *sensitive* and realizes he must constantly keep the buyers on his side. Communication through newsletters and letters also helps build a bond between buyer and seller. The stronger the communication ties, the less likely the buyer is to break the agreement or go elsewhere. This is especially important in the consulting field where communication with a client is paramount.

An examination of the first newsletter produced (Figure 9-1) shows some of the techniques the marketing firm utilized in order to help the builder accomplish his goals.

From the builder. This is similar to the column from the consultant discussed earlier. It gives the builder a chance to say things in a nonnews manner. That is, he or she can editorialize, talk about the development, its location, and so forth. In several of the columns the builder discussed building in the past, how things had changed, but how his quality had remained the same.

Main news story. "Springwood I and II Under Construction." That lets the buyers know about the progress of the development.

Page 1 feature. Once someone buys, you reinforce the buying decision, by giving him or her information about additional benefits. In this issue the marketing consultant talks about the city's park program—which is near the top—and gives the buyers something else to feel good about.

Looking inside the newsletter (Figure 9-1) buyers get a glimpse of their future neighbors. Notice the neighbors selected were chosen because of their stature in the community. Most would enjoy living next to a police officer or attorney. On the last page is another look at the community. The same approach runs throughout the other Park Del Amo newsletters.

Each issue of the newsletter reinforces the community benefits and gives future residents the idea that they are, indeed, fortunate to be able to live in Park Del Amo.

As a result of the newsletter, Park Del Amo lost only a handful of buyers when the time came for them to go through escrow. It is an example of how important effective communications can be to a company—or a consultant.

Executive Briefing, which is published by the CPA firm of Coopers & Lybrand (C&L), has a different format, but has much in common with Park Del Amo's newsletter. *Executive Briefing* (Figure 9-2) is targeted at potential and present clients of the CPA consulting firm. The prospects are businesspeople, which is one of the reasons the table of contents is highlighted on page 1. Businesspeople do not spend much time on material that is sent to them. Consequently, if they are not immediately grabbed by a headline (or contents) they are lost.

The contents act as a group of headlines designed to intrigue the reader. The first headline ("Commodity Market Tells Inflation Tale") is specific, but could be improved. For example, suppose it said, "Commodity Market Tells Inflation Tale for 1986" (or 1980s).

Inside Park Del Amo

Vol. I No. 4

From The Builder

by Ray Watt

Interested in a job that requires you to rise before sunup and gets you home long after sundown?

Frankly, neither was I. Years ago, however, those hours formed my initial introduction to the construction business. Both my father and brother were in it and, after working with them for a short time (I was a teenager at the time), I decided I was going to pursue another line of work.

I'm reminded of those early days whenever I see one of our superintendants at work on a project. A good superintendant puts in long hours because he cares about the project and how it will turn out. Springwood is fortunate to have three of these talented individuals—Gary Herschel, Tom Plumleigh and their supervisor, Ernie Lavoie.

The three spend countless hours at Park

From left, Tom Plumleigh, Ernie Lavoie and Gary Herschel at Springwood

Del Amo, making sure the Village will be a place you can enjoy—and one we can be proud of.

How many hours? Well, they drive nearly

(cont. on pg. 3)

COMING TOGETHER—In the foreground, framing for Springwood's recreation building nears completion. Just behind it are the five models that are under construction. The models are on schedule as is the recreation area.

Springwood I And II Under Construction

Phases I and II of Springwood are all under construction with framing on Phase I nearly completed.

Trenching and foundations on Phase II were started in March and trenching on Phase III will begin in April.

Construction of Springwood's five models is moving rapidly with completion scheduled around May 1. Phase I occupancy is slated for this summer.

Torrance Parks, Programs Near The Top

Within walking distance of Park Del Amo is Wilson Park, one of 27 parks in the City, and a 44-acre facility that is unparalleled in what it offers area residents.

Aside from the traditional baseball diamonds (Wilson has four, each with lights), the Park also has two soccer fields, 8 championship horseshoe courts, three nightlighted tennis courts and five nightlighted paddle tennis courts.

But that's only the beginning of what Springwood residents will find in their next door park. There's also a lake, gazebo, a picnic area that will accommodate 1,000 people, an outdoor pavilion and an exhibit area.

Interestingly, Wilson still has 17 acres of undeveloped land—"plenty of room for

(cont. on pg. 2)

Springwood Reports Arrive From State

The final subdivision report on Phase I and Phase II of Springwood has been issued by the Department of Real Estate. It is now available at the Information Center for those who purchased homes in the first two phases.

The report will allow purchase and sale agreements to be signed and escrow opened by buyers.

The sales representatives at the Information Center are in the process of contacting those who made reservations, however, if you need additional information, call the Information Center (212-5466) anytime between 10 a.m. and 5 p.m. daily.

FIG. 9-1. *Inside Park Del Amo.*

238

AT WORK—Ken Poole, who is General Counsel for Del Amo Fashion Center, enjoys a light moment with his secretary, Jenny. Poole will be moving into Springwood.

Would You Believe $99 A Month For A Home?

The house cost $16,500, his monthly payments were $99—and he did not have much left by the time he paid his taxes and utilities.

The year was 1960 and young Ken Poole was teaching history and English at Bishop Montgomery High School. The house he purchased was in Southwood, a tract of homes just West of Park Del Amo . . . homes that today are in the $250,000 range.

Today, 25 years and six children later, Ken and his wife reside in a home on an acre of land in Rancho Palos Verdes. Later this year, he will be packing his bags and moving into Springwood—and for good reason.

Ken only taught school for a year before entering the Loyola University School of Law. Today, he is Corporate Counsel for Del Amo Fashion Center, the world's largest indoor mall and the second-highest dollar volume shopping center in California.

The mall, of course, is only two short blocks from Springwood "and," adds Ken, "there are only a couple of stop signs. It's going to be quite a change . . . and an easy walk."

Proximity, however, was not the only thing that sold the Pooles on Springwood. "Convenience was the other. It's nice to have a single-family residence, but after 25 years of mowing lawns, pulling weeds and maintaining a residence, I am looking forward to someone else doing the work in a fully-maintained community. Oftentimes,

we forget how much time we spend in the yard."

Obviously, not all of the Poole's six children will be moving into Phase IV (Plan A) with their parents.

"Three are away at college and a fourth will graduate high school shortly. The fifth will be finishing up high school but the sixth still has a number of years to go."

Less commuting time also means more hours to handle the complex problems he faces at Del Amo. After spending ten years with a law firm (Hitchcock, Bowman & Milano) in Torrance, Ken finds his role has changed with the Center.

"About 25% of the time I spend practicing law. The other 75% is interviewing prospective mall tenants, putting together leases and handling some of the other things that come up on a daily basis."

Despite the busy schedule, Ken still finds time to participate in community activities. He's on the Board of Directors of Little Company of Mary Hospital; a member of the Advisory Board of the Salvation Army; and a Director of the Torrance Area Chamber of Commerce.

That might seem like quite a load but there's one other organization that Ken intends to join. And, he hopes to do it as soon as possible.

It's called the Springwood Homeowner's Association.

(Torrance Parks from Pg. 1)

expansion," says Gene Barnett, the City's Parks & Recreation Director.

Equally as impressive as the Park, are the programs that are offered through the Parks/Rec Department. Under Barnett's direction, the City has built programs that are not only innovative, but they serve every segment of the community as well.

For example, through Barnett's department, residents will find everything from "tiny tot" classes and after school programs to senior citizen programs (more than 3,000 seniors are enrolled) and youth and adult sports programs.

Last year, for instance, the department had more than 500 adults competing in softball. It also had 124 youth basketball teams.

Additionally, there are year-round gymnastics and one of the finest programs for the disabled of any department in California.

Much of the credit for the high standing Torrance has belongs to Barnett, who has run the department for the past seven years. The genial, outgoing director knows the community well. He has lived in the City for more than 20 years, watched it grow and is keenly aware of what kind of activities those

NEEDED REPAIRS—Torrance Parks & Recreation Director, Gene Barnett, right, shows worker an area on Wilson Park's tennis courts that need repair. The three courts, which are all equipped with lights, have just been added to the park which is across from Park Del Amo.

in the City need.

"We've tried to be innovative in our programming," explains Barnett. "We want to make sure the programs are diverse and there is something for every segment of the community. I think those people moving into Springwood will be quite surprised and happy with what we have to offer at Wilson."

And, as one of Barnett's assistants said, "if you can't find it at Wilson, it probably does not exist."

FIG. 9-1. (continued) (Figure continued on p. 240.)

A Quick Shopping Spree . . . Or Where To Spend Your $ In The Torrance Area

If you're looking for a place to spend that extra dollar, there's no better area than Torrance and the South Bay with its abundance of world famous malls and unique shopping centers.

First, within walking distance, is the world's largest indoor mall, the Del Amo Fashion Center. This mammoth center has every store imaginable—Bullock's, Broadway, Sears, Robinson's, J.C. Penney's, Orbach's and Montgomery Ward's.

In-between are more than 300 specialty shops. You'll even find shops that specialize in stuffed animals. For something different, look at the stuffed, natural mink bear.

For a change of pace, travel a few miles south to Peacock Alley, a quaint group of stores (Silver Spur and Hawthorne Blvd.) in

Del Amo . . .

Palos Verdes.

One of the oustanding features of Peacock Alley is its gift-oriented shops. You'll find one-of-a-kind items. A great place for a gift for someone who has everything. Next to Peacock, are Peninsula Center and the Courtyard Mall. For those with strong ankles (and enough breath), Courtyard has an ice skating rink.

Now, come back down the hill and go a few miles north of Del Amo (and Park Del Amo), to the Galleria. This center is only partially opened, however, in September it will be fully operational with close to 200

stores, including the May Co. and Nordstrom's.

In the same neighborhood is Old Towne. This mall which is between the Galleria and Del Amo, has several specialty shops that make it a worthwhile stop.

For some great bargains, try downtown Torrance. The area, which has hardly changed since the City was founded, has a variety of stores that you don't find often. For example, there's a taxidermy shop (Carson and Cabrillo) and down the street is a shop that manufactures flags.

The streets are a maze and among them you'll find recording studios, some of the best baked goods in the South Bay and numerous independent retailers.

Downtown Torrance . . .

The Galleria . . .

The Villages of Park Del Amo
22300 Maple Avenue
Torrance, CA 90503

FIG. 9-1. (continued)

Coopers & Lybrand

Executive Briefing

In This Issue

Commodity Market Tells Inflation Tale

With inflation down, business should have an easier time keeping costs down. That's the good news about commodity prices.

The precipitous drop in oil prices—50% in a two-month period—has brightened the outlook for inflation watchers. The impact of lower oil prices has already begun to show up at gasoline pumps, in heating fuel bills and in major inflation indices.

But news about inflation wasn't gloomy even before the descending price of oil became a front-page story. One perspective is that the drop in oil prices made a bright picture even rosier. Commodities besides oil have been logging results that have turned the inflation

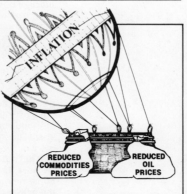

April 1986 © 1986 Coopers & Lybrand (USA) Communications Department 1251 Ave. of the Americas NYC 10020

FIG. 9-2. *Executive Briefing.* (Figure continued on p. 240.)

downward movements in commodity prices could lead to an unstable economic situation, both for the countries producing the commodities as well as for the countries and banks holding their debts.

What This Means to Business

The current environment allows business to plan ahead with a high degree of certainty concerning the inflationary outlook. And it also means that customers are likely to remain price conscious—so the highly competitive pricing environment will probably remain.

Says Bartz, ''The buyer's market still continues. Commodity prices aren't going up, and aluminum, synthetic rubber and other prices are falling. There are virtually no commodity items in short supply.''

It looks like a good year for cost-containment in 1986. ∎

Tax Advisory

Deduction Allowed for Office at Home Even Though Income Earned Elsewhere

Some stiff requirements have to be met before the IRS will allow deductions for office space or work space in the home. First, that space must be set aside only for work. So if you work in a den, where the family also watches TV, you can't take the deductions.

Second, unless the space is used to meet customers or clients, the home work space must be the *principal place of business* for that particular source of income. Thus, no deductions are allowed if you go to the office on weekdays but bring work home evenings and weekends.

In recent years the courts have provided some rather surprising interpretations of what constitutes a principal place of business. One of the most unusual cases involved a Metropolitan Opera violinist who spent 30 hours a week practicing in a room in his apartment because the Met did not provide practice rooms. Because the time spent practicing at home was considerably more than the number of hours spent in

rehearsals and performances, the Second Circuit Court of Appeals allowed the violinist to take deductions for his practice room at home.

The court also allowed deductions for an office at home by a philosophy professor who, in addition to teaching duties, was required to do research and write in his field. An office was provided on the campus, but it was crowded and lacked privacy; and inadequate security

FIG. 9-2. (continued)

"Tax Advisory" can be improved as well. Remember the need to offer readers benefits. A headline reading, "Tax Warning for Those Taking Their Homes as Deduction" would be more specific.

The next three headlines could be more precise, too. Do they relate to the readership? For example, would typical businesspeople be interested in what the chairman of the Interstate Commerce Commission has to offer? If he has something business related to say, it should be mentioned in the head.

Heads in newsletters should read much like heads in the newspaper. Each should have a hook or angle in it designed to get you to read beyond the bold-faced type that caught your eye.

The Coopers & Lybrand newsletter is not targeted just at the corporate employee. Coopers & Lybrand is after the executive, as evidenced by at least one of the topics, "Complex Tax Rules Govern Personal Use of Company Cars and Planes." It is only the high level or senior executive who enjoys perks in these two categories.

Both Park Del Amo and Coopers & Lybrand do an outstanding job of writing in practical, easy-to-understand terms. The reader does not have to be involved in building (for Park Del Amo) or finance (for C&L) to understand the content.

Graphics inside the Coopers & Lybrand newsletter are well done. They are easy to read; the heads punch out; the type is not crowded or too small; and the typeface is related to a helvetica.

Although there are no photos on these first few pages, Coopers & Lybrand uses graphics to break up the body copy. Incidentally, in many cases, especially where there is clip art available, graphics can be cheaper than photos. (Clip art is artwork that usually comes in a book. Many ad and PR agencies have it on hand, as do numerous printers. Artwork can be clipped and used. It can save many dollars.)

Employer's Newsline (Figure 9-3) is a quarterly that is well-targeted. It is aimed at two audiences—the personnel director or the person in charge of hiring for companies, or the president of a company. It is published by the PIC. The PIC is funded by the federal government. Companies that hire through it can obtain tax credits as well as on-the-job training subsidies.

Page 1 offers benefits designed expressly for employers; the $650,000 available in subsidies and the $5100 in tax credits. Notice how specific the heads are on these stories and how they stress those benefits.

In creating this newsletter, editors were aware of the needs and motivation of buyers. From a company's standpoint, few things are more important than money. That issue is addressed.

There is, however, another important issue that the newsletter subtly covers—the private company working with the public (governmental) sector. Many employers have nightmares regarding paperwork and red tape when it comes to government. Despite the benefits, they would rather not be involved in many programs because of those issues.

The PIC newsletter confronts those doubts. In the column by the chairman—who is a member of the private sector—the relationship between the public and private sector is discussed. The chairman lets the reader know that if the PIC performs poorly it suffers through a removal of funding.

There is another point the chair addresses—how good these workers are. That is another concern of the firms that may hire. The chair discusses a

EMPLOYER'S NEWSLINE...

Vol. 1 No. 1

Carson/Lomita/Torrance
Private Industry Council

From the Chairman

By
William
Johnson

Memories. All of us have them.

For me, one of the happiest occurred earlier this year when I picked up a copy of the local newspaper. In it was a story about a young man who had been out of work and, with no place to go, he decided to try the Carson, Lomita, Torrance, Private Industry Council.

Today, thanks to PIC's placement and the Broadway's training program, that young man, who is married and lives with his wife and young child in Carson, has been promoted to manager of the Broadway's Gourmet Department.

Reading about Darrell Lock gave me a great sense of pride. I felt good about the PIC and the work it is doing. I'm sure it also made those at the Broadway—who trained and hired Darrell—feel good, too. And I'm sure they feel equally as good about the 18 other PIC candidates they hired and put through a training and on-the-job program.

What's especially satisfying to me as a businessman is the knowledge that the PIC's funding is based upon performance. No placement, no funds. It's that simple. Thus the PIC works on the same principle as private industry. It has to produce in order to exist.

The PIC has produced for Darrell and thousands of others. But there are still many, many talented unemployed individuals in this three-city area. They come through our doors daily.

With the turnaround in the economy, the drop in inflation and unemployment, we

Cont. on page 4

Carson/Lomita/Torrance PIC

Nearly $650,000 No-Strings Training Subsidies Offered Local Employers

FROM MARRIOTT TO SIGMAPOWER—*On-the-job training funds in excess of $100,000 have been set aside for the new Torrance Marriott which may hire as many as 125 qualified, prescreened workers. Sigmapower of Carson is an example of a small company that is participating in the PIC program. The firm, which also provides on-the-job training, has two PIC applicants employed.*

On-the-job training subsidies amounting to nearly $650,000 have been set aside for fiscal 1985-86 by the Carson, Lomita, Torrance Private Industry Council.

The funds will go to underwrite programs of employers who offer on-the-job training to pre-screened and qualified PIC applicants.

Companies can qualify for the funds with either an existing training program or a new one. PIC personnel are also available to help firms create an on-the-job program if none exists.

Companies can qualify for funding irregardless of how small (one employee) the on-the-job-training program happens to be.

One of the largest was the recent Torrance Marriott program which has a potential underwriting of nearly $132,000 for the training of 125 workers. Another major program was undertaken by the Broadway which included both on-the-job and classroom training.

Information on the program can be obtained from the Carson, Lomita, Torrance PIC, (213) 618-2985.

$5,100 in Tax Credits per Employee

Companies hiring applicants from the Carson, Lomita, Torrance PIC can qualify for up to $5,100 in tax credits per employee. Companies interested in the credit program and the qualifications required, should contact the PIC (618-2985).

FIG. 9-3. *Employer's Newsline.*

FROM RACING HORSES TO RACING ENGINES

PURR—*Pat Hume, a Carson, Lomita, Torrance PIC applicant, was sent to school and then received on-the-job training by Sears (Del Amo). Pat has already been promoted into the tune-up department of the local department store and she will soon have her mechanic's license. Her supervisor regards her as "one of the best workers he has seen in 9 years."*

Pat Hume felt as if she was going nowhere. For 12 years she had worked hard as a groomer and assistant trainer of thoroughbred horses, but there was no advancement or even a promise of one.

To top it off, the groomer/assistant trainer position was far removed from a typical 9-5 job. Usually, she worked seven days a week, 13-hours a day. Pat was burned out.

"I wanted to find a normal job—one with a future. But, I had no idea of where to go. Besides, I didn't have any skills aside from my knowledge of horses."

Then, one Sunday, while browsing through the want ads in the Breeze, she saw it. It was an ad that brought her to the Private Industry Council.

"They gave me a bunch of aptitude tests," Pat recalls. "As it turned out, my greatest ability was in an area that I had loved since I was a kid—auto mechanics." PIC sent Pat to school and paid for her auto training. While still in school, she started working for Sears (Del Amo) in the auto repair department on Saturdays. When she graduated she became a trainee in Sears' battery and electrical department.

That was August, 1984. Today, after several promotions, Pat has been promoted to the tune-up department and she is about to receive her mechanic's license. Her boss, Lew Carnello, says she is "one of the best employees the department ever had."

"It's funny," says Pat, "I was always under the impression that I lacked skills. But, when I think back to when I was a kid I can remember my interest in automobiles. When I was in grammar school, I would steal away from my home and run down to the local auto repair shop and watch them work on cars. It fascinated me. But, it wasn't until I went to the PIC that those skills were brought out."

Pat's boss agrees. Carnello, who has been with Sears nine years and trained many employees, says Pat is an example of someone who has found a niche and loves what they are doing.

"In a short time she'll become a tune-up mechanic. After that, who knows? With her determination, she could go on to the Chicago Tower and be the Chairwoman of the Board."

Employer Says . . .

"Petite" Workers Doing Grand Job

"They are eager, extremely anxious to work, and highly motivated," says Sharon Parker enthusiastically.

Ms. Parker, plant administrator of La Petite Boulangerie, the Carson-based Pepsi Cola subsidiary, was talking about the PIC applicants her company has hired during the past year.

"I think," she says, "they differ from many applicants in their approach to the job. They look at their position as more than a job. Most of them can see the potential if they do well. That's a trait you do not find in many employees today."

Ms. Parker says her company is especially pleased with the prescreening the PIC provides. As a result, nearly every applicant that has been sent to La Petite has been well-qualified—and hired.

She feels so strongly about PIC's ability to prescreen that when someone walks in the door looking for a job, she automatically refers them to the PIC.

"We're relatively new and we still have some problems in our plant. The PIC employees seem to understand and they've worked well during those problem periods. It's an example of their conscientious attitude and their excellent work ethic."

THE BEST—*Sharon Parker, La Petite Boulangerie plant administrator, says PIC applicants stand out "with their work ethic and their motivation."*

FIG. 9-3. (*continued*) (*Figure continued on p. 246.*)

DAYS OF EMPLOYER'S COMPLEX PAPERWORK A THING OF PAST

Remember what happened when you hired a worker who enabled your firm to earn tax credits and an on-the-job training subsidy?

Along with the worker, your personnel people found themselves bogged down with forms that were so complicated they took a professional interpreter a year to unravel.

All that, however, is a thing of the past.

For any employers who hire a PIC applicant either as an on-the-job or classroom trainee, there is no longer any cumbersome, time consuming forms to fill out.

Thanks to the personnel departments of the Carson/Lomita/Torrance PIC, the paperwork is now handled by PIC staff workers. Thus those tax credits and other employer subsidies can be obtained with a minimum of time expended by your personnel department and/or others who handle your hiring.

———

Employer's Newsline is sponsored by the cities of Carson, Lomita and Torrance.

PIC High Tech Applicants Go Through Rigorous Schooling

Control Data Institute, the 20-year-old school that ranks near the top in the nation insofar as high tech training is concerned, has produced more than 50 graduates for PIC in the fields of computer technology and automated office skills, during the past three years.

Ninety-two percent of the graduates have been placed in jobs within private industry.

The school offers two programs, an 8½ month long class, and one that is 4 months in duration. Both cost approximately $5,000, which the PIC pays for.

The long course is designed for computer technology and repair specialists. The short for mastering automated office technology as well as word processing.

Prior to admission, the candidates are given rigorous aptitude and math tests by the PIC personnel department. These tests are followed by additional screening conducted by Control Data.

Rita McCutchan of CDI says that "PIC's applicants are all well-qualified before they ever walk in our doors. Their success ratio is certainly evidence of that."

EXTENSIVE TRAINING—PIC applicants spend up to 8½ months in training at Control Data Institute in order to master computer technology and service skills. They are prescreened before they are enrolled.

FIG. 9-3. (continued)

246

typical worker and his accomplishments. Inside, there is a success story about a worker and testimonials from other companies, all designed to alleviate any concerns that a firm might have before coming to the PIC.

South Bay Business Report (Figure 9-4) is an example of a newsletter that misses the mark. The "Dean's Message" says that the newsletter was designed to cover, "a broad range of management topics." And it was. But the range is so broad that it fails to hit home with any audience.

South Bay Business Report is published by a university and designed to try to build an image and following for the university's school of management. The intent is good, the execution could be better.

Why? Let's look at some of the elements in the newsletter.

"The Continuing Insurance Crisis," is the theme of the main news story. Which insurance crisis? Business? Personal? Both? Be specific.

Inside there is a story on the U.S. trade deficit with Japan. Once again, there is nothing specific about it. Will it impact on jobs? on industry? Is it growing, shrinking, or a problem for some reason? Will it impact on recent management graduates? None of these questions are addressed.

On page 2 are faculty and staff notes. Are these of interest to anyone— except those who happen to be faculty and staff members? The newsletter is designed to attract business-people, not the faculty or staff. Notes of this type fit much better when they are put on the last page. Keep the news up front.

Graphically, the newsletter could be improved. There is no art. The only thing that breaks up body copy is a few subheads and bold-face type. This makes it difficult to read. From a graphic standpoint, the newsletter can be improved with little trouble. There should be more heads, more variety, and either some photos or illustrations.

Editorially, the publication should be more focused. The lead story goes on for two more pages, entirely too much copy for the lead story in a four-page newsletter.

The next newsletter (Figure 9-5) is from a bank. It is targeted at the bank's prime customers (businesspeople) and does a good job of selling itself to that audience.

The president's column addresses an issue that every depositor, businessperson or not, is interested in hearing about—why there are an inordinate number of bank failures and why this bank will not fail.

The lead story tells about an important news development, the building of a new bank. Inside are features on two of the bank's business customers. This serves two purposes. First, it shows the present (and potential) customers the market to which the bank is catering. Second, it allows the bank to say (with help from those two customers) how helpful it can be.

The photo at the bottom of page 1 tells an important story as well. It pictures the bank president with the mayor of the city of Los Angeles. That says the bank's president is important, also.

There are features on employees of the month, and these stories give present and potential depositors an idea of how anxious the employees are to serve them.

There is also a spotlight on one of the bank's officers, which stresses the banking background of the executive.

On the back page is a profile of one of the bank's directors, a successful businesswoman. One point of the story is that the director is not a figurehead.

California State University
Dominguez Hills

South Bay
BUSINESS REPORT

Vol. 1, No. 1   **April 1986**

Published by the Bureau of Business Research and Services ■ *School of Management* ■ *California State University, Dominguez Hills* ■ *Carson, CA*

THE CONTINUING INSURANCE CRISIS —

POSSIBILITIES FOR A CURE

by Aaron Liberman, Ph.D., Associate Professor of Public Administration **FACHE**
Director, Bureau of Business Research & Services

When insurance rates began their upward spiral during 1985, there were some righteously indignant businessmen and political leaders who hoped that the crisis would dissipate with a minimum amount of discomfort.

As this hoped for scenario was dashed by sustained cost escalations, the concern and disappointment turned to anger and resentment. The emotions resulting from these premium increases were further aggravated by several insurance carriers' efforts to purge from their roles risks which were deemed to be excessive or undesirable. Mid-term policy cancellations quite literally created a panic environment for a large number of policy holders, who, after several years of competitive pricing, suddenly found themselves without any available alternatives.

Some municipalities, burdened by rate increases ranging from 100% to 1,000% in some cases, began self-insuring or curtailing needed service programs. Many businesses have opted

to accept higher deductibles and, in certain instances, have gone the same self-insured route.

At the same time, several state insurance departments have instituted interim rules precluding the use of mid-term cancellations. Meanwhile numerous inquiries are under way at the Federal and State levels to determine both the causes of the problem and the possibility of resolution.

DEAN'S MESSAGE

In conjunction with our university's 25th Year Celebration, I am very pleased to introduce the first issue of *South Bay Business Report.* Since its founding in 1974, the School of Management has developed truly excellent undergraduate and graduate programs in business and public administration. We are particularly proud of the quality of our faculty and the impressive accomplishments of our alumni. One goal of the newsletter will be to keep you updated on these and other items of information relating to the School of Management.

However, our main intent is to provide you with articles of direct professional interest that cover a broad range of management topics. Because your time is important, we will present information that is relevant to you in a concise format that focuses upon key and useful facts. In this issue you will find an article by Dr. Aaron Liberman

ORIGIN OF THE PROBLEM

The profound changes in the insurance market during 1985 were the result of a combination of events which have occurred during the past six years. The three most prominent causes related to: (1) **Price Cutting** which resulted in cash-flow underwriting (premiums from new accounts to cover mounting deficits from adverse claims

cont. pg. 3

on the liability insurance crisis and its impact on management. Also, while articles on the national economy can be found in numerous publications, I think you will find the perspective presented in this issue by Dr. Martin Blyn to be particularly interesting.

The quality of an institution is defined by the quality of the faculty. Therefore, we would like to also utilize this newsletter to highlight our very fine faculty. In addition to brief summaries of faculty activities, each issue will profile an individual faculty member. In this issue we present Dr. R. Bryant Mills, who has extensive experience in management and labor relations.

Welcome once again to our premier issue. I look forward to your continuing interest and support of our school and university.

Ronald S. Lemos
Ronald S. Lemos
Dean

FIG. 9-4. *South Bay Business Report.*

FACULTY NOTES

Charles (Ken) Jameson, professor of Marketing, is conducting a study on consumer images of supermarkets in the South Bay region.

Richard Ulivi, professor of Finance, has recently completed a paper for publication entitled "The Financial Plan: A Trojan Horse?" The paper discusses whether or not the public benefits from such plans or whether these plans are merely covers to help salespersons sell more financial products.

Raoul Freeman, professor of Computer Information Systems, has had his paper entitled "Implementation Plan Documentation of Large Scale Systems," accepted for publication in the Winter issue of the AEDS JOURNAL.

Seymour Wolfson, professor of Computer Information Systems, has been nominated for the Presidency of the Association of Computing Machinery.

Milton Pine, professor of Computer Information Systems, is currently conducting research for a Gardena distributor of copy machines and products. His work involves advising on hardware and software acquisitions, systems analysis, and staff training.

Donald Barnett, professor of Accounting, and Dr. Brhane Tesfay, Professor of Management, recently participated in a symposium on effective advising of minority business students. The symposium was held at the University of Wisconsin.

C.E. Zoerner, Jr., professor of Marketing, has completed a book entitled *How To Take The Pain Out Of Managerial Writing.* The book will be published by Del Amo Press.

Kosaku Yoshida, professor of Quantitative Methods, presented a paper at the 17th Annual Conference of the American Institute for Decision Sciences in Las Vegas. The paper was published in the conference proceedings and was entitled "Long-Run ARIMA Model Building."

Bryant Mills, associate dean and Martin Blyn, professor of Finance, presented a paper at the national conference of the Association for Human Resource Management recently held in Boston. The paper was published in the Proceedings of the conference and was entitled "Academic Culture and University Mismanagement."

Ronald S. Lemos, dean of the School of Management, published an article entitled "Microcomputers and the SBI Program" in the Summer 1985 edition of the *American Journal of Small Business*

Burhan Yavas, professor of Quantitative Methods, will present two research papers at the July 1986 meeting of the Western Economics Association. Titles of the papers are: "A Simulation Model of Interregional Growth," and "The Adjustment Process of the Mexican Economy." ■

STAFF NOTES

R. Bryant Mills, Ph.D., is the associate dean of the School of Management, California State University, Dominguez Hills. Prior to joining CSU Dominguez Hills in 1983, Mills was the assistant dean in the F.E. Seidman School of Business, Grand Valley State University, Grand Rapids, Michigan. A graduate of Cal Poly-San Luis Obispo and the University of Iowa, Mills is active in numerous civic organizations and professional societies in the fields of human resource management and labor relations.

Mills has been a regular attendee at the South Bay Business Roundtable since 1983. Members may recall that Mills presented the January 15, 1985, program entitled; "Promises Made, Promises Broken: the Employment (Termination) At-Will Doctrine and the Implied Employment Contract." Employment practices is a topic that is very familiar to Mills. He is a well-known consultant to businesses and law firms and has testified as an expert witness in numerous employment related court cases in both state and federal courts. He has written extensively in the field of human resource management and is the author of several articles that have appeared in several professional journals. Also, he has chaired panels and presented research papers at many professional conferences during the last fifteen years.

As the associate dean, Mills is actively involved in a variety of School of Management activities including the South Bay Business Roundtable and the Bureau for Business Research and Service. Despite his busy schedule, Mills finds time to teach one graduate course per term in the school's Master in Business Administration program.

Over the last year, Mills has been researching and writing on a variety of topics including office dissidents and how managers might better deal with the dissident and dissatisfied employee.

Mills is married to Lanyce Kay Mills, a CPA and Tax Manager for Alexander Thornton and Company. The couple make their home in Fountain Valley. ■

South Bay BUSINESS REPORT

Questions regarding material printed in South Bay Business Report should be referred to:

Aaron Liberman, Ph.D., Director
Bureau of Business Research
and Services
California State University,
Dominguez Hills
Carson, California 90747
(213) 516-3661

Ronald S. Lemos, Ph.D., Dean
School of Management

Bryant Mills, Ph.D., Associate Dean
School of Management

FIG. 9-4. (continued)

Vol. 1, No. 2

NEWSLINE

Pacific
Business
Bank

From the President

*By
Michael I. Mitoma*

The recent number of bank failures has caused a great deal of concern among the general public. This concern is justified, since the banking industry handles a commodity very dear to most people — their money!

The banking industry is no different from most industries in terms of why companies succeed or fail. A loan to a bank is the same as an account receivable to a commercial business. These loans are profitable, since points and interest are charged. The bank, however, does not have the large profit margin of a manufacturing business. The normal profit is only 2%-5%. This means that any loan losses have a severe impact on profitability.

The key to success is in the company's **management** — not only its officers, but also its Board of Directors. Many of the California financial institutions that have failed were led by individuals who thought they were real estate developers and not bankers. Many were headquartered in Orange County and were caught in the real estate crash that took place there. Other financial institutions were joint venturing and developing property for themselves. They forgot the purpose for their existence — that of making loans to individuals and businesses.

We are fortunate in having Directors who are really concerned about our Bank. They are always out looking for new customers and thinking of ways to improve the Bank. They are supportive of management and do not allow their egos to interfere with what is best for the Bank. They provide an environment that encourages the Bank's management and personnel to give all they can to ensure the Bank's success.

Another common factor in bank failures is the investment in elaborate quarters. The purchase of real estate for a bank's use may be a good strategy in many instances, provided the cost per square foot is reasonable. However, any excessive investment in furniture, fixtures, and quarters can cause the problem of illiquidity. This means no money is available to lend. This is like a manufacturer running out of inventory.

The recent industry problems have created a tremendous opportunity to Pacific Business Bank. We have the diversity of resources and management that is the hallmark of all successful banks. Our Board of Directors is comprised of individuals from varied business backgrounds, and our management team has both major and independent bank experience. We have emphasized a loan portfolio to a variety of businesses. With this loan diversification and good loan underwriting, we will avoid the financial problems that have affected other banks in Southern California.

Pacific Business Bank's New Home on the Way

UPCOMING — *Construction of Pacific Business
Bank's new 11,000 square-foot building, is slated to begin this Fall. The
new facility, which will occupy the site adjoining Pacific's present headquarters, will triple the Bank's existing space.*

Pacific Business Bank's new 11,000 square-foot home is being designed so that it will offer customers special conveniences as well as an ideal environment in which to bank.

The Bank will have an 8,000 square-foot bottom floor and a 3,000 square-foot mezzanine. Throughout the structure there will be additional natural lighting provided by skylights.

The administrative and operation areas of the Bank can be opened and closed separately. Thus, if the Bank's officers have late meetings scheduled, the administrative area can be left open while the operation area is closed.

The mezzanine will be equipped with a conference room, staff room and kitchen. It will overlook the administrative area.

The building, which was designed by the architectural firm of Kato-Shimasaki & Associates, was designed to give those inside the Bank a feeling of openness, as well as comfort.

WORTHY CAUSE— *Los Angeles Mayor Tom Bradley, right, joins Pacific Business Bank President Michael I. Mitoma, left, and Taizo Watanabe, the Consul General of Japan, for lunch following the Asian Rehabilitation Service Charity Golf Tournament. The tournament, which is held yearly, is sponsored by the Bank, and all proceeds go to the charity.*

FIG. 9-5. Pacific Business Bank *Newsline.*

Albert Londino and Stacey Spagon look over list of new accounts.

Sparks Rapid Growth

Albert Londino Spearheads PBB's Business Approach

Doctors may not make "house calls" any longer, but Albert Londino, PBB's Vice President in charge of business development, certainly does.

Londino makes it a practice to get acquainted with every business account that is opened, regardless of the company's size. Londino may set up an interview with the new account at the Bank or he may visit them at the business location.

"We want to know as much about the customer and his or her industry as possible," Londino explains. "That way, if the customer ever has need for a loan, we don't have to spend additional time trying to analyze the industry and the company's prospects. We can respond immediately."

That service is one of the reasons why PBB has become one of the fastest-growing banks in the South Bay. "Every industry is unique and in order to service them, a bank should familiarize itself with as many customers as possible."

Londino, a banker with more than a decade of experience, has worked in banks from coast to coast. A native of New York and a graduate of NYU, where he earned a BA in Management and MBA in International Business, Londino worked for Citicorp and The Bowery Bank on the East Coast.

In California he worked for Crocker, where he was Assistant Vice President of Business Development, and Republic Bank. In each of his positions, his specialty has been business development and determining customer and industry needs.

When Pacific opened in 1984, the Air Force veteran, and father of three girls (9, 7 and 2 months), decided to "join because of its philosophy. I had worked in large and small banks, but Pacific made a serious and definite commitment to business. It's a commitment that has become one of our cornerstones and, I believe, the reason for our rapid growth."

From Baseball to Classroom to Building— Plaster's Triple Play Is Winner

He was a tall, skinny shortstop with a great deal of natural ability.

So much ability that the Pittsburgh Pirates signed him right out of high school and sent him to the baseball club's AAA farm club in the Texas League.

The South Bay has another attraction for Bud—Pacific Business Bank. Despite being headquartered 90 miles away, he has been a customer of the bank since it opened.

"And for good reason," he says. "This bank is like a big family. They take an interest in what

CONSTRUCTIVE CONFAB— *Bud Plaster, center, shows plans for his newest project to Bank Officers Albert Londino, left, and Glen Higuchi. Plaster, who is doing most of his building in the high desert, has developed more than $16 million worth of property. He commutes to PBB because, as he puts it, "the service has certainly been worth it."*

The kid, however, did not go on to the Hall of Fame or the Major Leagues. Instead, Bud Plaster went on to fulfill a long-time ambition— teach school.

What made him move from a kid's dream (the baseball diamond) to a kid's nightmare (the classroom)?

"I always wanted to teach," he recalls. "Even when I signed with Pittsburgh, there was a clause in the contract that provided for a college education through a masters degree. As soon as I completed school, I quit baseball."

For 19 years Bud was a teacher, administrator and principal in districts throughout California. Then, eight years ago, he moved to the high desert and found a new vocation... building and development.

"It was another career that appealed to me. So much so, that I decided to leave teaching."

Today, Bud is no longer clearing classrooms. He's too busy heading Arlen Real Estate Development Company, one of the fastest-growing, most successful young real estate development firms in Southern California.

Bud's firm has constructed nearly $16 million in residential housing. He's also built some apartments and commercial buildings in the Gardena area, an area that brings back memories. He was a graduate of Leuzinger High School and later returned there to teach.

their customers are doing.

"On several occasions I've brought in a development package and building associates with me to the bank. Glen (Higuchi) and Albert (Londino) have been exceptional; they've rolled out the carpet and given me an enormous amount of personal attention. You don't find that at banks today."

Pacific has also answered Bud's financial needs with several construction loans. "They get to know you... and your business. Even though I live 90 miles away, it feels like home every time I walk into the bank."

Stock Information

Gary R. Fournier, Vice President, Kidder, Peabody & Company, is the market maker for Pacific Business Bank's stock. For those interested in the stock and its price, Mr. Fournier is located at 333 S. Grand Avenue, Suite 2300, Los Angeles, CA 90071. Or, he can be reached at (213) 485-1100. According to Mr. Fournier, the most recent price for PBB was (as of July 31) 13½-14.

FIG. 9-5. (continued) *(Figure continued on p. 252.)*

These Two Are Cleaning Up

After 20-plus years as aerospace engineers, Bert Swearinger and Armando Figueroa did two things no one ever figured would happen.

First, they tossed their experience and careers aside—and quit their jobs.

Then they opened a business of their own . . . a car wash.

That was 13 years ago, and since then the pair have not only made a success of their business (Carson Car Wash), but they have also created an ideal life-style, one that includes golf and leisure—two of their goals when they left aerospace.

"Many people believe that going into business requires a great deal of risk and thinking before you take the plunge," says Bert. "But Armando and I just decided to do it. We weren't even sure what kind of business to go into."

COMING CLEAN — Bert Swearinger and his partner, Armando Figueroa, discuss some of the new, innovative car wash equipment that Carson Car Wash has installed during the past two years with Bank Officer Albert Londino (center). PBB did the financing.

"We decided," explains Armando, "that we did not want to work all night. We even thought about construction, but decided against it."

Armando, who lived in Carson, suggested the car wash. "We had some doubts," says Bert, "but we took the plunge."

From the outside, a car wash may appear to be a simple operation, but the machinery needs constant attention and cleaning. It also needs change and updating.

Bert and Armando have pioneered many of those changes. They were the first car wash in the South Bay to replace plastic and neoprene brushes with cloth (1980). "Recently," explains Bert, "brushless has become the in-thing." Their

(Cont. on pg. 4)

Employees of the Month

Miss June: Stacey Spagon

Which would you rather do—vacation in Europe or go to work in a bank?

Stacey Spagon had that choice, and, believe it or not, she chose work over play. That gives you some insight on Stacey's attitude, the enthusiasm she has for her job, and one of the reasons why she was chosen PBB's June "Employee of the Month."

It's not that Stacey doesn't appreciate fun. In fact, if you were to ask fellow employees, they would unquestionably name Stacey, a native of Westchester, one of the Bank's most outgoing and carefree employees.

At the same time, however, Stacey—who works with Albert Londino in the loan department—is excited about her work and what she has seen at the Bank.

"The Bank has a great philosophy when it comes to customers and employees. One of the first things I learned when I came here (March, '85), was that customers are individuals and each deserves individual attention.

"There's a warm, friendly relationship between customers and the Bank employees. If someone has a question, they can ask any employee for the answer. If that employee does not know, he or she will find out and direct the customer to the right party. No one shrugs you off or gives you a blank look. I don't think you find that at many banks."

Stacey, who is single, bilingual (Spanish) and a photography buff, is equally enthused about her opportunity at the Bank. A graduate of USC in Public Administration, she discovered a number of things when she joined Pacific.

"This is a small, but rapidly growing bank. It's the kind of place where an employee can learn to do more than one thing. I also found that the officers were all willing to train and teach you. That makes the chances for advancement much greater."

The contact with customers and the things she has learned about banking during the past few months have convinced her of two things.

"I want to make banking a career, and I'm especially interested in a career in bank marketing. I know at Pacific, I'll have the opportunity to pursue that goal."

Miss July: Roeena Law

"Unquestionably, at this Bank you will find more personalized service . . . more of a one-on-one relationship. It is a Bank where the customers not only get to know the officers and employees, but they can benefit from that relationship as well."

Roeena Law, PBB's New Account Representative, and its July "Employee of the Month," was talking about the difference in banks.

And Roeena knows what she is talking about. She spent nearly a decade in the banking industry before coming to PBB. During that time she worked for several different banks in the new account area.

"Each bank has a personality of its own," she says. "Some banks let you open an account, order your checks and then forget about you. At PBB, there is a heavy emphasis on customer involvement, more so than anywhere else I have worked.

"For example, although there are some people who come in and know exactly what kind of account they want, there are others who are not aware of some of the special interest-earning opportunities that exist.

"That's where involvement comes in. We explain every option available. Banking has become more complex in the past few years, and there are numerous earning opportunities available today that did not exist before. Our policy is to try and point out each option to the new account. We try to help people put their money to work . . . and that's fun."

Roeena's interest in helping customers was one of the prime reasons she was named "Employee of the Month." She has also brought a great deal of expertise with her.

A native of Gardena (she graduated from Gardena High and L.A. Business College), Roeena entered the banking field as soon as she left school. She worked with several large Los Angeles banks and came to PBB last January.

Part of the reason for the move was it was closer to home (Compton), her husband (Fred, who works for Shell Oil), and her nine-year-old son, Aaron.

When she's not busy at the Bank or at home, you can usually find her out dancing or at the bowling alley—where she carries an average that would make most men envious—160-170.

FIG. 9-5. (continued)

Profile
Mary Mann—A Director And Entrepreneur

To some, Mary Mann is known as one of the most successful businesswomen in Southern California.

To others, she is known for her ability to pound nails, pour cement, or handle a plumbing problem.

She even used to patch tires ("when we used patches," she laughingly recalls), clean plugs, and even adjust carburetors. Her father was a contractor and builder, and he raised Mary "so I could do anything."

With that background, it's no surprise that Mary is an entrepreneur's entrepreneur—she had one of the first Honda motorcycle dealerships in Pasadena, then she became a Honda auto dealer, and today she is owner of a half-dozen other businesses ranging from an office leasing company to a manufacturing facility.

Despite a busy schedule, Mary has found the time to travel from Pasadena to Carson to serve as one of Pacific's Directors.

"I love it," she says. "Being a Director has changed greatly from what it used to be. In the past, a Director was usually just a title. Today, if you are a Director, you have responsibilities and obligations.

"Pacific Directors are responsible for the Bank's actions. In the future, I think you're going to find Directors in every industry becoming more responsible for their company's decisions. Just as it is a good thing for banking, it will be good for other fields."

Mary's duties at the Bank include the chairing of two committees (audit and nominating), plus the serving on a third (loan).

She smiles when she talks about her role at the Bank and her business enterprises. "When I first started in business, I was an oddity. After all, a woman's place was in the home, not under a car hood . . . and especially not on a motorcycle."

(These Two/cont. from pg. 3)

wash is the only one in the area that utilizes soft water and steam for whitewalls.

Whatever innovation the two put into their business, it takes capital. When they first took the business plunge, they had to come up with $50,000. That meant mortgaging their homes. That was 13 years ago, and since then the business has not only prospered, but the two have created an ideal partnership "because," laughs Armando, "we seldom see each other."

Actually, their paths do cross occasionally. Bert works Friday, Saturday, Sunday and every other Monday. Armando has Tuesday-Thursday and every other Monday.

"With those weekdays off," smiles Bert, "I get all the golf I want. In fact, since we've been in this business, I've worn out more golf than work shoes."

Although Bert and Armando constantly joke about their efforts, the two former engineers worked hard, long hours to get their business off the ground.

"The one piece of advice I have for anyone who wants to go into business," says Armando, "is be prepared . . . to do anything and everything."

Be prepared for financial problems as well. That was one of the reasons the pair chose Pacific Business Bank.

"I've always felt this community needed a bank that responded to the needs of the local community. Pacific does, and that's why we are with them."

Pacific responded to the pair two years ago when it provided the financing for $130,000 worth of new equipment. The equipment is computerized, and allows Bert and Armando to run a more efficient, dependable wash that gets cars cleaner.

"The bank has been there every time we have needed them," says Armando. "That's great for our business and this community as well."

WATCHING PROGRESS—Michael I. Mitoma, Pacific's President, and Director Mary Mann, examine the rendering of the Bank's new 11,000 square-foot structure.

Pacific Business Bank
438 West Carson Street
Carson, California 90745

FIG. 9-5. (continued)

This bank's directors are working directors. They take an interest and responsibility in the bank.

In today's financial environment where so many company actions are rubber stamped by boards of directors, the bank stands out as a carefully run firm that takes input and advice from every area.

Graphically, the newsletter could be improved. The type is too small. Newsletters should utilize 10 or 12 point type for readability.

CHAPTER 10

CREATING AUDIO/VISUALS

We live in a visual-oriented society where the images on a 60-second television spot have become just as influential—if not more—than the spoken word on that same spot.

Video can sell millions of dollars worth of goods in a few seconds, and it can help the consultant sell his or her services and programs equally as fast.

Whether we are talking about 35 mm slide shows or videocassette productions, there are keys to good videos. Regardless of which configuration is used, if you want to sell something via video it should be entertaining as well as sales oriented.

The best video presentations are equal to good books. That is, they have a beginning, middle, and end. Like a good ad, they appeal to the needs of the audience. They tell a story, move logically along, and take the prospective client along with them.

The most effective videos are not the most expensive, either. Put together a good script (which constantly educates, informs, and addresses the needs of the potential buyer), keep the client moving with frequent changes (if you are using slides they should change about every 5 to 10 seconds), add a musical soundtrack that enhances the story, a professional announcer who knows how to sell, and you have an effective production.

Time

Keep your videos under 10 minutes. The attention span of most people is excellent to five minutes, but begins to fade after that.

Music

Make it fit the mood of the production, but stay away from familiar music when you have dialogue on the soundtrack. A well-known tune will distract the viewer when he or she should be listening to the announcer's voice. There is, however, nothing wrong with using an effective, familiar song at the beginning or end of a production when you want to make an emotional impact. Music can be used throughout the film (or audio/visual); however, if you are making an important point, the music should be toned down considerably.

Emotion

Videos that sell move people emotionally. Just as a good sales pitch causes the buyer to make an emotional buying decision, a carefully crafted video will lead the prospect to an emotional buying decision as well.

From a practical standpoint, a 35 mm slideshow can be the most cost-effective production put together. It is practical when making changes. Let's say you add a service to your consulting practice (or drop something from it); a 35 mm film is easy to edit and change. It is also inexpensive compared to video.

People

Our interest in people is greater than our interest in machinery. Thus whenever possible use people in your video. The most interesting people are, of course, the little people—kids. Everyone loves kids.

The following is a portion of a script that was used for a 10-minute video. The video was used to sell a local PIC to employers.

The film was put together as part of a sales package aimed at employers. Its goal was to sell employers on the idea of hiring these workers. Private sector employers, however, are not enthused with the idea of working with the public (government) sector. Many have had disastrous experiences and were deluged with required paperwork.

The film was supposed to allay those fears and make the employers aware of an opportunity to earn tax credits and reimbursement for on-the-job training. It was also designed to make them cognizant of the tremendous number of qualified, anxious workers in the job pool.

The hiring process through the PIC can be complex, however, you do not want your video to be intricate. Keep things simple. If there is a detailed explanation or process, be general about it. Leave it up to the conversation that follows to explain any missing ingredients. You will not be able to keep the attention of viewers if you get too involved.

Imagine, for example, watching a replay of a football game. If the announcer analyzed the move of every player in every play, he or she would put the audience to sleep within a few minutes. Examine the following PIC script. Comments are on the right hand side of the script.

Sample Audio/Visual Script/Comments

Script	Comments

(music intro)

This ran 28 seconds. It was upbeat and title slides were shown.

Dialogue

Remember January 1980? Inflation was 18 percent, unemployment was rising as rapidly as gasoline prices, and the country was near economic chaos.

Starting with a question sparks viewer curiosity. The announcer is also talking about something that viewers identify with almost instantly.

1980 also marked the debut of a new administration and revised economic policies. One of those policies was a revolutionary new direction that the administration would be taking when it came to finding work for the semiskilled, unskilled, or unemployed worker.

Music is brought up slightly, to give feeling of hope with the intro of the new administration. To give you an idea of pacing, there are three slide changes in this section.

For years, government had tried to solve the unemployment problem with a variety of programs. Most were programs in which job seekers were given government jobs or other public sector employment. Unfortunately, many were temporary positions and when the funding ran out, workers were back on the street.

Three slide changes in this section.

The new administration had other ideas. One was to involve private business and businesspeople in a program that would concentrate on placing the unemployed in permanent, private industry jobs.

Notice how simple and easy to understand the story is. Of course, the program and the decision was more complex, but it does no good (and you will lose them) to try to give complex explanations to viewers.

The thrust would be to retrain the unemployed. Retraining would come in the form of schooling or even on-the-job training. Either way, the emphasis was going to be on taking the semiskilled, unskilled, and unemployed and placing them in local private sector jobs.

Six slides are in this section.

Obviously, both the present and future employment needs of local businesses had to be accurately deter-

(*Continued on p. 258.*)

Script	Comments
mined. In order to monitor those needs, a committee familiar with private industry would be established.	
The government decided the best group to monitor these needs would be the people already working in the private sector . . . in other words, the businesspeople themselves.	To the audience—a group of private industry employers—this is a wise decision. They agree with it and will find it easy to agree with other portions of the slide show.
Thus private industry councils were created in local areas throughout the country. Each PIC, as it is called, is composed of business owners, CEOs, presidents of prominent companies, or other private sector executives who know their communities. By law a majority of the PIC's membership must be from private industry. Those who agree to serve are not compensated.	Within 2 minutes the PIC has been explained in lay terms. Keep in mind that people will never resent you explaining something in a video that they already know about—as long as you do it in a mature way. This audio/visual is educating and informing. It is not talking down to anyone.
These PICs meet on a regular basis and they do four things. First, they evaluate the needs of the local labor market. They may do this through surveys or other similar methods. Second, they fund and monitor training programs. They do not just put someone in school or a training program without checking on their progress.	There are three slides in this section. It is not rushed because the writer wants those viewing to listen to the four things. He does not want to rush them with the rapid movement of slides.
In fact, schools that train PIC applicants are never paid in full until the program is completed and the student is placed on a job.	
The PIC even has staff workers who occasionally monitor the training and provide technical assistance whenever necessary, in order to ensure the success of each trainee.	
Third, the PIC tries to find jobs and job training opportunities in the area. Fourth, it sets policies and goals for the overall PIC program.	The pace is slowed here as well. Only three slides between this section and the one above.
The Carson, Lomita, Torrance PIC is both typical and atypical of PICs throughout the state. It is typical insofar as our goals are concerned. Our	Notice the change in the tone. When the announcer starts to talk about Carson, Lomita, Torrance he goes from third person (they) to first person

Script	Comments

Script

job is to place qualified workers in private industry jobs. And we certainly have done that. Since our founding, we have placed thousands of workers in occupations ranging from word processing and cable TV installation to auto mechanics, sales, computer technology, and computer repair.

Amazingly, when these people came to PIC, most were considered unemployable. The Carson, Lomita, Torrance PIC, however, does more than find jobs for people. When someone walks in the door looking for a position, he or she goes through a complete pre-employment screening operation. They are interviewed and given a variety of aptitude tests.

In other words, PIC does the job of a personnel department. We interview, test, and evaluate potential employees before we send them to a company to be hired. If the potential employee needs classroom training, PIC sees that they get it. If they are ready for on-the-job training, PIC arranges that too.

By the time we send a potential employee to a company, he or she is not only prepared, but a ready and willing worker.

The Carson, Lomita, Torrance PIC has also created an employment program for youth. It is called YES (Youth Employment Summer) and through it we provide willing, capable young workers to fill private industry jobs during the summer months. Last year, more than 400 youngsters between the ages of 16–21 were placed in the private sector by PIC. These young people are screened and their aptitudes are determined as well.

Now, the question is, how good are these employees? And what benefits

Comments

(we, our) for greater impact with the viewing audience. He is one of them.

Aside from addressing needs, a good slide show (like a good ad) should address all the doubts that a potential client has—in this case, the PIC admits that, "Yes, they weren't too good when they came to us but we remedy that situation through the process we put them through."

We will never send you a slouch. We only send you the best.

And we do the same with youngsters. If you need summer staff, why not come to us and get qualified, screened workers.

Key paragraph. This is what every potential employer in the room wants
(*Continued on p. 260.*)

Script

does hiring a PIC candidate offer to you, the potential employer?

Before we answer that last question, let's take a look at the Carson, Lomita, Torrance PIC. Remember, we said it was both typical and atypical.

How are we atypical? Primarily through our reputation and standing in the state. Of the 50 PICs in California, Carson, Lomita, Torrance is ranked number one in the percentage of applicants that have been hired by local private companies.

More than 90 percent of our applicants have been interviewed and hired by private industry for permanent jobs. That gives you an idea of the quality of the PIC job seeker—as well as the way the Carson, Lomita, Torrance PIC operates.

Let's take a closer look at some of those applicants and some of the companies they work for. There's the Broadway. Nineteen applicants were trained and placed in sales positions. How well have they done? Well, take Darrell Lock. After three months, he was promoted to manager of the Broadway's Gourmet section. A similar program has worked with the Marriott Hotel in Torrance.

Then there is Pat Hume. A short time ago, she came to our offices after spending 12 years as a groomer and assistant trainer of horses. She wanted to embark on a new career. We gave her an aptitude test, enrolled her in school, and today she is with Sears—in its auto repair department.

Pat is more than just another employee. She has progressed from battery and electronic tester to the tune-up area. Lou Carnella, her supervisor,

Comments

answered. Slide shows are no different than ads or a good direct mail piece. They must promise and deliver benefits and answer needs.

In slide shows, as in direct mail, it never hurts to reiterate a point that the audience may have forgotten.

Important point. This is emphasized on the screen with a graphic slide with the number one imprinted. Everyone wants to be associated with the best.

This is really saying, "Your peers recognize how good we and our applicants are. They have hired more than 90 percent of those we have sent to them. Maybe you should be taking a closer look at us." If someone else on the block is doing it maybe you should, too.

Case study of actual workers. Now we are getting specific. This is the kind of testimony the viewers can identify with and appreciate.

Another well-known employer to those in the room.

Testimonial from an employer. The words need not be spoken by the person who said them. An announcer can say them just as well, and keep the

Script

says she has the best attitude of any worker he has had in 9 years. And he says she could even go on to become chairperson of the board.

We could tell you about Steve Moore, who has become one of the top cable installers at Storer Cable or Marlene Copperman and Bob Kinslow who have become technicians with the Coherent Company and Interglobal Technology.

Or we could tell you about Regina Sims or Linda Brown, both successful word processing operators. Or we could tell you about the hundreds and hundreds of others we have trained for companies throughout Southern California.

Each was trained on the job or learned their skills in school and owe their new careers to the Job Training Partnership Act (JTPA). It is the JTPA that provides PIC with training monies. Funds flow from the U.S. Department of Labor to the states where it is distributed to local areas. The funding is based on community needs and how well we perform.

Thus just as private industry is rewarded with higher profits when it performs well, the PIC is rewarded with additional funding when it does the job.

Now, what does this all mean to you—the potential employer? What do you get out it aside from an employee that we can virtually guarantee. Well, let's discuss those employer benefits, benefits that mean dollars and cents to your company.

First, whenever you want, we are ready to lend our staff's expertise to your company in reviewing its needs. Whether you need one worker or an entire crew, whether you need entry

Comments

slide show from slowing. When a nonprofessional takes the microphone, it not only slows the show but can break the sales rhythm that has been established.

Throughout this section and the previous ones which mentioned employees names music was utilized and there was a slight rise in the volume.

Now that the basics of the program are understood, the program goes more in-depth. However, it will not tackle complex explanations. Notice, too, the use of acronyms only after the full meaning of the initials have been explained. Never use an acronym unless it is clear what it refers to.

Once again, a tie between the private sector (the audience) and the PIC. We operate just as you do.

In the event you went to sleep, let's wake up and cover some basic points that will mean a great deal to you— benefits . . . dollars. This is what the announcer is stressing. It is back to the benefits for those in the audience.

(Continued on p. 262.)

Script	Comments

Script

level or skilled workers, we can meet those needs.

We can help you set up a training program or work with a program that you may already have.

Now, let's look at some of the financial benefits. Under the PIC system, if you train one of our applicants on the job, a portion of his or her compensation is reimbursed to you by us. That portion can be as high as 50 percent of the employee's wage.

Or suppose you want to send one of our applicants to a special school. Or perhaps you want to train them in one of your own classroom situations. We'll pay for the tuition, books, and supplies.

But that's not where it ends. Full-time PIC applicants may qualify for up to $5100 in tax credits the first year and the nice thing about it is you do not get saddled with the paperwork. We do it for you.

There is, of course, one other thing *about* hiring one of our applicants. You're looking *at* someone who is not just looking for a job, you're looking *at* someone who has made a special effort to find us, come *to* our offices, undergone a battery of tests and interviews *and* answered hundreds of questions about his or *her* hopes and desires for the future.

At PIC *our* applicants are not just job seekers, they *are* people like you and me who are willing to work and work hard for a share, *a* piece of that great American Dream.

Each one of you has the capability of opening the door to that dream *for* these people and, at the same time, adding *a* capable, loyal, productive worker to your company. So don't wait, do it today, and do it *with* PIC.

Comments

Every company is interested in this. Notice how the best benefits (from the potential client's standpoint) have been saved for the end.

And even more benefits. . . .

Music begins to come in stronger. Under each underlined word there is a new slide. Each slide is a candid shot of a ready, willing worker, hard at work.

The call for action. Ask for the sale. Following this section, the music comes in full volume, and lasts an additional 29 seconds. During this time there are shots of workers.

CANDIDS AND GRAPHICS IN AUDIO/VISUALS

Candids and graphics are the two most effective types of photographs to use in an audio/visual. For example, in the PIC slide show the actual names of employees who came from the ranks of PIC applicants are mentioned. Instead of shooting the typical head shot, the photographer shot candids of each of the people while they were at work. Most of his shots were taken while they were on the job. The cable TV installer was shown climbing a telephone pole; the auto mechanic was shown working under the hood of a car. Candids—they give the slide show an extra visual attraction and are certainly more interesting than the standard posed photo.

Projected Costs

Graphics are effective but can be expensive and almost every slide show needs them. In the preceding show, the producer spent $800 on graphics, or approximately 35 percent of the total cost of the show. (This show was put together with $1100 in photography; $280 in announcer fees; $100 in studio time; and $800 in graphics. The consultant wrote the script himself. If you had to purchase a script, it could run from a minimum of $1000 on up.) This is an extremely low cost and gives you an idea of how reasonable an audio/visual can be if the consultant is involved and does not contract everything to an outside service.

Graphics are expensive because usually an artist has to draw or design the graphics (whether it be a map of the United States or an arrow going from one city to another), and then it is photographed. Thus you pay for a photographer as well as an artist.

Computers and software designed to create graphics are making this phase of a slide show more reasonable. There are number of programs that will design both color and black-and-white graphics. This saves the producer the expensive step of hiring an artist to draw or design the desired graphics.

Music can be obtained through any recording studio. Many have songs that are in the public domain and there are no fees required for usage. Surprisingly, there are thousands of songs to pick from. If you wish to use a recognizable, copyrighted song, then you must negotiate with the publisher where fees are concerned.

To be effective, slides should coincide with the spoken word that refers to the image on the slide. Slide projectors do not change instantaneously. There is usually a gap of 1–1½ seconds, requiring the slide advance to be hit from one to two words early.

There are, of course, dozens of projectors that are reasonably priced. One of the most dependable is a projector that will handle both the 35 mm slide tray and also has a slot for cassette tape playback. These units can usually be synchronized and silent tones—heard only by the projector—can be put in place on one side of the tape. This enables you to start the projector and forget it. The tray advances when it hears the tones. These tones can be put on in a studio or in your living room when the show is completed and ready for viewing.

As a rule, the larger the visual image, the more effective it will be. If you are in a room with one or two people, most of the 35 mm cassette projectors have self-contained screens that would be sufficient for a limited showing. If you get more than three people, try to show the film on a large screen. Most of the 35 mm cassette projectors have a lens that is usually mounted in the rear and designed for showing on a full-size (6 × 9 or larger) screen.

If you should put the show on for a large audience, investigate the possibilities of using rear-screen projection. This is effective for a large group and enables you to hide the projector behind the screen.

Volume is important in every slide show. You do not want to blow people away by turning the audio volume up too high. At the close of the show, if there is no announcer's voice, it may be advisable to turn the volume up, especially if you have an emotional ending. If you turn it up, do not make it overpowering to the point where it will annoy anyone in the room.

A step-by-step checklist for putting together an audio/visual follows.

Audio/Visual Production Checklist

1. Decide on the audience for the A/V.

2. Determine the needs of those in the audience. What is in your presentation that will answer those needs?

3. Write the slide show with those needs in mind.

4. Make sure the slide show has a beginning, middle, and end.

5. Try to design the slide show as a story, not a lecture.

6. Examine the script to see if it informs the audience; entertains; and answers the needs they have.

7. If it does not, change the show.

8. Time the script. A page of copy (double-spaced) can be read by a professional in about 90 seconds.

9. Keep the slide show under 10 minutes.

10. Reread the slide show script. Make sure there are not any elements that have been forgotten.

11. Review the audience needs once again. Does the slide show address them?

12. Book studio time for the audio portion of the show.

13. Go through the script and list all photo possibilities.

14. If you have photos that may require location shooting, see if you can substitute another picture that will not require location but will tell the same story.

15. Compile a complete list of all needed photos.

16. Compile a list of needed graphics. Wherever possible substitute photos for graphics.

17. Plan a shooting schedule.

18. Get photo approval wherever necessary.

19. Conduct the photo shooting.

20. Go over possible music selections to back the announcer's voice.

21. Decide on whether you will use music in the public domain (no fees) or music which requires a fee.

22. If you need to pay a fee, make sure you settle the fee arrangements with the publisher before you go into the studio and put the music to the tape.

23. Look for music that will help emphasize key passages.

24. Avoid using music with vocals in a slide show. The vocal will take away from the announcer's voice.

25. Select parts of the show that will make a dramatic impact—beginning and usually the end.

26. Select music that is appropriate for these emotional sections. The engineer in the studio can be of great help here.

27. Avoid putting well-known music in key parts of your show. People will find themselves listening to the music instead of the dialogue.

28. Record the vocal (announcer) portion of the show. This should not take more than 90 minutes for a 10 minute show, including the editing.

29. Allow another 90 minutes to put the music on the other track of the tape.

30. Put one version of the audio track on cassette tape while in the studio. The cassettes are used in 35 mm projectors.

31. Select 35 mm photos that will match the dialogue on the audio.

32. Arrange slides so that none stays on for any prolonged period.

33. Try to change slides every 5 to 10 seconds.

34. Tone the cassette so slides change automatically when audio track is played.

CHAPTER 11

LETTERS, SALES, AND TELEPHONE TECHNIQUES

Communication is the backbone of consulting. It is also the most important thing to master in business.

You may be doing a phenomenal job in your company or for your clients but how do they know? Do you communicate with them frequently? Do you send them copies of correspondence so they can see the effort you may be putting forth on their behalf? Do you drop them notes?

Communication is especially important in an intangible business such as consulting. If you are selling shoes, your client or boss only has to look at sales to determine if you are doing a good job. That is not the case with consulting. A consultant may spend two or three weeks (or longer) on a project with no visible results. If the client only sees him or her when a contract is signed, and then a bill is presented, anxiety and suspicion develops.

Every successful consulting firm develops its own technique of communicating. Some have a policy that the person who generated the contract makes a weekly call to the executive within the company who signed it. The call updates the firm and lets them know the consulting firm is at work.

This does not mean that all consultants should be in daily contact with clients, but it does indicate that communication should be on a regular basis, both written and verbal.

Communication is important when it comes to prospecting, too. There are consultants who scour the daily newspaper, local magazines, and trade papers for news concerning potential clients. When they see someone's name mentioned (promotions or awards), they cut the item and mail it to the person with a congratulatory note.

Others read for industry news. If they find something new, something that might be of interest to a present or prospective client, they cut and paste it, reprint it (examples of reprints are in Chapter 5), and mail it.

Some consultants have "tickler" files. Every three months a prospect's name comes up and they mail him or her something. That something may be a report they found that relates to the prospect's industry or it may be a copy of an article. It could also be a note in which the consultant outlines some new and interesting technique that is being utilized in the field. And some consultants simply send thank you notes. There are few things that have greater impact than a thank you.

Correspondence is a sales call. It lets the present and prospective clients know you are out there. A prospect may say no to your services but a few months later his or her situation may change. He or she may suddenly be in the market for services. If you have maintained communication, you will have a stronger bond—and a better chance—for the business than your competitors who may sit by their telephones waiting for the call, never bothering to initiate the communications.

All correspondence should be personalized. Do not send form letters to prospects or clients—it is a turnoff. Think of the impact form letters have when you receive one. Notes and letters will not close the sale, but they keep the door open and your name is constantly in the prospect's mind.

A list of possible communication messages follows.

Important Letters/Notes to Clients

1. Thank you note following potential client meeting
2. Follow-up note reiterating conversation in a meeting
3. Note to prospect/client about item in newspaper/magazine
4. Note to prospect/client regarding his or her promotion
5. Note to prospect/client regarding new development in field
6. Note to prospect/client with article of interest
7. Note to prospect/client reminding him or her you will call
8. Progress report to client on regular basis
9. Blind carbon copy of letter you may be sending to someone on behalf of the client; the blind copy goes to the client
10. Reminder note to client about a program or something you have engineered that is about to take place. For example, you may be giving or be involved in a seminar
11. Note to prospect/client with reprint of article on you or your firm

No communication device has been overused and abused as much as the telephone. Through computers, telemarketing has become both a blessing and a nightmare to businesspeople (and the public). The sales call and pitch are commonplace. Most businesspeople (or their secretaries) field at least one cold call (or more) a day. More than one businessperson has developed frayed nerves and a short temper after taking a call from a salesperson who found one more ingenious way to get around the secretary.

Where does the consultant fit in this environment?

Should he or she spend an hour a day making cold calls; trying to set appointments? That approach may still fly for people selling supplies, charities, or other similar products, however, it does not bode well for the consultant. The former is usually selling low-priced, impersonal items to the masses in business. The latter is trying to reach a narrow audience with a specialized, high-priced, personalized service.

In this environment, the consultant who spends an hour a day on cold calls may wind up turning off more prospects than getting appointments. The telephone, however, can be a potent sales tool for the consultant who uses it in conjunction with some other techniques.

FINANCIAL BROKER CASE STUDY

An east coast financial broker despised cold calling. The hour a day he forced himself to put in on the telephone became a nightmare and his results were negligible. Finally, he decided to do something else. Instead of making an hour of daily calls, he began to go out into his territory. He would stop by offices, retail outlets, and any other places that appeared to house potential clients. He introduced himself and dropped off a card along with a brochure or handout. Before leaving, he would let them know he would call to see if he might be of service. He always asked if there was any best time to call; a time when the businessperson was least busy.

On the surface, personal visit cold calls appear to differ little from the telephone. There is a difference. First, the prospect sees you in-person. He or she knows you are taking time to make a special trip to their place of business—without the promise of a sale—and it is much easier to avoid the call than the personal visitor.

The broker (and any consultant) made it clear from the beginning that he realized they were busy, and he only wanted a minute or two of their time. He qualified the length of the visit from the beginning. By doing so, he alleviated any fear that the prospect might have in terms of the length of the consultant's visit. That initial conversation and visit took less than 3 minutes. Every businessperson he talked to appreciated his brevity.

The financial broker always picked up a card when he was in the prospect's office. He would follow with a short thank you note reminding them of his visit and the fact that he was going to call the following week.

The broker made two powerful impressions. First, an in-person, brief visit, and then a thank you note. When he made the call, he found most prospects willing to listen.

From the call the broker made appointments. In more than 70 percent of the cases he was able to set an appointment via the telephone. Today, that financial broker is one of the most successful consultants in the country. He pyramided his hour-a-day visits into a healthy practice. Take a hint from the financial broker. Make sure the calls have been warmed before dialing. For those consultants who do use the telephone, keep the following in mind.

12 Key Telephone Steps

1. Do not waste the prospect's time. Get to the point.
2. If the prospect is not available, find out what time he or she will be.
3. Find out the best day and time to call back.
4. Friday afternoons are generally a good time for calls. The week is winding down and executives usually do not have the pressure that is found in normal daily routine.

5. Avoid morning calls. This is the time when many executives plan their day. An unscheduled call may throw them off and cause them to inadvertently put you off.

6. If the person you call is not available, do not leave your number. Leave your name and call back when you are given the best time to reach them. There are two reasons for making the call-back yourself. If the prospect returns your call and you are out or busy, he or she throws the message away and feels the obligation has been fulfilled. Also, if you are busy and the call comes in, you may not immediately recognize the prospect's name. There is nothing worse than having a prospect return your call, and you've forgotten why you called or who he or she is.

7. Learn to read voices. If you detect a prospect is rushed or harried, say so. Suggest to him or her that perhaps it would be better if you called back. Is there a convenient time? Businesspeople will appreciate this courtesy.

8. Always make sure to identify yourself and your business. Do not assume because you met the prospect once, he or she will remember your name when you call. Give them your name, occupation, and a reminder about your last conversation. Many of us may remember names, but we forget when we met the person, the circumstances, and what the person's business was.

9. Do not degrade competitors on the telephone (or for that matter, anywhere else).

10. Utilize your USP in your telephone conversations. This helps remind the prospect of your unique service and abilities.

11. Be honest. If you cannot deliver by a certain time, say so.

12. Be courteous to everyone—including secretaries or anyone else who prod you with screening questions. Many of these intermediaries have the confidence and respect of their bosses.

SOURCES OF PROSPECTS

In addition to personal and telephone calls, consultants scour the newspaper for DBAs. These are the names of new companies being formed. The DBAs appear almost daily in local newspapers. These new businesspeople have needs just as established businesspeople do. Send the new businessperson a congratulatory note. Follow up (about four or five days after the note arrives), with a telephone call. Outline your services; your USP. If you can be of service, set an appointment.

Most DBAs do not run telephone numbers when they are filed. This requires the consultant to do some research and track the new number through the telephone company. With a congratulatory note preceding the call, your time may be well spent.

Some consultants subscribe to two or three trade papers that cover their industry. They look for specific news that they know will interest certain clients. They cut, paste, and mail the clips along with a brief note. Although you may have clients within an industry, many do not have time to read the weekly (or monthly) trade papers that cover their field. Most just scan the trades and the paper usually winds up sitting.

Set aside time to read for your prospects. Finding something that interests them is only one reason to read. You may also discover something about the industry that will help you redirect or improve your marketing efforts or other skills. You may suddenly develop an idea for a new service to offer to the industry. Staying familiar with your industry is important.

Consultants—like any businessperson—must sell if their practice is to grow and prosper. Remember, selling is not arm twisting. It is serving, educating, and informing people. It is communicating with them.

SAMPLE LETTERS

Figures 11-1 through 11-12 are examples of letters and client correspondence that can be copied verbatim. You will find everything from thank you notes to complex pitch letters, designed to interest a prospect in your services.

To many, letter writing is an arduous chore. Gary Halbert, a professional copywriter who has penned some of the best sales letters ever composed, has put together a short course on letter writing which will give you insight into the type of material that should be contained in correspondence to present and potential clients. The course will also give you insight into what and why people buy when it comes to a consulting service or, for that matter, any product.

When Halbert put it together, he pretended it was a conversation (in the form of correspondence) between father and son (Bond). The points Halbert makes are revealing and if followed will enable any consultant not only to communicate better with his or her clientele, but increase sales as well.

Dear Bond:

This letter is going to be the first in a long series of letters in which I will attempt to communicate to you a lot of the important things that I have learned in the last 46 years.

I am going to teach you what I have learned about selling by mail, getting and staying healthy, how to get along with people, and in general, how to have a good life without getting yourself all messed up. I'm going to try to write to you every day of the week (except Sunday) and spend about one hour on each letter.

Let's start by looking at customization. For example, suppose you get a letter in the mail that says:

Dear Occupant:

Here is news about a great new way to make money. Etc., etc., etc.

Mildly interesting, but compare it to this . . .

Dear Bond:

Here is a great new way for 16-year-old kids to make money. Etc., etc., etc.

There is a great difference between the two. Just imagine that you were to receive such a letter on or right after June 26. It would get your attention much more than the first letter, wouldn't it?

Notice this, too. The second letter is not only customized (it is for 16-year-olds), it is also personalized because it refers to you by name.

The "Dear Bond" and the "16-year-old kids" part of the letter zeroes in on the reader. Here is another example of customization. Suppose you were writing an ad about a book that tells how to buy real estate with no money down. Your headline might look something like:

How to Buy Real Estate with No Money Down

```
(This should go on your letterhead)


                                        Date


Name
Title (if any)
Company
Address
City, State, Zip

Dear

Just a short note to say many thanks for the time you
spent the other day discussing (name of company).
As I mentioned, it is a fascinatng venture with a $million
worth of publicity potential.

We're in the process of putting together the proposal,
and it should be in your hands within the next week.

I think you will find it addresses areas that are critical
to (name of company) growth.

Once again, many thanks for your time and the insight.

                                        Sincerely,


                                        (your name)

YN/si

cc:  (Name of person carbon copy sent to)

(Note:  This is the type of note you might send to a
prospect following an initial meeting.  It shows you
are not only interested, but enthused about the
project.)
```

FIG. 11-1. Sample Letter

Now, look at this . . .

How to Buy New York Real Estate with No Money Down

It is another example (New York) of customizing. Examine some of the letters you receive in the mail. See if they are customized and personalized. The most effective ones are:

Dear Bond:

How is my favorite youngest son? Today, we are going to get started on the subject of how consultants (and others) can make money.

Usually, when someone asks me what is the number one secret to a consultant's success, I tell them that they should get involved in whatever excites them the most.

```
(This should be on your letterhead)


                                        Date


Name
Title (if any)
Company
Address
City, State, Zip

Dear

Thought you might be interested in the enclosed.  These
ran in last Sunday's (Times) business section, and are
examples of what I meant when I talked about articles
that "are written specifically for the newsaper about
some current, hot topic."

This sets the company up as an authority--and it makes
a great reprint for potential (and existing) clients.

This is one way for a CPA firm to "publicize" itself and
get some incredible, positive feedback.  (The clients,
of course, do not realize that someone wrote it for the
firm.  They believe the Times approached the CPA firm
and asked for it.)

Hope it is of interest.

                                        Sincerely,


                                        (your name)

YN/si

encl.


(Note:  This was sent by a public relations consultant,
but the same thrust could be used by a consultant who
found a technique or procedure that a prospect could
use.)
```

FIG. 11-2. Sample Letter

```
(This should be on your letterhead)


                                               Date


Name
Title (if any)
Company
Address
City, State, Zip

Dear

In the event you have not seen it, the enclosed
is a tear sheet from the spring Torrance Magazine
with your story in it.

Thought you might enjoy a copy.

                                        Best Regards


                                        (your name)


YN/si

encl.


(Note:  This is the type of short note that can be
sent to a prospect when you see something about him
or his company in a newspaper, trade paper or magazine.)
```

FIG. 11-3. Sample Letter

This is good advice. Money, especially big money, is most often a byproduct of enthusiasm. If a person secretly in his or her heart wants to be an architect, he or she should not go into selling real estate just because it is said that that is where the money is.

The money is where the enthusiasm is. Remember this when you hire someone, too. Always look for the most enthusiastic person, not necessarily the best qualified.

Attitude is the most important thing of all. Usually, when I discuss money making with a consultant, I spend a lot more time on attitude because it is so important. But you already have a great attitude, so I will save my discussion for later.

Now, the very first thing a consultant must do in order to become successful, is to become a "student of markets." Not products, not technique, not copywriting. Of course, all of these things are important, and a consultant must know about them, but first a consultant must understand what people want to buy. The way to deduce what people want to buy is simply observe what they do buy.

But be careful. You want to know what people actually do buy, not what they say they buy. Here's a true story. Once a beer company did a survey to determine which products their customers preferred. To their astonishment they found 80 percent of the people they surveyed preferred their premium beer as opposed to their regular beer.

Why were they astonished? Because their sales figures showed that most people bought their regular beer, not the premium. What was going on? There was an easy explanation. The surveyed people were trying to give the "right" answer so they put down the beer they felt they should drink.

Response like that happens all the time. For example, how many people read the *National Enquirer*? Almost everybody you talk to puts it down, and will say they never read it. But the *National Enquirer* is the largest selling newspaper in the world. More than 5 million copies a week.

What do people read? If you took a survey, one of the best read books would be the *Bible*. That, however, is not true. Many people own a *Bible*, but few actually read it. And who can blame them. The *Bible* is repetitive and hard to read. Yet people feel guilty in their attempt to give the *right* answer.

If you want to successfully market your consulting practice you have to know how it is. How it really is. Not how people wish it was or how they think it is. You must become a student of reality.

How do you find out what your customers and potential customers will buy? And, more particularly, how do you find out what they will buy via your letters?

```
      (This should be on your letterhead)


                                        Date

      Name
      Title (if any)
      Company
      Address
      City, State, Zip

      Dear

      Just a short note to express my appreciation for the
      time you and Orlan took in discussing Orion and Smokey
      Mountain--which is certainly going to be a winner.

      I'm in the process of putting together a proposal that
      I think you will find quite interesting.  It should be
      in your hands within the next week or so.

      In the meantime, once again, many thanks for your time
      and interest.

                                        Sincerely


                                        (your name)

      YN/si
      cc:  (name of person carbon copy sent to)

      Encl.
```

FIG. 11-4. Sample Letter

```
                    (This should be on your letterhead)


                                                        Date


        Name
        Title (if any)
        Company
        Address
        City, State, Zip

        Dear

        Just a short note to express my appreciation
        for the slide show reference with the City of
        (name of city).  I talked to Charles Smith
        who said they had almost completed the show;
        i.e. slides were in existence and the script
        had been virtually finalized.  Thus, there
        would be no need, at this time, for our ser-
        vices.

        Still, I certainly appreciate the reference.
        Once again, my thanks.

                                            Sincerely,


                                            (Your Name)


        YN/si


        (Note:  Obviously, this was sent by a consultant
        following a reference.  It shows the person who
        supplied the reference that you appreciate his
        time and efforts--whether you got the client or
        not.)
```

FIG. 11-5. Sample Letter

As we go along, I will supply those answers. The most important concept for now, however, is to be realistic and understand that your customers will not always buy what they say they will. They will buy, however, what they have been buying.

That is proven.

Let's get back to the subject of being a student of markets.

Dear Bond:

Once in a while I give a class on copywriting and/or selling or introducing your services by mail. One of the questions I like to ask is . . .

If you and I both owned a hamburger stand and we were in a contest to see who would sell the most hamburgers, what advantages would you most like to have on your side?

The answers vary. Some people say they would like to have the advantage of having superior meat from which to make their burgers. Others say they want sesame seed buns. Others mention location. Someone usually wants to be able to offer the lowest prices, and so on.

My answer is "I will give you every single advantage you have asked for. I only want one. If you give it to me, I am a sure winner."

What advantage?

The only advantage I want is a *starving crowd*.

Think about it. What I am saying is when you write letters to potential clients, you must be on the lookout for clients who are starving (or at least hungry) for your particular service.

How do you measure this hunger? Let's look at an example. Suppose you want to sell a book on how to invest money and you write a letter. Who do you mail it to? Here are some possibilities.

Possibility 1.   Mail to people whose names you get out of the telephone book.

Comments: Terrible idea.   There are too many nonprospects in this group. Some will not have money to invest. Some never purchase anything by mail. Some are too busy to read your letter. In short there is too much wasted circulation. It is like shooting with a shotgun instead of a rifle.

Possibility 2. Mail to people whose name you get from a telephone book, but limit the mailing to people in high-income areas.

```
    (This should be on your letterhead)



                                    Date


    Name
    Title (if any)
    Company
    Address
    City, State, Zip

    Dear

    Hope you received the "final version."

    Incidentally, if you are thinking about a
    seminar, I have one in mind that I think
    would draw a considerable number of clients
    as well as bankers, etc.

    Next time we sit down we can kick it around.

                                    Best Regards


                                    (Your Name)

    YN/si
    cc:  (Name of person carbon copy sent to)
```

FIG. 11-6. Sample Letter

```
(This should be on your letterhead)


                                                     Date


Name
Title (if any)
Company
Address
City, State, Zip

Dear

Enjoyed the brief chat about publicity, promotion and
your proposed venture.

I've enclosed some information which will give you some
insight into the kind of work we do, and the clients
with whom we have worked.

Look forward to meeting with you.

                                               Sincerely,

                                               (Your Name)

YN/si

Encl.

(Note:  This could be sent by any consultant to a
prospect following an initial meeting.  It would
be a note and packet with a brochure, and other
items of "credibility.")
```

FIG. 11-7. Sample Letter

Comments: Better, but not good enough. High-income areas are, incidentally, easy to identify because several companies have compiled statistics on every U.S. zip code and they can tell you the average age, education level, how much they spend on autos, and so on. This still is not good enough. For one thing, not everyone who lives in a high income area has a high income. Some might be maids or gardeners or some other type of servant. Some may have money but are not interested in your investment service. Some may be interested in investing only in areas in which they already have expertise.

Possibility 3.   Mail to people who have above average incomes (doctors, lawyers, architects, top executives, accountants, owners of Rolls Royce automobiles, and so on).

Comments: Not bad. We are getting into an area where we at least have a chance. Most of these people have a high income, and may be interested in investing. We do not know if they are. However, they probably have the financial ability to invest. This group is more likely to respond. Now, let's improve the odds.

```
(This should be on your letterhead)


                                        Date


Name
Title (if any)
Company
Address
City, State, Zip

Dear

Just a short note to say many thanks for the show the
other day.

The questions were great, and the exposure for the book
was super.

Hope we can do it again.

                                   Sincerely,


                                   (Your Name)


YN/si
```

FIG. 11-8. Sample Letter

```
(This should be on your letterhead)


                                        Date


    Name
    Title (if any)
    Company
    Address
    City, State, Zip

    Dear

    Thought you might like to see how (name of
    company) came out in the upcoming Franchise
    500.  It could be used as an excellent fran-
    chise selling tool.

    Hope you had a happy turkey day.

                              Sincerely,


                              (Your Name)

    YN/si

    Encl.
```

FIG. 11-9. Sample Letter

```
  (This should be on your letterhead)


                                              Date


  Name
  Title (if any)
  Company
  Address
  City, State, Zip

  Dear

  Thought you might be interested in the enclosed.
  This is a local CPA firm we've been representing
  on a few projects.

  Hope everything's going well.

                                              Sincerely,

                                              (Your Name)


  YN/si

  Encl.


  (Note: This refers to some positive results that
  the consulting firm obtained for a client.  The
  firm is passing the results along to a prospect
  so they can see first-hand the type of results
  that this firm gets.)
```

FIG. 11-10. Sample Letter

Possibility 4. Mail to a list of upper-income people who are proven buyers. Buyers of what? Actually for the purpose of selling by mail, it is generally true that mail-order buyers of anything are better than almost any group of nonmail-order buyers. In other words people who have bought a similar service previously are better prospects than people who have never bought.

Comments: Now we are getting close. This is the first group that gives us a reasonable shot at success. But we can do better.

Possibility 5. Mail to a list of wealthy people who have already ordered a similar investment product by mail, and they have purchased it several times.

Comments: Even better. They are buyers, wealthy, and have purchased a product similar to ours several times.

Possibility 6. We could mail to wealthy people who have purchased a product similar to ours several times, and they have paid a great deal of money for what they bought.

Comments: These are close to the best. But we can qualify our market even better.

```
(This should be on your letterhead)


                                            Date


Name
Title (if any)
Company
Address
City, State, Zip

Dear

Enjoyed the brief chat the other day and I think there
is a definite promotional program that could be put to-
gether for dealers that would increase sales significantly.

If there is some interest, I'd like to discuss it with you
in greater detail.  I'll give you a call to see what you
think.


                              Best Regards


                              (Your Name)


YN/si


(Note:  Notice how all follow-up is left to the
consultant who is trying to sell his or her services.
Never leave it to the prospect to call you after he
or she receives correspondence.)
```

FIG. 11-11. Sample Letter

Possibility 7. We could mail our promotion to a list of wealthy people who have purchased a product similar to ours, and have done so repeatedly. They have also paid a great deal of money for their purchases, and recently they made a similar purchase.

Comments: This is a top list. It is certainly the best list we are likely to be able to rent. But there is one more step we can take.

Possibility 8. We can mail to our own customers.

Comments: All things being equal, your own customers—people who have bought from you recently or people you are presently dealing with—will respond better than any leads.

We've spent a good deal of time discussing who to mail to. Now let's look at the mailing piece, especially the outside envelope. This is where most consultants make a mistake.

Everyone divides their mail into "A-pile" and "B-pile" correspondence. The "A-pile" contains letters that appear to be personal. They are from friends, relatives, clients, business associates, and so on.

The "B-pile" contains letters that obviously contain a commercial message. Everyone opens "A-pile" mail first. "B-pile" envelopes are set aside. Sometimes

```
(This should be on your letterhead)


                                            Date


Name
Title (if any)
Company
Address
City, State, Zip

Dear

Many thanks for the time you took discussing the "Super Shuttle."

Briefly, here's the type of launch I envision:

(1)  First week in January a news release along with photos of
the Super Shuttle.  This would go to all media in the South Bay
area including the South Bay section of the Times, etc.  This
would be the announcement of the Shuttle, its tentative schedule,
the area it would cover, etc.

(2)  At the same time, I propose we have a "Super Shuttle Week"
(Jan. 19-26).  There are a number of possibilities in ths area.
During the week, we might designate each day for a different com-
munity and/or group.  For example, the first day might be "busi-
nessman's day" and all businessmen throughout the area could ride
for free or half-price.  The second might be Senior Citizens,
hotel day, etc.

For example, perhaps the 19th is P.V., the 20th Torrance, the
21st El Segundo, etc.  On those particular days, people going to
the airport would get either a reduced (or free) fare.  By recog-
nizing each community, we might be able to get each Mayor to
recognize (and proclaim) "Super Shuttle Week" in his (or her)
community.  To commemorate the week, we could set up photo ses-
sions with Mayors presnting plaques, "driving" the Super Shuttle,
etc.  This would give us additional material for the media.

Since part of the area involves L.A. City, we might be able to
get the Mayor to proclaim the same thing through the area and,
perhaps, get him to pose and drive one of the "Super Shuttles."

The recognition would enable us to get continuous exposure for
Super Shuttle during its inaugural period.  At the same time, it
would also spread goodwill for the company--(name of company) is
providing a free service (if only for a day) for various com-
munties.  You're showing the company is interested in the com-

                            -More-
```

FIG. 11-12. Sample Letter

munity. This, of course, could benefit you later in other deal-
ings.

At the same time, we would be servicing stories and pictures to
Chamber of Commerce publications. There's a possibility of trying
to "sell" one of the local papers on a story pegged around "a day
in the life of a driver." There might also be a TV possibility
pegged around the same theme.

There would, of course, be a number of other promotional and PR
opportunities ranging from follow-up new releases to even a possible business story on (name of company), how it operates and
how it benefits the community.

The program would be designed to call as much attention as possible
to the Super Shuttle during that first week. At the same time, we
would try to get civic recognition and, by doing so, attract maximum exposure in the local media. There could be other promotional
elements--"Super Shuttle" buttons, stickers, t-shirts that could
go along with even a "Ms. Super Shuttle." We could kick these
around and utilize the ones that make sense. Much depends on the
budget.

For designing and carrying out the launch, our fee would be
(amount) plus expenses. No expenses, incidentally, of more than
(amount) would be incurred without prior approval.

I'll call you to see what you think. Once again, many thanks
for your time and interest.

                                        Sincerely,

                                        (Your Name)

YN/si

-2-

FIG. 11-12. (continued)

they are thrown away immediately without the envelope ever being opened, and at best they are opened usually when the recipient has nothing else to do.

To increase your chances of your letter being opened and read, here are a few tips:

Type the name and address of the recipient. Avoid using labels.

Use a first-class stamp, instead of the meter.

There is one other step you can consider. Use your company's address on the outside, not its name. Thus the recipient cannot guess that it comes from "John Jones Personnel Services" or "Mary Smith Management Consulting."

Now, here are some hints as to what should go inside your letters.

Attention, Interest, Desire, Action (AIDA).

Attention comes first. We must get the reader's attention before he or she can become interested in our letter or offer. Remember, however, that you must be relevant with your attention getter. If you use a lead sentence that has nothing to do with the rest of the body copy, it will turn off the prospect. The first few paragraphs should tie-in with the attention-getting introduction. For example, an attention getter could be a sentence leading off with a question, or one that outlines how the prospect can save (or make) money.

Next you have to catch the reader's interest. This can be done with information and facts, by educating the prospect.

Desire follows and can be created by describing the benefits our potential customer can derive if he buys our service. Benefits may seem obvious but they should always be stated. Repeat the obvious. The benefit of owning a new home is not owning a new home, but living in comfort, luxury, and having improved status.

The benefit of a prospect going for your offer or investment is not riches, but peace of mind and never worrying about bills or financial emergencies. In other words, look for the underlying phrases and meanings of the benefits. Life insurance is protection for one's family, not a $100,000 death benefit.

And no letter to a prospect is complete without a call-to-action. Either you call the prospect, or he or she calls you or something is mailed into your office.

One last thing—appearance. Make sure your letter is easy to read. Use short paragraphs and make sure there is plenty of white space between the words and the borders of the page. Short paragraphs and white space give letters the appearance of being easy to read. That's what you want, a letter that the prospect perceives as being easy to read.

Follow these hints and your letters and direct mail solicitations will have a much greater chance for success. Remember, the object of a letter, especially in a service business like consulting, is to give the recipient the visual impression that you can provide personalized, quality service.

CHAPTER 12

CREDIT, COLLECTIONS, AND ACCOUNTING

Good credit, prompt collections, and an accurate accounting system which aids you in forecasting your overhead and expenses are the lifeblood of a consultant's practice. You may be the best consultant in your field, but if you are poor at collecting and paying bills, and live a lifestyle above your means, you will not be in business for long.

Many consultants despise the rigors of bookkeeping. They hate asking clients for money, especially if it is overdue. If you are one of those, the best thing is to hire a bookkeeper or accountant who will do your billing, call when receivables are outstanding, and will be objective, as well as set a standard for collections and billing.

Some consultants use assistants, secretaries, or other office personnel if it becomes necessary to call a client and ask for overdue monies.

BILLING AND COLLECTION PROCEDURE

There are tactful approaches. Someone can call (your wife or husband, if need be) your client, ask for the accounting department, and introduce themselves as your bookkeeper. They can ask if the client received the bill. If so, is there a question? Does the client have any idea when payment will be made? When collecting funds, it is always a good idea to credit the call to your bookkeeping department. In other words, you never call for the funds, the bookkeeper does.

Every bill and/or invoice that goes out should have a notation on it as to the terms, such as net 10; due the 1st; whatever. A bill should never be sent without a due date. If one is, the client may give it to his or her accounting department, and they could hold it for 90 days or more. A date gives the invoice a sense of urgency.

Expenses should be backed with receipts. You can photocopy a telephone bill and highlight the client's long-distance calls with a pen. If you duplicate materials for a client, get a receipt from the printer, and have the job spelled out.

If you rent a car, take someone to lunch or dinner, or whatever, always get a receipt and include it in the client's bill.

It is poor policy to bill and estimate expenses such as telephone, duplicating, and so on. This can become annoying to the client and cause him or her to question other aspects of your bill.

Clients should be billed on a timely basis. That is, if your bills are due on the 1st, make sure the client gets your bill at least 10 days in advance of the due date. Do not send the bill on the 30th and expect to get the check on the 2nd.

Your billings should be part of a regular cycle. If you send them out on the 15th, make sure you are consistent and always send them on the 15th.

If you are a consultant that is paid a monthly retainer, your retainer (typically) should be paid before the work is done. In other words, if you work for a client during the month of June, your retainer is due June 1st.

If you bill on an hourly basis, make sure you keep close track of the hours (each employee should mark a time sheet which has room for the client's name and the hours spent). When the bill is sent it should break down the hours and days on which the work was done.

Before establishing your billing procedures, go through the following checklist.

Billing and Collection Procedure Checklist

1. Establish a definite credit and collection policy.
2. Bill promptly.
3. Put due date and terms on each bill that leaves your office.
4. Have receipts for all expenditures; include copies with bill.
5. Do not estimate expenses.
6. Have someone within your office be responsible for collections.
7. Have the responsible party call when overdue bills exceed the "grace" period. (A grace is a period of time allowed between the due date, a second notice, or a telephone call. A consultant, for example, may have a client's bill that is due on the 10th. Between the 10th and 17th the consultant may establish a grace period. Nothing is done—no reminders or the like—until this period passes.)

Equally as important as collecting funds is paying your bills. Payables form the basis for your credit rating. Although you may not foresee the need for loans and so forth, there may come a time when you decide you want to expand, purchase an expensive piece of equipment, or something similar. You may not want to drain your capital. If that is the case, credit becomes extremely important.

Handle bills from vendors in a timely manner. A good policy is to pay bills within 30 days. Your credit habits can become an asset or liability in business. If you get in the habit of paying vendors on time, you will find they will go out of their way to serve you. If you have a problem and need something from a vendor immediately, you have a good chance of getting it—if your payments have been timely.

There is an interesting adage in business: Get all the credit you can when you *do not need it*. Establish credit lines early because if you are faced with attempting to establish credit when you do need it, chances are it will be difficult to obtain the funds.

At the same time, make your money work for you. We live in volatile economic times. Interest rates may be up or down at anytime. A consultant's cash-on-hand can be significant. For example, he or she may incur major expenses on behalf of the client; the client pays, the consultant finds himself or herself with thousands of dollars of revenue on hand. The revenue will go to pay the expenses but the expenses may not be due. The consultant may be able to work with the money for 30 days. If so, be aware of the options you have through the bank and/or an investment service. Through one of these services you may be able to earn additional interest income.

This brings up an important ingredient in any business—a banking relationship. Consulting, of course, is not an enterprise like automobile or steel manufacturing. The only thing tangible about consulting is the consultant. There are no products, inventory, or similar materials to put up for collateral.

Consultants will find, whether they incorporate or not, that bankers will usually require them to put up personal assets when borrowing money. Still, a consultant can establish a credit line. Even if you do not need the credit line it is important for one reason—you may need it one day.

Banking relationships are often misunderstood. Banks are service businesses. They are in business to grant loans and serve customers. If they never extend credit, they will never make money for their shareholders or depositors.

You want to establish a relationship and account with a bank and banker you can communicate with on a regular basis. This may not be the branch of a large chain. Branch banks may be restricted in the authority they give to managers. At the same time, executives within branch banks may change frequently or be transferred to other branches in the system.

It is important to find a bank where the manager or executive you deal with understands your business. If they understand it, they can more readily accommodate credit requests. Try to avoid a bank where they show little understanding or patience with your field of expertise.

Find a good, local community bank (if there is one in your area). Find one where you can establish rapport with the banker. When you look for a bank, spend time interviewing the banker. To some, this is confusing because they are intimidated by bankers. There is no reason to be. Remember, the banker is going to be selling you a service, much as you sell a client a service. He or she is going to take your money and make money from it.

Banking is a major investment for the small businessperson. Before you invest any funds in a bank, make sure you and the banker can communicate. Make sure you can see him or her whenever you need to and that the future needs of your business are addressed at the beginning of your relationship. Developing a relationship with a banker can help consultants in other ways. Generally bankers know the financial condition of companies within their area or they can find out. If you have been dealing with a client and are worried about payment, you may gain valuable insight from your banker—if you have a good confidential relationship with him or her.

It pays to put all your funds in one bank. The deposits give you more muscle and will enhance your importance. It is all right to shop around for banks and bankers, but once you find one, stick to it.

Some hints on selecting a bank and banker follow.

10 Guidelines for Selecting Bank/Banker

1. Survey banks in area; types of services they offer; businesses and industries they serve.

2. Ask other businesspeople for references and insights into local banks.

3. Narrow selection of potential banks and make appointments for interviewing bankers at banks that deal with your profession or industry.

4. Narrow this selection to banks that understand the cash flow and accounting of a consulting and/or service business.

5. Look for banks that have autonomy. That is, they can make loan and credit line decisions in-house.

6. Talk to bankers about credit lines.

7. Talk to bankers about special services; interest bearing accounts.

8. Narrow selection to banker with whom you have rapport.

9. Make bank selection.

10. Obtain credit line.

Budgeting is important in any business. Look at your accounts, receivables, rent, telephone, other overhead, and do some forecasting. If you have a computer there are numerous software programs that will help in this area.

Even without a computer, budgeting is simple in the consulting field. You can easily isolate your fixed and variable expenses. Add the fixed expenses. Variable will be more difficult, but you might take an average of three or four months to get an idea what you normally spend. Do not forget to include taxes, which can be substantial especially in states which have both corporate and individual tax rates. These figures should include all your expenses and your salary.

At the same time, look at your sales (or income). Are you taking in more money than you are spending? Silly question? Not really. In some businesses a firm may go in the red for six months before they discover they are not making money. Magazine publishing is an example. A consultant may be fooled, too, unless he or she has carefully detailed all overhead and looked closely at his or her client base and the income derived from them.

From a tax standpoint, many businesses lose money. Do not, however, confuse the paper loss of funds with an actual loss.

In the remainder of this chapter you will find a variety of forms (Figures 12-1 through 12-12) pertaining to finance, banking, personnel, and credit.

The questions on the financial statement and bank loan application will give you insight into the type of requirements bankers seek.

Personnel background is often overlooked. However, if a consultant is going to have a firm that grows with dependable help, the questions and background check of potential employees is necessary. The bookkeeping forms will give you an idea of how entering of income and expenses should be handled. There is also a postage form which enables the consultant to keep track of any mailing activity that is performed on behalf of the client.

TO: **The Torrance National Bank**

RESOLVED: That this organization establish in its name one or more deposit accounts with THE TORRANCE NATIONAL BANK upon such terms and conditions as may be agreed upon with said Bank and that the

_____ and _____ of this
TITLE   TITLE

organization be and they are hereby authorized to establish such an account.
RESOLVED: That

_____ (Title)
(PRINT OR TYPE NAME)

and/or _____ (Title)
(PRINT OR TYPE NAME)

and/or _____ (Title)
(PRINT OR TYPE NAME)

and/or _____ (Title)
(PRINT OR TYPE NAME)

and/or _____ (Title)
(PRINT OR TYPE NAME)

of this organization be, and they are hereby authorized to draw checks on said account of this organization, signed as provided herein with signatures duly certified to said Bank by the Secretary of this organization and said Bank is hereby authorized to honor and pay any and all checks so signed, including those drawn to the individual order of any officer or other person authorized to sign the same.

I hereby certify that the foregoing is a full, true and correct copy of the resolution adopted by the Board of the

_____
(NAME OF CORPORATION)

_____
(ADDRESS)

at a meeting of said Board regularly held on the _____ day of _____, 19___ and that the signatures appearing on the reverse side of this card are the signatures of the persons duly authorized to withdraw funds of said organization from said Bank in accordance with the above resolution until such authority is revoked by giving written notice thereof to said Bank signed by the officers of said organization thereunto duly authorized by its Governing Body.

WITNESS my hand and seal of the organization.

(SEAL)
_____
(SIGNATURE)   SECRETARY

We hereby certify the foregoing to be correct: **(FOR LODGE, ASSOCIATION)**

1. _____   2. _____
   RETIRING OFFICER (TITLE)   RETIRING OFFICER (TITLE)

FOR BANK USE ONLY

Previous Bank _____   Savings Account _____
or Branch

Opened   Original
By _____   Opening Date _____   Amount _____

Closed   Date
By _____   Closed _____   **Reason** _____

NA-404 FINANCIAL SUPPLIERS

1. _____
   SIGNATURE

2. _____
   SIGNATURE

3. _____
   SIGNATURE

4. _____
   SIGNATURE

ACCOUNT NUMBER

ACCOUNT NAME

FIG. 12-1. Bank signature card agreement/corporation. (*Figure continued on p. 290.*)

289

THE TORRANCE NATIONAL BANK

Corporation, Association, Society
SIGNATURE CARD AGREEMENT

Date: _____

☐ CHECKING ☐ NOW ☐ MONEY MARKET ☐ SAVINGS
☐ TIME CERTIFICATE OF DEPOSIT ☐ OTHER _____

STATEMENTS: ☐ MAIL ☐ HOLD FOR PICK-UP

BY SIGNING THIS AGREEMENT, THIS ☐ CORPORATION ☐ ASSOCIATION ☐ SOCIETY

★ Opens the type of account indicated above and agrees to be bound by the Bank's rules concerning the account.

★ Promises to pay the Bank's service charges and fees as disclosed in the SCHEDULE OF FEES and CHARGES and any overdrafts on the account under the terms of the DEPOSIT ACCOUNT AGREEMENT.

★ Acknowledges receipt of the current DEPOSIT ACCOUNT AGREEMENT, SCHEDULE OF FEES and CHARGES, signature card and any other disclosure required for the type of account.

★ (CHECK BOX IF APPLICABLE) — Under penalty of perjury, the undersigned certify:

☐ 1. That the taxpayer identification number (or social security number) shown on this form for each account-holder is the correct number of the accountholder shown.

☐ 2. That each accountholder is not subject to backup withholding either because such accountholder has not been notified that they are subject to backup withholding as a result of a failure to report all interest or dividends, or the Internal Revenue Service has notified such accountholder that they are no longer subject to backup withholding.

_____ (INITIAL)

(Do not check Box 2 if any accountholder has been notified that they are subject to backup withholding and such accountholder has not received notice from the IRS that backup withholding has terminated. **Also, if Box 2 does not apply, strike out that paragraph and initial it.**)

NAME OF ACCOUNT (To be filled in by Bank)

ACCOUNT NUMBER _____
OPENING DATE _____

The Bank is authorized to pay out funds with any _____ NUMBER of the authorized signatures below.

NAME (TYPE)	SIGNATURE	TAXPAYER IDENTIFICATION NUMBER (TIN)	OFFICIAL TITLE
1.			
2.			
3.			
4.			
5.			
6.			

NA-404 FINANCIAL SUPPLIERS

NA-14/8

FIG. 12-1. (continued)

THE TORRANCE NATIONAL BANK   Partnership, Sole Ownership, Joint Venture

SIGNATURE CARD AGREEMENT

Date: _____

☐ CHECKING ☐ NOW ☐ MONEY MARKET ☐ SAVINGS
☐ TIME CERTIFICATE OF DEPOSIT ☐ OTHER _____

OWNERSHIP: ☐ JOINT VENTURE ☐ PARTNERSHIP ☐ LIMITED PARTNERSHIP ☐ SOLE OWNERSHIP

STATEMENTS: ☐ MAIL ☐ HOLD FOR PICK-UP

BY SIGNING THIS AGREEMENT, The Firm

★ Opens the type of account indicated above and agrees to be bound by the Bank's rules concerning the account.
★ And each of the undersigned in his undivided capacity promises to pay the Bank's service charges and fees as disclosed in the SCHEDULE OF FEES and CHARGES and any overdrafts on the account under the terms of the DEPOSIT ACCOUNT AGREEMENT.
★ Acknowledges receipt of the current DEPOSIT ACCOUNT AGREEMENT, SCHEDULE OF FEES and CHARGES, signature card and any other disclosure required for the type of account.
★ (CHECK BOX IF APPLICABLE)—Under penalties of perjury, the undersigned certify:
  ☐ 1. That the taxpayer identification number (or social security number) shown on this form for each accountholder is the correct number of the accountholder shown.
  ☐ 2. That each accountholder is not subject to backup withholding either because such accountholder has not been notified that they are subject to backup withholding as a result of a failure to report all interest or dividends, or the Internal Revenue Service has notified such accountholder that they are no longer subject to backup withholding.
(Do not check Box 2 if any accountholder has been notified that they are subject to backup withholding and such accountholder has not received notice from the IRS that backup withholding has terminated. **Also, if Box 2 does not apply, strike out that paragraph and initial it.**)

_____ (INITIAL)

  This account is opened and held by the undersigned as the sole owner or by the undersigned in their representative capacities as all the general partners or co-venturers of this firm.

  This authorization shall remain effective until the Bank receives written notice to the contrary signed by all of the undersigned. All previous authorizations heretofore given with respect to said account are revoked. The revocation of this or previous authorization shall not affect the validity of any item signed or endorsed by any person or persons at the time authorized to act. Each of the undersigned in his individual capacity guarantees payment of any overdraft created in this account.

  ☐ If the adjacent box is checked, the Firm shall continue in existence after the death of any of the undersigned provided that a) if this is a limited partnership, at least one of the undersigned survives, or b) if this is a general partnership, at least two of the undersigned survive.

  All items shall be signed for the Firm by the required number of authorized signers indicated below. The Bank or undersigned (with minimum signatures required to transact business) may terminate this banking relationship at any time.

NA-403 FINANCIAL SUPPLIERS

FIG. 12-2. Bank signature card partnership/sole proprietor. *(Figure continued on p. 292.)*

ACCOUNT NAME

ACCOUNT NO.

Checks to be signed by nos. _____ Checks to be countersigned by nos. _____

1. _____ 2. _____
   Authorized Signature   Authorized Signature

3. _____ 4. _____
   Authorized Signature   Authorized Signature

Street Address _____ City _____

Business _____ Telephone _____

| TAX ACCT. |
| NUMBER |

1. _____ 2. _____
   (Signature)   (Signature)

3. _____ 4. _____
   (Signature)   (Signature)

FOR BANK USE ONLY

Previous Bank
or Branch Office _____ Sav. Acct. Number _____
   ☐ Ck
   ☐ Cs

Opened
By _____ Date _____ Amount _____

Introduced
By _____ Date Closed _____ Reason _____

(Page 2)

ACCOUNT
NUMBER

ACCOUNT
NAME

Checks to be signed by Nos. _____ Countersigned by Nos. _____

1 _____
   SIGNATURE

2 _____
   SIGNATURE

3 _____
   SIGNATURE

4 _____
   SIGNATURE

FIG. 12-2. (continued)

FINANCIAL STATEMENT

INDIVIDUAL FORM

If married, you may apply for a separate account.

FILL ALL BLANKS, WRITING "NO" OR "NONE" WHERE NECESSARY TO COMPLETE INFORMATION

	NAME	
To: **The Torrance National Bank**	From:	

For the purpose of procuring and establishing credit from time to time with you, each of the undersigned furnish the following as a true and accurate statement of the **FINANCIAL CONDITION OF THE**

UNDERSIGNED ON _____ , 19 ___

The undersigned agree to and will notify you immediately in writing of any material change in the financial condition of the undersigned and in the absence of such notice or of a new and full written statement, this may be considered as a continuing statement and substantially correct; and it is hereby expressly agreed that upon application for further credit, this statement shall have the same force and effect as if delivered as an original statement of the financial condition of the undersigned at the time such further credit is requested. In consideration of the granting of such credit the undersigned and each of them agree that if the undersigned or any or either of them, or any endorser or guarantor of the obligations of the undersigned or any or either of them at any time fail or become insolvent or commit an act of bankruptcy, or if any deposit account of the undersigned or any or either of them with you, or any other property of the undersigned or any or either of them held by you be attempted to be obtained or held by writ of execution, garnishment, attachment, or other legal process, or if any of the representations made below prove to be untrue or if the undersigned or any or either of them fail to notify you of any material change as above agreed, or if any such material change occurs, then and in either case all obligations of the undersigned or any or either of them held by you shall immediately become due and payable without demand or notice. All sums at any time in any deposit account shall be subject to Bank's right to set-off for liabilities owed to the Bank by any of the undersigned, to the fullest extent permissible by applicable law, and upon any other personal property of the undersigned or any or either of them in your possession, from time to time, to secure obligations of undersigned and each of them, either as borrower or guarantor, held by you, and further agree that all obligations or any part thereof, of the undersigned or any or either of them held by you, both matured and unmatured, may at any time be charged against the balance of any deposit account of the undersigned or any or either of them with you, without notice to the undersigned.

If you are married, complete all information for yourself and your spouse. You do not have to list spouse's separate property unless this is an application for a joint account. You do not have to list income from alimony, child support or maintenance unless you want the Bank to consider it for purposes of the application for credit.

ASSETS	$		LIABILITIES	$	
CASH IN TTNB–CHECKING ACCOUNT			NOTE PAYABLE TO _____ BANK . .		
CASH IN TTNB–SAVINGS ACCOUNT			OTHER NOTES PAYABLE, DUE WITHIN ONE YEAR		
CASH IN _____ (OTHER–GIVE NAME)			ACCOUNTS AND BILLS PAYABLE–NOT DUE		
ACCOUNTS RECEIVABLE–CURRENT			ACCOUNTS AND BILLS PAYABLE–PAST DUE		
NOTES RECEIVABLE–CURRENT			DUE TO RELATIVES		
STOCKS AND BONDS LISTED ON EXCHANGES (DETAIL ON SCHEDULE)			TRUST DEEDS, MORTGAGES OR OTHER LIENS ON REAL ESTATE, DUE WITHIN ONE YEAR		
OTHER CURRENT ASSETS: DESCRIBE			NOTES SECURED BY PERSONAL PROPERTY		
			OTHER LIABILITIES: DUE WITHIN ONE YEAR		
TOTAL CURRENT ASSETS			**INCOME TAXES DUE AND/OR ACCRUED**		
			TOTAL CURRENT LIABILITIES		
NOTES SECURED BY FIRST TRUST DEEDS, MORTGAGES OR OTHER LIENS ON REAL ESTATE, ALL GOOD .					
NOTES SECURED BY SECOND TRUST DEEDS, MORTGAGES OR OTHER LIENS ON REAL ESTATE, ALL GOOD .			TRUST DEEDS, MORTGAGES, OR OTHER LIENS ON REAL ESTATE, DUE AFTER ONE YEAR		
ACCOUNTS AND NOTES RECEIVABLE, SLOW			NOTES AND BILLS PAYABLE, DUE AFTER ONE YEAR		
DUE FROM RELATIVES			OTHER LIABILITIES; DESCRIBE		
STOCKS AND BONDS NOT LISTED ON EXCHANGE (DETAIL ON SCHEDULE) . . .					
REAL ESTATE (DETAIL ON SCHEDULE) . . .					
PRESENT CASH SURRENDER VALUE OF LIFE INSURANCE (REPORT AMOUNT BORROWED IN OTHER LIABILITIES) . . .					
AUTOMOBILE: MAKE_____ YEAR _____					
OTHER ASSETS; DESCRIBE			TOTAL LIABILITIES		
			NET WORTH		
TOTAL ASSETS	$		**TOTAL**	$	

ARE YOU CONTINGENTLY LIABLE FOR ANY ENDORSEMENTS OR GUARANTEES? ☐ YES ☐ NO

IF YES, GIVE DETAILS _____

ANNUAL INCOME AND EXPENSE FOR PERIOD FROM _____ TO _____

INCOME:

		EXPENSE:	
EARNINGS	$ _____	INTEREST	$ _____
RENTALS	$ _____	TAXES AND ASSESSMENTS	$ _____
DIVIDENDS	$ _____	UPKEEP ON REAL ESTATE	$ _____
INTEREST	$ _____	PAYMENT UPON MORTGAGES, CONTRACTS, ETC. . . .	$ _____
OTHER INCOME (YOU DO NOT HAVE TO LIST INCOME FROM ALIMONY, CHILD SUPPORT OR MAINTENANCE UNLESS YOU WANT THE BANK TO CONSIDER IT FOR THE PURPOSE OF THIS APPLICA- TION FOR CREDIT.)	$ _____	RENT	$ _____
		PERSONAL LIVING EXPENSE	$ _____
(If you are married, your earnings, your spouse's earnings and all other income is presumed to be community property unless you indicate otherwise.)	$ _____	OTHER EXPENSE	$ _____
TOTAL INCOME	$ _____	TOTAL EXPENSE	$ _____

ARE ANY OF YOUR ASSETS HELD IN JOINT TENANCY, TENANCY IN COMMON OR COMMUNITY PROPERTY? ☐ YES ☐ NO

IF YES, GIVE DETAILS _____

CL-304   3-78L

FIG. 12-3. Sample financial statement. *(Figure continued on p. 294.)*

INSURANCE

TYPE	AMOUNT	COMPANY	BENEFICIARY
LIFE	$		
OTHER	$		
AGENT – Name and Address			

SCHEDULE OF STOCKS AND BONDS

NUMBER OF SHARES OR PAR VALUE OF BONDS	DESCRIPTION	ISSUED IN NAME OF	COST	MARKET VALUE	LISTED OR UNLISTED
			$	$	

ARE YOU AWARE OF ANY RESTRICTIONS DEALING WITH THE TRANSFER OR SALE OF THE ABOVE SECURITIES? ☐ YES ☐ NO	IF YES, GIVE DETAILS
ARE ANY OF YOUR STOCKS OR BONDS IN JOINT TENANCY TENANCY IN COMMON OR COMMUNITY PROPERTY? ☐ YES ☐ NO	IF YES, INDICATE HOW YOUR STOCKS ARE HELD

SCHEDULE OF REAL ESTATE

LEGAL DESCRIPTION & ADDRESS (ALSO GIVE BRIEF PHYSICAL DESCRIPTION)	DATE ACQUIRED	TITLE IN NAME OF	COST	MARKET VALUE	TRUST DEED, MORTGAGE OR OTHER LIENS			
					UNPAID BALANCE	MONTHLY PAYMENT	RENTAL INCOME	HELD BY
		TOTAL	$	$	$	$		

IS ANY OF ABOVE REAL ESTATE SUBJECT TO DECLARATION OF HOMESTEAD? ☐ YES ☐ NO	IS ANY OF YOUR REAL PROPERTY HELD IN JOINT TENANCY, TENANCY IN COMMON OR COMMUNITY PROPERTY? ☐ YES ☐ NO
ARE YOU LEASING ANY REAL OR PERSONAL PROPERTY? ☐ YES ☐ NO	IF YES, GIVE DETAILS AS TO TERMS OF LEASES

BANKING CONNECTIONS

NAME OF BANKS IN WHICH YOU CARRY ACCOUNTS

HAVE YOU PREVIOUSLY BORROWED FROM OTHER BANKS? ☐ YES ☐ NO	WERE YOUR BORROWINGS ☐ UNSECURED ☐ SECURED ☐ ENDORSED	PREVIOUS MAXIMUM AMOUNT BORROWED FROM BANKS $

PAST AND PRESENT BUSINESS CONNECTIONS

NAME OF EMPLOYERS OR ASSOCIATES	LOCATION	DATE OF CONNECTION	DATE CONNECTION TERMINATED

GENERAL INFORMATION

AGE	☐ MARRIED ☐ UNMARRIED ☐ SEPARATED	OCCUPATION	TELEPHONE Work ( ) Home ( )	SOCIAL SECURITY NUMBER
STREET ADDRESS			CITY	ZIP CODE

HAVE YOU EVER FAILED IN BUSINESS OR COMPROMISED DEBTS WITH YOUR CREDITORS? ☐ YES ☐ NO	IF YES, GIVE DETAILS	DO YOU HAVE A WILL? ☐ YES ☐ NO
ARE ANY OF YOUR ASSETS PLEDGED OR IN ANY OTHER MANNER UNAVAILABLE FOR PAYING DEBTS? ☐ YES ☐ NO	IF UNAVAILABLE OR PLEDGED, GIVE DETAILS	
ARE THERE ANY SUITS, JUDGEMENTS, EXECUTIONS OF ATTACHMENTS AGAINST YOU PENDING? ☐ YES ☐ NO	IF YES, GIVE DETAILS	

COMPLETE THIS PART ONLY 1. IF YOU ARE MARRIED. 2. YOU ARE RELYING ON ALIMONY, CHILD SUPPORT OR MAINTENANCE AS INCOME.

NAME AND ADDRESS OF SPOUSE OR FORMER SPOUSE	SOC. SEC. NO.	AGE	BUS. PHONE NO. ( )
NAME AND ADDRESS OF SPOUSE'S OR FORMER SPOUSE'S EMPLOYER	POSITION	HOW LONG YR.- MO.-	MO. SALARY $

APPLICANT'S SIGNATURE DATE	CO-APPLICANT'S SIGNATURE (IF THIS IS TO BE A JOINT ACCOUNT) DATE

YOUR SPOUSE'S SIGNATURE IS NOT REQUIRED IF THIS IS TO BE YOUR SEPARATE ACCOUNT

YOUR SPOUSE'S OR FORMER SPOUSE'S AUTHORIZATION MAY BE NEEDED IF YOU ARE RELYING ON HIS OR HER INCOME OR OTHER COMMUNITY PROPERTY.	(OPTIONAL) SIGNATURE—TO AUTHORIZE VERIFICATION OF INCOME OR CREDIT HISTORY **ONLY**

FIG. 12-3. (continued)

GENERAL LOAN APPLICATION

To: The TORRANCE NATIONAL BANK

TYPE OF CREDIT DESIRED: ☐ AUTOMOBILE LOAN   ☐ PERSONAL   ☐ EVER-REDI   ☐ OTHER _____

Specify

Amount Requested $	Terms Requested	Collateral Offered (if any)	Office

EVEN IF MARRIED YOU MAY APPLY FOR A SEPARATE ACCOUNT. This application covers a request for (check one) ☐ Separate Credit ☐ Joint Credit

IF CO-APPLICANT IS OTHER THAN APPLICANT'S SPOUSE, CO-APPLICANT MUST COMPLETE A SEPARATE GENERAL LOAN APPLICATION

IF JOINT CREDIT, STATE NAME OF CO-APPLICANT: _____

The Federal Equal Credit Opportunity Act prohibits creditors from discriminating against credit applicants on the basis of sex or marital status. The Federal Agency which administers compliance with this law concerning this bank is the Comptroller of the Currency, Consumer Affairs Division, Washington, D.C. 20219.

PART A — YOUR PERSONAL INFORMATION

Name		Age	Social Security No.	Driver's License No.

CHECK ONE ☐ Married   ☐ Unmarried   ☐ Separated

	No. Dependents	Home Phone

Current Address Street	City	State	Zip	How Long? Yrs. Mos.

☐ OWN HOME ☐ RENT	Mo. Pmt. or Rent $	Mortgage Bal.	Lienholder Name and Address

Previous Address Street	City	State	Zip	How Long? Yrs. Mos.

Name and Address of Nearest Relative not Living with You	Relationship	Home Phone

PART B — YOUR EMPLOYMENT AND INCOME

NOTE: All income of married individuals will be considered as community property unless you indicate otherwise.

Name of Employer	Position	How Long?	Mo. Earnings	Phone
Address of Employer	Previous Employer			How Long?

OTHER INCOME   NOTE: You do not have to list alimony, child support, or maintenance unless you want us to consider it in evaluating this application.

Source of Other Income	Amount $	Check One: ☐ Monthly ☐ Quarterly ☐ Annually

PART C — YOUR SPOUSE

Complete this part ONLY IF:
1) Your spouse will use the account or will be contractually liable for the account, or
2) You are relying on child support or maintenance income in applying for this account or
3) You want us to consider your spouse's income or other community property in order to obtain credit.

Name		Age	Social Security No.	Driver's License No.

Current Address Street	City	State	Zip	How Long?

Name and Address of Employer	How Long?	Mo. Earning?	Bus. Phone

PART D — OBLIGATIONS AND CREDIT REFERENCES

Please indicate name account is carried in if other than your own. If you are married we will assume all obligations are ones for which the community is liable unless you indicate otherwise.

NAME AND ADDRESS OF CREDITOR	ACCOUNT NUMBER	ORIG. AMT.	BAL. OWING	MO. PAYMENT
(Last home/auto financed)				

IF YOU NEED ADDITIONAL SPACE PLEASE LIST ON A SEPARATE PIECE OF PAPER AND ATTACH.

PART E — BANKING RELATIONSHIP

CHECKING	Bank Name and Location	Account No.
SAVINGS	Bank Name and Location	Account No.

OPTIONAL:
If the loan is granted, you are hereby authorized to charge the payments to my checking

account # _____ at _____ OFFICE # _____

Signature	Date	Signature	Date

REVOKED: _____   _____

Date   Signature

PLEASE DISBURSE LOAN PROCEEDS AS FOLLOWS:
☐ CREDIT CHECKING
   ACCOUNT NO. _____
☐ OTHER _____
☐ ISSUE CASHIERS
   CHECK TO _____

CREDIT INSURANCE DESIRED: ☐ Joint Life   ☐ Single Life   ☐ Disability (Single)
APPLICANT: YOU ARE NOT ELIGIBLE IF YOU HAVE REACHED YOUR 65TH BIRTHDAY.

I have completed this Application to obtain credit, and certify that the above statements and those on the reverse are true. I authorize the Bank to check my credit references and to verify my employment. I also authorize the Bank to provide credit information arising from this transaction to others. Applicant must sign below. If applicant is married, applicant's spouse must also sign if jointly applying for this loan. Signing this application will not make the signors contractually liable to repay the Loan.

APPLICANT'S SIGNATURE	DATE	SPOUSE'S SIGANTURE, IF REQUIRED — See immediately above.	DATE

L-100 Financial Suppliers

FIG. 12-4. Sample loan application. (_Figure continued on p. 296._)

SIMPLE INTEREST PERSONAL LOAN
WORKSHEET AND DISBURSEMENT INSTRUCTIONS

NAME(S) OF BORROWER(S)

PROPERTY IMPROVEMENT WORKSHEET

CHECK-OFF LIST	DATE REQUESTED	DATE RECEIVED OR COMPLETED	PROPERTY EQUITY	
1. INCOME TAX RETURN OR FINANCIAL STMT			APPRAISAL	$
2. CREDIT CLEARANCE			PRICE PAID	$
3. APPRAISAL			T.D. BALANCES	$
4. LOT BOOK REPORT			EQUITY (BASED ON APPRAISAL OR PRICE PAID)	$
5. DEALER NOTIFIED	APPR	REJ	**INCOME**	
6. LOAN DOCUMENTS				
7. DEED OF TRUST—RECORDED			APPLICANT'S INCOME	$
8. REQUEST FOR NOTICE—RECORDED			OTHER INCOME	$
9. FEES PAID			OTHER INCOME	$
10. DISCLOSURE STATEMENT (SEPARATE COPY TO EACH CUSTOMER)			TOTAL INCOME	$
11. NOTICE OF RIGHT OF RECISSION (TWO COPIES TO EACH CUSTOMER)			LESS: FIXED PAYMENT—OUR PAYMENT—INC. TAX	$
12. FLOOD HAZARD INSURANCE			NET EXCESS	$

VEHICLE INSPECTION REPORT

REGISTERED OWNER				LEGAL OWNER	

YEAR/CYL.	MAKE	MODEL	SERIAL OR I.D. NUMBER	LICENSE NUMBER	SPEEDOMETER READING

CONDITION - EXPLAIN (PAINT, BODY, GLASS, MOTOR, TIRES, UPHOLSTERY, ETC.)

☐ P/B ☐ P/S ☐ P/W ☐ A/T ☐ AIR ☐ AM-FM STEREO RADIO ☐ SMOG DEVICE ☐ OTHER

INSPECTED BY	DATE INSPECTED

CASH SALE PRICE	BOOK RETAIL	BOOK WHOLESALE	LOAN VALUE: SEE CURRENT BASE RATE GUIDE AND SUPPLEMENT
$	$	$	$

PAYMENT AMOUNT (ROUNDED UP) $ _____ X NUMBER OF PAYMENTS _____ = TOTAL OF PAYMENTS $ _____

TOTAL OF PAYMENTS $ _____   TOTAL OF PAYMENTS $ _____

LESS NET LOAN AMOUNT – _____   LESS ____ PYMNTS OF $ _____ = – _____

EQUALS: FINANCE CHARGE $ _____   EQUALS FINAL PAYMENT $ _____

LOAN DISBURSEMENT INSTRUCTIONS

ISSUE CASHIERS CHECK - (CHECK NUMBER)		DATE FIRST PAYMENT DUE
1.	$	
2.	$	FIGURED BY / VERIFIED BY
3.	$	ANNUAL PERCENTAGE RATE ____ %
4.	$	
CREDIT ACCOUNT OF (INCLUDE TYPE AND NUMBER)	$	
PAY EXISTING LOAN BALANCE OF LOAN NUMBER	$	
OTHER	$	
FEES ☐ APPRAISAL ☐ D.M.V. ☐ MISC.	$	
TOTAL NET PROCEEDS	$	

BORROWER'S SIGNATURE	DATE
BORROWER'S SIGNATURE	DATE

LOAN OFFICER'S SIGNATURE	DATE

LOAN OFFICERS COMMENTS:

FIG. 12-4. (continued)

FORM 611R

Ideal

THE IDEAL SYSTEM, REG. U.S. PAT. OFFICE. MADE IN U.S.A.

Line	Date 19__	Memo	(1) Total Cash Receipts	(2) Retail Sales	(3) Wholesale Sales	(4) Other	(7) Cash Received on Account	(8) Sales Tax	(9) Charge Sales	(10) Other Income & Balance Sheet Items — Name	(11) Amount
1	5-1	Days Receipts	406.60	180.00	150.00	50.00		26.60			
2	2	"	1438.70	200.00	1100.00	110.00		28.70			
3	3	"	422.65	195.00	75.00	125.00		27.65			
4	4	B. Carson Co.	50.00				50.00				
5	4	P.G. Shavers Co.	68.00				68.00				
6	5	Days Receipts	326.35	160.00	70.00	75.00		21.35			
7	6	N.W. Gas Co.	37.33							Refund	37.33
8	6	Days Receipts	502.90	235.00	100.00	135.00		32.90			
9	7	A. Reynolds	27.82	26.00				1.82			
10	8	Leonard Co.	75.00				75.00				
11	9	Days Receipts	299.60	50.00	130.00	100.00		19.60			
12	10	Max Langan	20.00				20.00				
13	11	Days Receipts	334.89	58.00	146.07	108.00		22.82			
14	13	Days Receipts	454.75	220.00	50.00	155.00		29.75			
15	18	State Ins. Fund	25.00							Refund	25.00
16	23	Werba Receipts	6239.24	486.41		891.03		48.80			
17	24	Days Receipts	385.20	145.00	90.00	125.00		25.20			
18	26	Days Receipts	428.00	125.00		275.00		28.00			
19	30	White Assoc.	40.00				40.00				
20											
21											
22											
23											
24											
25											
26											
27											
28											
29											
30											
31											
32											
33		Total	11582.03	2029.07	2029.07	2149.03		746.19			62.33

FIG. 12-5. Receipts journal/forms. (Figure continued on p. 298.)

CASH DISBURSEMENTS
GENERAL BUSINESS

	DATE 19__	CHECK NUMBER	TO WHOM PAID	AMOUNT	PURCHASES & MATERIALS	CASH PAID ON ACCOUNT	OTHER COSTS	SALARY & WAGES	SALARY & WAGE DEDUCTIONS
1	3.1	240	M.L. Realty Co.	400 00					
2	2	241	N.Y. Telephone	145 50					
3	4	242	Southside Printers	35 00					
4	5	243	Pacific Trucking	200 00					
5	6	244	Weekly Payroll	600 00				800 00	200 00
6	8	245	Postmaster	20 00					
7	10	246	J.A. Plumbing	56 50					
8	11	247	L.M. Furnishings	80 00					
9	13	248	Atlantic Inc.	500 00	500 00				
10	14	249	Weekly Payroll	550 00				700 00	150 00
11	16	250	Century Stationery	23 00	23 00	23 00			
12	16	251	R. Smith Co.	248 00	248 00				
13	19	252	Southside Printers	18 00					
14	19	253	National Bank	9 50					
15	20	254	Weekly Payroll	600 00				800 00	200 00
16	22	255	J.B. Supplies	119 00	119 00				
17	23	256	Grow Best Landscape	45 00					
18	23	257	Green Delivery Co.	26 00					
19	24	258	Aema Inc.	350 00	350 00				
20	25	259	N.Y. State Sales Tax	69 00					
21	26	260	West Water Co.	32 00					
22	28	261	N.Y. State Unempl. Tax	95 00					
23	28	262	Weekly Payroll	550 00				700 00	150 00
24	29	263	Internal Revenue Ser.	415 80					
25	29	264	Internal Revenue Ser.	428 00					
26									
27									
28									
29				5657 50	1240 00	23 00		3000 00	700 00
30									
31									
32									
33									

FIG. 12-5. (continued)

CASH DISBURSEMENTS

	ADVER-TISING & INSURANCE	AUTO & TRUCK EXPENSES	RENT & INTEREST	SUPPLIES & POSTAGE	REPAIRS & MAINT.	UTILITIES & TELEPHONE	TAXES & LICENSES	OTHER EXPENSES (name)	OTHER EXPENSES AMOUNT	BALANCE SHEET ITEMS NAME OF ACCOUNT	BALANCE SHEET ITEMS AMOUNT	
1			400 00									1
2												2
3	35 00					14 50						3
4		200 00										4
5												5
6				20 00								6
7					56 50							7
8										Furniture	80 00	8
9												9
10												10
11												11
12												12
13	18 00											13
14			9 50									14
15												15
16												16
17					45 00							17
18								Delivery Exp.	26 00			18
19												19
20										N.Y. Sales Tx.	69 00	20
21						32 00	95 00					21
22												22
23												23
24										Tx. Payable	486 00	24
25							214 00			Tx. Payable	214 00	25
26	53 00	200 00	409 50	20 00	101 50	177 50	309 00		26 00		821 00	26
27												27
28												28
29												29
30												30
31												31
32												32
33												33

THE IDEAL SYSTEM, REG. U.S. PAT. OFFICE. MADE IN U.S.A.

FIG. 12-6. Disbursements journal/forms.

AC ALADDIN COMMUNICATIONS

2259 Torrance Blvd., Torrance, CA 90501
(213) 320-1122 ● (213) 775-1288 ● (213) 530-"BEEP"

Firm Name _____ Date Established _____

Firm Address _____

Trade Style or Name _____

Type of Business

☐ Professional Corp.   ☐ Proprietorship   ☐ Partnership   ☐ Corporation

	Bank Name	Phone Number	Business Account Number	Contact
1.				
2.				

	Credit or Finance Reference	Phone Number	Contact
1.			
2.			
3.			
4.			

PERSONAL INFORMATION ON PROPRIETORSHIPS, PARTNERSHIPS, PROFESSIONAL CORPORATIONS, AND BUSINESSES UNDER 2 YEARS OLD.

	(1)	(2)	(3)
Name			
Home Address			
Spouse's First Name			
Social Security No.			

Additional Comments _____
_____
_____
_____
_____
_____

C5/CRI (2/84)

FIG. 12-7. Commercial credit form.

POSTAGE & SUPPLIES

_____
  Type Of Mailing

_____
  Company

_____

_____
  Publication(s) mailed to

_____
  Date mailed

_____   _____   _____
No. Sent   Cost (each)   Total

_____   _____   _____
No. Sent   Supplies   Total

    Total Cost of Mailing----_____

POSTAGE & Supplies

_____
  Type Of Mailing

_____
  Company

_____

_____
  Publication(s) mailed to

_____
  Date Mailed

_____   _____   _____
No. Sent   Cost (each)   Total

_____   _____   _____
No. Sent   Supplies   Total

    Total Cost of Mailing--_____

POSTAGE & SUPPLIES

_____
  Type Of Mailing

_____
  Company

_____

_____
  Publication(s) mailed to

_____
  Date mailed

_____   _____   _____
No. Sent   Cost (each)   Total

_____   _____   _____
No. Sent   Supplies   Total

    Total Cost of Mailing -----_____

POSTAGE & Supplies

_____
  Type Of Mailing

_____
  Company

_____

_____
  Publication(s) mailed to

_____
  Date Mailed

_____   _____   _____
No. Sent   Cost (each)   Total

_____   _____   _____
No. Sent   Supplies   Total

    Total Cost of Mailing-----_____

FIG. 12-8. Mailing/postage tracking/billing forms.

Application For Employment

Applicants are considered for all positions without regard to race, color, religion, sex, national origin, age, marital or veteran status, or the presence of a non-job-related medical condition or handicap.

(PLEASE PRINT)

Date of Application _____

Position(s) Applied For _____

Referral Source: ☐ Advertisement ☐ Friend ☐ Relative ☐ Walk-In

☐ Employment Agency ☐ Other _____

Name _____
      LAST   FIRST   MIDDLE

Address _____
      NUMBER   STREET   CITY   STATE   ZIP CODE

Telephone ( )_____ Social Security Number _____|_____|_____
     Area Code

If employed and you are under 18, can you furnish a work permit? ☐ Yes ☐ No

Have you filed an application here before? ☐ Yes ☐ No   If Yes, give date _____

Have you ever been employed here before? ☐ Yes ☐ No   If yes, give date _____

Are you employed now? ☐ Yes ☐ No   May we contact your present employer? ☐ Yes ☐ No

Are you prevented from lawfully becoming employed in this country because of Visa or Immigration Status? ☐ Yes ☐ No
(Proof of citizenship or immigration status may be required upon employment.)

On what date would you be available for work? _____

Are you available to work ☐ Full Time ☐ Part-Time ☐ Shift Work ☐ Temporary

Are you on a lay-off and subject to recall? ☐ Yes ☐ No

Can you travel if a job requires it? ☐ Yes ☐ No

Have you been convicted of a felony within the last 7 years? ☐ No ☐ Yes
(Conviction will not necessarily disqualify applicant from employment.)

If Yes, please explain _____

_____

AN EQUAL OPPORTUNITY EMPLOYER M/F/V/H

FIG. 12-9. Application for employment. Applicant data record (employment) form.

Veteran of the U.S. Military service? ☐ Yes ☐ No   If Yes, Branch _____

Indicate languages you speak, read, and/or write.

	FLUENT	GOOD	FAIR
SPEAK			
READ			
WRITE			

List professional, trade, business or civic activities and offices held.
(You may exclude those which indicate race, color, religion, sex or national origin): _____

_____

_____

_____

Give name, address and telephone number of three references who are not related to you and are not previous employers.

_____

_____

_____

Special Employment Notice to Disabled Veterans, Vietnam Era Veterans, and Individuals With Physical Or Mental Handicaps.

Government contractors are subject to 38 USC 2012 of the Vietnam Era Veterans Readjustment Act of 1974 which requires that they take affirmative action to employ and advance in employment qualified disabled veterans and veterans of the Vietnam Era, and Section 503 of the Rehabilitation Act of 1973, as amended, which requires government contractors to take affirmative action to employ and advance in employment qualified handicapped individuals.

If you are a disabled veteran, or have a physical or mental handicap, you are invited to volunteer this information. The purpose is to provide information regarding proper placement and appropriate accommodation to enable you to perform the job to the best of your ability in a proper and safe manner. This information will be treated as confidential. Failure to provide this information will not jeopardize or adversely affect your consideration for employment.

If you wish to be identified, please sign below.

☐ Handicapped Individual   ☐ Disabled Veteran   ☐ Vietnam Era Veteran

Signed _____

FIG. 12-9. (continued) (Figure continued on p. 304.)

Employment Experience

Start with your present or last job. Include military service assignments and volunteer activities. Exclude organization names which indicate race, color, religion, sex or national origin.

1	Employer	Telephone ( )	Dates Employed From / To	**Work Performed**
	Address			
	Job Title		Hourly Rate/Salary Starting / Final	
	Supervisor			
	Reason for Leaving			
2	Employer	Telephone ( )	Dates Employed From / To	**Work Performed**
	Address			
	Job Title		Hourly Rate/Salary Starting / Final	
	Supervisor			
	Reason for Leaving			
3	Employer	Telephone ( )	Dates Employed From / To	**Work Performed**
	Address			
	Job Title		Hourly Rate/Salary Starting / Final	
	Supervisor			
	Reason for Leaving			
4	Employer	Telephone ( )	Dates Employed From / To	**Work Performed**
	Address			
	Job Title		Hourly Rate/Salary Starting / Final	
	Supervisor			
	Reason for Leaving			

If you need additional space, please continue on a separate sheet of paper.

Special Skills and Qualifications
Summarize special skills and qualifications
acquired from employment or other experience _____

_____

_____

_____

FIG. 12-9. (*continued*)

Education

	Elementary	High	College/University	Graduate/Professional
School Name				
Years Completed: (Circle)	4 5 6 7 8	9 10 11 12	1 2 3 4	1 2 3 4
Diploma/Degree				
Describe Course Of Study:				
Describe Specialized Training, Apprenticeship, Skills, and Extra-Curricular Activities				

Honors Received:

State any additional information you feel may be helpful to us in considering your application.

Applicant's Statement

I certify that answers given herein are true and complete to the best of my knowledge.

I authorize investigation of all statements contained in this application for employment as may be necessary in arriving at an employment decision. I understand that this application is not and is not intended to be a contract of employment.

In the event of employment. I understand that false or misleading information given in my application or interview(s) may result in discharge. I understand, also, that I am required to abide by all rules and regulations of the Company.

_____ _____
Signature of Applicant   Date

For Personnel Department Use Only

Arrange Interview ☐ Yes ☐ No

Remarks _____

_____
                                                    INTERVIEWER   DATE

Employed ☐ Yes ☐ No   Date of Employment _____

Job Title _____ Hourly Rate/Salary _____ Department _____

            By _____
                        NAME AND TITLE   DATE

This Application For Employment and Applicant Data Record is sold for general use throughout the United States. Amsterdam Printing and Litho Corp. assumes no responsibility for the inclusion in said form of any questions which, when asked by the employer of the job applicant, may violate State and/or Federal Law.

FIG. 12-9. (continued) (Figure continued on p. 306.)

Applicant
Data Record

Applicants are considered for all positions, and employees are treated during employment without regard to race, color, religion, sex, national origin, age, marital or veteran status, medical condition or handicap.

As employers/government contractors, we comply with government regulations and affirmative action responsibilities.

Solely to help us comply with government record keeping, reporting and other legal requirements, please fill out the Applicant Data Record. We appreciate your cooperation.

This data is for periodic government reporting and will be kept in a <u>Confidential File</u> separate from the Application for Employment.

(PLEASE PRINT)

Date _____

Position(s) Applied For _____

Referral Source: ☐ Advertisement ☐ Friend ☐ Relative ☐ Walk-In

☐ Employment Agency ☐ Other _____

Name _____   Phone (___) _____
     LAST   FIRST   MIDDLE   Area Code

Address _____
     NUMBER   STREET   CITY   STATE   ZIP CODE

Affirmative Action Survey

Government agencies require periodic reports on the sex, ethnicity, handicapped and veteran status of applicants. This data is for analysis and affirmative action only. Submission of information is voluntary.

Check one:

☐ Male ☐ Female

Check one of the following:

Race/Ethnic Group: ☐ White ☐ Black ☐ Hispanic

☐ American Indian/Alaskan Native ☐ Asian/Pacific Islander

Check if any of the following are applicable:

☐ Vietnam Era Veteran ☐ Disabled Veteran ☐ Handicapped Individual

---

Re-order Form #23960 From Amsterdam Printing and Litho Corp., Amsterdam, N.Y. 12010
©copyright 1984 Amsterdam Printing and Litho Corp., Amsterdam, N.Y. 12010

FIG. 12-9. *(continued)*

FOR PERSONNEL DEPARTMENT USE ONLY

Position(s) Applied For Is Open: ☐ Yes ☐ No

Position(s) Considered For: _____

_____

Date _____

NOTES:

FIG. 12-9. (continued)

CONFIDENTIAL EMPLOYEE HISTORY

EMPLOYEE NAME																											EMPLOYMENT DATE	STATUS		
																													☐ REGULAR ☐ PART TIME ☐ TEMPORARY		
YEARS OF SERVICE	1	2	3	4	5	6	7	8	9	10	11	12	13	14	15	16	17	18	19	20	21	22	23	24	25	26		SECURITY CLEARANCE	LEVEL	DATE GRANTED

PAYROLL DATA

BIRTHDATE	SEX	SOCIAL SECURITY NO.			MARITAL STATUS	NAME OF SPOUSE			NO. OF CHILDREN
FEDERAL WITHHOLDING:	EXEMPTIONS CLAIMED								
	ADDITIONAL AMOUNT WITHHELD								

	DATE ELIGIBLE	DATE JOINED	DATE WITHDRAWN		INSURANCE	DATE ELIGIBLE	DATE JOINED	DATE WITHDRAWN
UNION STATUS					LIFE			
PENSION PLAN					MEDICAL - SELF			
CREDIT UNION					DEP.			
					MAJ. MED. - SELF			
					DEP.			

GENERAL INFORMATION

ADDRESS	CITY	STATE	ZIP	PHONE
ADDRESS	CITY	STATE	ZIP	PHONE
ADDRESS	CITY	STATE	ZIP	PHONE
ADDRESS	CITY	STATE	ZIP	PHONE

IN EMERGENCY NOTIFY	RELATIONSHIP	CITY	STATE	ZIP	PHONE
	RELATIONSHIP	CITY	STATE	ZIP	PHONE

RELATIVES OR FRIENDS EMPLOYED BY THIS CO.	NAMES	RELATIONSHIP	NAMES	RELATIONSHIP

EDUCATION	ELEM. _____ J H S _____ S H S _____	SPECIAL SKILLS OR TRAINING	
	COLLEGE 1 2 3 4 MAJOR _____		
	OTHER _____		

TERMINATION RECORD

☐ RESIGNATION DATE _____	REASON
☐ DISMISSAL DATE _____	REASON
RECOMMENDED FOR RE-EMPLOYMENT ☐ YES ☐ NO	REASON

FORM #08340,1 1972   AMSTERDAM PRINTING AND LITHO CORP., Amsterdam, N. Y. 12010   (over)

FIG. 12-10. Confidential employee history form.

PERSONNEL RECORD

W. T.

Name   Clock No.   Status

Address   Social Security No.

City and State   Phone No.   Citizen Yes ☐ No ☐   Sex M ☐ F ☐

Marital Status S ☐ M ☐ W ☐ Date of Birth   No. of Dependents

Date Employed   Department

Occupational Classification: Starting Rate

Schooling and Previous Working Experience

Date	Salary or Hourly Rate	Occupation	REASON FOR CHANGE	Authorized By

Date Left Employ   Reason For Leaving

FORM #00851   AMSTERDAM PRINTING AND LITHO CORP., Amsterdam, N. Y. 12010

FIG. 12-11. Personnel record form.

309

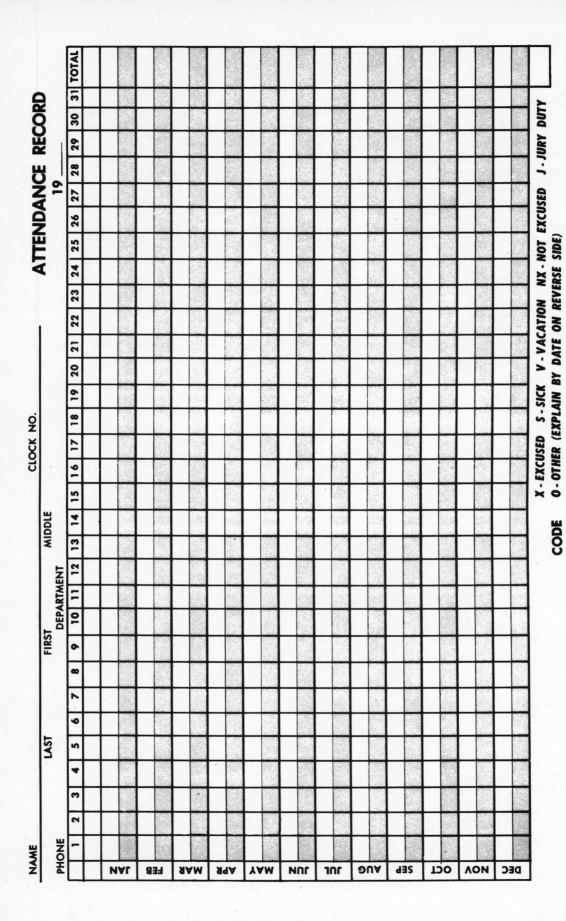

FIG. 12-12. Attendance record form.

CHAPTER 13

KEY ELEMENTS OF A SUCCESSFUL PRACTICE

What enables a consultant's practice to grow? The most important ingredient is a positive attitude. Attitude is critical to the consultant because regardless of your chosen field, you risk rejection ("No, I do not want any today") more than any other professional.

Consultants run a higher risk of rejection than even salespeople. In sales, you sell the client a product and/or service. It is delivered, you receive your commission check, and you are on to the next customer. Occasionally there is a cancellation, but for the most part when the goods are ordered and delivered, the salesperson turns his or her attention elsewhere.

In consulting, you sell the prospect on a service. Then you have to *keep* selling the consultant on your value and ability and the program and approach you have developed.

Case in point: The management consultant spends time selling a prospect on his or her services. Finally, the prospect becomes a client, then the consultant has to continue selling the client on the program he or she has developed and his or her ability to implement the program.

The same is true for others. Imagine you are a money manager. You have just spent two months convincing a prospect with a significant portfolio to become a client. The day after he or she signs, you put him or her into a stock, and pass on a real estate deal. A week later the stock has dropped 15 points and the real estate has climbed 10 percent in value.

As bad as that sounds there is one thing that could be worse. Your upset client calls and asks, "Why? What happened?" Then he or she decides to take his or her portfolio elsewhere.

Regardless of the consulting profession you have chosen, rejection will be part of your life. Every consultant has to pursue clients and there is the chance they will say no.

Every consultant has to formulate plans and there is the possibility the client will either reject them or they will go wrong.

Every consultant has to sell the potential client on his or her ability and even after the client has been sold the consultant must continue the sales process. That is why communication is so important in business.

Attitude becomes the critical factor. The consultant who does not hold up well under criticism or adversity had best find another profession. That does not mean you should never be disappointed or depressed. On the contrary, you would not be human if you did not occasionally display those characteristics. Every consultant does. The important thing, however, is not to let depression take control. When you lose a client, it is an unfortunate experience and there isn't a consultant who does not feel badly about the loss. But do not let the loss bother you for days on end. If you cannot shake the blues, you will find they will impact every other phase of your business and personal life. Certainly you can be depressed for a few minutes—but then go on. Forget about the past. There is nothing you can do about it. You should, however, learn from it.

When successful consultants lose a client they analyze (objectively) what went wrong. Was the job finished? If not, why was the account severed? Was there a personality conflict? Could it have been avoided? Did they do the job? Was there a communication failure? Was it the fee? The billing? Could any of those procedures have been improved?

If the consultant objectively analyzes the situation, he or she will soon begin to understand why the client left. Most important, what he or she learns will help in the future.

Consulting, like sales, is a profession that counts heavily on the law of averages. Consultants will not sell every prospect, but if you were able to hit 1 out of 10, you would be a winner. The key is to remember to keep swinging. If your attitude gets out of kilter and you stop, that is when business slides downhill rapidly.

Consulting, of course, is not the same as sales but sales is an important part of the profession. The consultant who wants to sit back and wait for people to call or come in the door is in the wrong business.

Consultants spend up to 25 percent (and sometimes more) of their time prospecting for new clients. Whether they go to civic meetings, club groups, put on seminars, send letters, or work the telephone, they are *selling*.

Good consultants never stop prospecting. Good consultants are also flexible. Being intransigent is fine for someone who is holding all the cards, but in the consulting business it is the beginning of the end. Your ideas may be superior and you know it, however, a client may have his or her own way of approaching a problem. To throw it out without consideration is a mistake. You not only alienate the client but you may be tossing away a solution.

When working with a client, introduce your ideas slowly. If you are working with a group of employees who report to your client, listen to their input, and give them credit whenever possible. This is particularly true if you have sessions with a group of employees when you are analyzing a problem. If the answer comes to you first, see if you cannot induce one of the employees to develop the answer with a little prompting. A solution that is seemingly developed from within a company is certainly more acceptable to the employees you deal with than one from without.

In consulting, the important thing is to get the job done right. If you give others a share of the credit along the way, you will create allies within the client company and goodwill that will ultimately lead to additional assignments and clients. Running roughshod over a client's employees is not the way to get things done. Be flexible and move slowly.

Every consultant should have goals. There are, of course, thousands of books that have been written on the importance of goal setting. The consultant should monitor his or her progress as a businessperson. Is your business growing the way you anticipated? Are you able to afford the help you need? Are you becoming financially independent as you planned? If not, why?

For many businesspeople—as well as consultants—there is a five-year plan. That is, plan on spending 5 years in business before you are well-established. The toughest time will be years one through three, when you are getting established, adding clients, but still not in a position to hire as much help as you need.

It is during this time period that a consultant may spend 60–70 hours a week in the office. And it is during this period that many wonder if it was really worth leaving the 40-hour-a-week job with its vacations, sick pay, benefits, and so forth.

It is also during this period that a consultant discovers that he or she may lack skills. For instance, you may be an excellent electrical engineering consultant, but you may hate the bookkeeping part of the job.

If you find yourself lacking certain skills, hire someone—on a part-time basis—to handle those duties. There are part-time bookkeepers, CPAs, and salespeople. Part-timers have the advantage of not requiring benefits and can often be paid as an outside service so you are not saddled with additional tax payments as you would be for other employees.

TWO SECRETS TO SUCCESS

Is there a consultant's secret to success?

Yes, there is. In fact, there are two. In a survey of successful consultants in 14 different fields, there were two secrets that 90 percent of them felt were the keys to success.

Success was not contingent on the amount of knowledge of one's field (although a consultant should certainly know his or her profession). It was, instead, a matter of perseverance and/or hard work. That was secret number one. Each consultant said that one of the two elements that made him or her successful was willingness to work hard and to persevere in spite of what happened.

Success had nothing to do with brilliance. It was a product of hard work and long hours. The ability to keep going when things were not going well.

The second attribute the consultants selected was specialization. The message is to specialize. Pick any field but make sure you specialize in it. None tried to be all things to all clients; jack-of-all-trades. They established niches and reputations.

Those are the two secrets of success. Those points can best be illustrated by the following case study.

The Management Consultant Case Study

He was born in Tennessee and raised on a small farm outside of Nashville. As a youth, he did not have television or radio. He spent hours staring out the window using his imagination, and dreaming.

By the time he was in his twenties, most of his dreams had come true. He was a millionaire businessman and management consultant. His expertise was such that prospective businesspeople throughout the country sought his advice.

He was unable to talk personally to the vast numbers that sought his counsel, so he established a publishing company that sold the advice through mail order. The firm grew rapidly. Within a few years, his investment had grown into an enterprise that was grossing $10 million a year.

Problems, however, began to develop. The owner decided the company needed to expand. He began traveling, giving seminars, talking to others, and weighing opportunities for his burgeoning young firm.

While he was gone, he left the running of the firm to an experienced management team. In late 1982, he came back to his corporate offices after an absence of nearly six months. To his dismay, the company was in debt and on the verge of closing its doors. To save it, he retained attorneys and the company was placed in bankruptcy (Chapter 11), which is under the court's protection. Still, angry creditors hounded the firm and blamed the owner for the demise. The creditors were on the verge of forcing liquidation. The only way to save the company was for the owner to resign and leave the board and his firm in the hands of others.

In 1983, he resigned. His salary and fringe benefits were cut off. A number of creditors, still anxious to have him removed permanently from the firm, offered to settle; to buy the firm for a fraction of what it was worth.

The owner had a difficult decision to make. Should he take the money and gracefully bow out or should he stay, without compensation, fight for his company, and hope it would recover..

What would you do? Would you settle for a million dollars and live comfortably from interest payments? Or would you stay, fight for the ownership, and risk everything?

How did you—the present or prospective consultant—answer that question? Compare your decision with that of Chase Revel, the owner of Entrepreneur Group, Inc., and the company that publishes *Entrepreneur* magazine.

Revel stayed, and recovered. It took three years for him to regain control, but he did it. In doing so, he displayed many of the attributes that winning businesspeople—successful consultants—need in order to not only survive, but prosper as well.

Opening a practice is only the first part of the business battle. Successful consultants—that is, those who not only open a business but nurture it and make it grow—share a number of common characteristics in addition to that positive attitude.

The following ability inventory measures a number of those attributes. It is not a test to determine whether someone will be a success or failure in consulting. On the contrary, this is a test that already assumes you are in business. It is, however, a test that measures "growth attributes"—in other words, your ability to make your consulting practice grow. There are no right or wrong answers, no passing or failing score. However, the scale at the end of the test will give you an idea as to where you are on the "consultant's growth scale."

CONSULTANT'S ABILITY INVENTORY

PART I
ACTIVITY PREFERENCES

In the following questions, you are given a choice of two activities. You also have a total of 3 points that can be given to any one of the activities or you may divide the 3 equally (1½ and 1½), or give one activity 2 and the other 1.

		Score
1.	I would rather:	
a.	Fix something around the house	_____
b.	Attend a conference	_____
2.	I would rather:	
c.	Solve math or chess puzzles	_____
d.	Help others with their personal problems	_____
3.	I would rather:	
e.	Build things with wood	_____
f.	Meet important people	_____
4.	I would rather:	
g.	Drive a truck	_____
h.	Build a model of a rocket	_____
5.	I would rather:	
i.	Read on my own	_____
j.	Go to a sporting event	_____
6.	I would rather:	
k.	Take a course in business	_____
l.	Take a course in chemistry	_____
7.	I would rather:	
m.	Sell something to someone	_____
n.	Keep my desk and room neat	_____
8.	I would rather:	
o.	Write letters to friends	_____
p.	Write business letters	_____
9.	I would rather:	
q.	Belong to a social group	_____
r.	Play in a band or musical group	_____

Score

10. I would rather:

    s. Supervise others   _____

    t. Keep detailed records   _____

11. I would rather:

    u. Enroll in a math course   _____

    v. Take a course in art   _____

12. I would rather:

    w. Enroll in a mechanical drawing class   _____

    x. Lead a group   _____

13. I would rather:

    y. Go to a party   _____

    z. Operate my own business   _____

PART II
ACTIVITY PERFORMANCE

This portion of the aptitude test contains statements concerning how well you can do activities. If you can do a listed activity well, score from 1 to 3 points; 3 being the highest. If you cannot do the activity, do it poorly, or would prefer to avoid it, give yourself a low score, either a 0 or 1.

1. I understand simple chemical formulas.   _____

2. I have participated in a science fair.   _____

3. I can write poetry.   _____

4. I can repair the TV.   _____

5. I have operated power tools in a shop.   _____

6. I enjoy painting.   _____

7. I like to design posters and other art.   _____

8. I like to perform on stage.   _____

9. I like to use a computer for spreadsheet analysis.   _____

10. I can make electrical repairs.   _____

PART III
PREFERENCE TEST

Handle the next series of questions with the same scoring.

1. I have served as an elected official in high school or college.   _____

2. I have won an award as a salesperson.   _____

3. I am a good salesperson.   _____

Score

4. I like to plan entertainment for a party. _____

5. I like book work and handling accounts receivable. _____

6. I have worked in an office. _____

7. I have organized a group or club. _____

8. I have had my own business. _____

9. I know how to be a leader. _____

10. I keep accurate records of bills, payments, and sales. _____

PART IV
OCCUPATIONAL PREFERENCE

In the next section, there are occupations listed. You will be given a choice of two in each question. Pick the one you do (or would) prefer.

Score

(a) Plumber _____

(b) Electrician _____

(c) Biologist _____

(d) Surveyor _____

(e) Chemist _____

(f) Musician _____

(g) Science writer _____

(h) Commercial artist _____

(i) Buyer _____

(j) Budget reviewer _____

(k) Business executive _____

(l) Tax expert _____

(m) Television producer _____

(n) Clinical psychologist _____

(o) Stock and bond salesperson _____

(p) Quality control expert _____

(q) Financial analyst _____

(r) Promoter of events _____

(s) Political campaign chief _____

(t) Meteorologist _____

(u) Television talk show host _____

(v) Federal bank examiner _____

(w) Comedy playwright _____

	Score
(x) Marriage counselor	_____
(y) Professional speaker	_____
(z) Computer operator	_____

Scoring of Ability Test

For Part I, Activity Preferences, add the total points you gave to the following letters: b, d, f, h, j, l, m, o, q, s, v, x, and z.

For Part II, Activity Performance, add the total points as well.

For Part III, the Preference Test, add your total points.

For Part IV, Occupational Preference, add the following points you gave to each of these letters: b, c, f, h, i, k, m, o, r, s, u, x, and y.

SCORING OF ABILITY TESTS
Part I

There is no pass or fail, but this test does measure the type of activities you prefer—an important indicator of things and the possible growth of your consulting practice. This test actually measures your preference for activities in six different areas:

1. Practical
2. Curiosity
3. Creative
4. Social
5. Entrepreneurial
6. Conservative or traditional

The growth-oriented consultant will score high in entrepreneurial areas and lower in conservative and traditional activities.

The person taking the test should take a close look at the activities he or she prefers.

Part II

This is a measurement of your abilities. If you scored high you probably have an inquiring mind and are meticulous. Although both these abilities are admirable traits—and a consultant can use a touch of each—they are not critical when it comes to growth in business.

Consultants usually score low on this part. If you scored high you have definite abilities when it comes to details. Once again, although details are important in any business, they are not the most important determinant of growth.

Part III

Your preferences are as important as your abilities. If you do not want to do something, chances are you will do a poor job if you are forced into it. This part measures your entrepreneurial preferences.

Part IV

The last test pins down the type of occupational preferences you have. Scoring high shows a consultant with a growth-oriented personality.

INDEX